The Earth Is God's

FAITH AND CULTURES SERIES

The Earth Is God's

A Theology of American Culture

William A. Dyrness

Wipf & Stock
PUBLISHERS
Eugene, Oregon

Wipf and Stock Publishers
199 W 8th Ave, Suite 3
Eugene, OR 97401

The Earth Is God's
A Theology of American Culture
By Dyrness, William A.

ISBN: 1-59244-795-3
Publication date 8/19/2004
Previously published by Orbis Books, 1997

To the faculty of the School of Theology
at Fuller Seminary:
colleagues
mentors
friends

Contents

Foreword

Robert J. Schreiter, C.PP.S

Culture as a category for understanding human beings and human societies has taken on new significance in recent years. One of the reasons for this heightened importance has been the impact of globalization. Globalization is usually recognized in its powerful homogenizing forces as it has reshaped economies, society, and education, and in the way it has created a kind of global hyperculture whose icons are fast food, athletic clothing, music, and videos. But what has become increasingly evident is that those same homogenizing forces, rather than submerging local cultures, have evoked powerful responses of resistance and revitalization from local cultures. Around the globe cultures as particularities are reasserting themselves in the face of the homogenizing power of neo-liberal capitalist economy and the cultural icons it produces.

A second reason is the new situations of cultural production that are going on in the urban centers of the world. The rapidly urbanizing character of population flows around the planet are bringing together people from very different cultural backgrounds. In these new urban settings they must engage in shaping a new culture for themselves, born out of the multiple identifications that their new environments thrust upon them. Carrying with them memories of rural life, but now thrown in the midst of many cultures and struggling to find their way in an urban (and often alien) setting, people are forming new identities. As a number of authors are starting to suggest, culture is replacing class as the defining characteristic of many groups in such societies.

Third, the sheer pluralism to which people are now subjected makes matters of self-definition and group definition more pressing than may have been the case in the past. In multi-cultural cities of an earlier period, cultures were segregated into their own neighborhoods or quarters. Today they are more likely to be subjected to constant internal migration. Culture becomes not only a source of identification, but it becomes also a matter of survival.

Finally, how people choose to live together, and especially how they choose to relate to the finite resources of their physical environment have become increasingly important issues of, quite literally, life and death. It has become all too evident that lifestyles predicated on high levels of consumption of water, clean air, and energy sources will not be sustainable as lifestyles to be enjoyed by more than a few.

In the midst of all of these developments, it is clear that we need a theology of culture that can address especially how culture has been reconfigured by world and local events. The theologies of culture written in the 1950s—one thinks of those of Paul Tillich and Bernard Meland—could not have foreseen how culture itself would be pressed to the forefront of late twentieth-century concerns. A theology of culture today has to reach before marveling at the culture-producing capacities of human beings and their societies, and how these relate to religion. Theologies of cultures today have to take up questions of ethnicity, race, ecology, and sustainability. How cultures will interact, especially when sharing the same physical space as they now must do in so many cities, is also a matter that cannot be ignored. Given the way culture in its particularity is now being valued, some assessment needs to be made about how to rank this among other aspects of human life, especially as these come into competition with one another.

It is because of these challenges that we should welcome this book of William Dyrness. He sets out to give a thoroughly theological account of culture based on a theology of creation, and an anthropology rooted in human interdependence and sociability. In his words, "culture is what we make of creation." By establishing his theology of culture on this broad base, he can take up some of the urgent questions of culture of our time and give the answers a genuinely biblical and theological cast. His theology of culture does not get reduced to the questions of culture themselves. His evangelical background and commitments assure that the theology which emerges remains thoroughly theological and is not simply a cultural reading in theological disguise. In doing this, his work represents an important addition to the emerging evangelical theology in the United States, which has to be counted as some of the most incisive and thoughtful work going on in the discipline today.

I hope that readers will share my enthusiasm about the project that Dyrness has outlined here and in their reading will engage him in these important issues. What he helps us to do is step back for a moment from the particularities of any culture and ask just what it is about culture that is so significant for Christians and for Christian theology. His point of departure is evangelical, but Christian theologians of many different traditions will recognize his sensitive treatment of their positions in this work as well. It is my hope that this work will help us all reopen the discussion of an adequate and faithful theology of culture suited to the needs of the very changed circumstances of our time.

Preface

The challenges faced by North Americans in thinking about their culture were graphically illustrated for our family while returning to the States from the Philippines in 1982. In June of that year we left Manila, traveling for the first time with our newly adopted Filipino son. Stopping in Hong Kong en route to London and New York, we discovered that Jonathan needed a visa for our brief stopover in London. For two days we waited in long lines at the British Embassy in Hong Kong and sought to convince stone-faced officials that our two-and-a-half-year-old son would not seek to stay in Britain and add to the overburdened social service system. But they were unmoved. After years of living abroad, on three continents, and traveling unhindered with our American passports (and affluence!), for the first time we caught a glimpse of life from the other side of the fence. I had studied and taught theology for fifteen years, but I felt then economic, ethnic, and cultural issues that had not previously figured in my research and teaching. In the faces of those petitioners and those officials, I saw longings and fears that made the usual theological fare seem pale and irrelevant. I wondered how God's new creation and our call to proclaim the good news relate to these human dramas.

Since then the social estrangement and tensions have, if anything, grown worse. And one certainly does not have to travel abroad to experience them; they are a part of our daily experience in Los Angeles or St. Louis or Boise. It is no longer possible to ignore the increasing gulf between poor countries and the few wealthy countries; ethnic tensions and deep-seated animosities are beginning to appear intractable; and these economic and cultural issues are exacerbated by the push and pull of environmental factors and by immigration. But even more alarming than these problems is the fact that, in spite of the amazing growth of the Christian movement world wide, Christians often seem incapable of addressing, let alone having an impact on, such concerns.

This books seeks to stimulate a Christian discussion on culture by means of an examination of the recent history of theological reflection. We will argue that former ways of thinking about God—as sure knowledge or as a narrative of God's acts—have not provided the resources we need to address our corporate and embodied life in the world. Neat cognitive structures (what we have called the loci of theology) and the narratives of God's mighty acts are certainly important tools, but they call for an elaboration that will work them further down into the fabric of our corporate life—into issues of clean water and ethnic conflict. Happily, the most recent generation of theological scholarship has suggested some new ways of speaking of God that should prove helpful in addressing these geopolitical concerns. Grounded in the triune presence of God, we argue that the categories of relationship, agency, and embodiment provide windows that helpfully illumine our human life in the world.

In many ways the argument of this book is unoriginal. It follows up important advances made for example by David Tracy and Nicholas Lash in *Cosmology and Theology*, which called for a new paradigm in theology in which creation and history are integrated.[1] Jürgen Moltmann in his influential book *God in Creation* focused theological reflection on God's intimate presence in the world order.[2] These chapters are a modest effort to continue this particular line of theological reflection from an evangelical perspective, and to apply it to some specific issues of North American culture. After the discussion of our historical context we develop a theology of creation using these categories. This will in turn underlie the discussion of culture, ethnicity, ecology, and art that follows. Other areas could (and perhaps should) have been covered—for example, science or politics—but these modest discussions are offered as illustrations of the way this line of thinking may be applied.

It will be clear from the footnotes how much I owe to colleagues at Fuller and beyond who have been thinking about these things longer than I have—especially Miroslav Volf and Colin Gunton. Many of my colleagues and friends took time to read portions of the manuscript and make comments. Francis I. Andersen, Robert Banks, Robert K. Johnston, Richard Mouw, Nancey Murphy, and Stanley Mutunga all made helpful comments and continue to suggest far more bibliography than I could possibly read. My brother C. T. Dyrness has always been my teacher in matters ecological and was helpful here as well. All these must be thanked but not blamed for anything that I finally have said. I must also express gratitude to Dr. David Kasale, then Dean and now Principal of the Nairobi Evangelical Graduate School of Theology in Nairobi, Kenya, who invited me to give an early version of these chapters as lectures during my sabbatical in May 1996. Closer to home, Michael Beetley, Peter Smith, Terry Larm, and Susan Wood have given better support than I deserve in preparing the manuscript for publication. I am grateful to Bill Burrows, a friend as well as a publisher, for his helpful and encouraging comments on the manuscript when it was at a critical stage. Finally, I need to acknowledge with love my wife, Grace, and son, Jonathan (now with his American passport), who accompanied me to Africa and allowed me to spend as much time as I needed crouched over this little flickering screen. *Solo Deo Gloria*.

Introduction

The Earth Is God's

A Theology of American Culture

It is symptomatic of our century that a book which seeks to further theological reflection on our social and cultural life together should begin by pointing out the gulf that exists between theology and our corporate life. Christians in the twentieth century have not been able to make up their minds whether God and our corporate lives have anything to do with each other. In the first years of the century believers were arguing that God is busy bringing in the Kingdom through the events we see around us. When that became impossible, they insisted that these events showed that the return of Christ was near and we needed to spend our time preaching and living the gospel rather than seeking to reform society. Nor is it possible to predict which side of the theological spectrum will take which position. At the beginning of the century the liberal project exuded confidence that Christian social projects, like the sun rising in the east, held out hope for the future of the race, while the fundamentalists demurred; at the end of the century the roles appear to be reversed and the so-called Christian Right appears hopeful that God intends a kind of Christian America, while many of the neo-liberals are not so sure. In both cases the theological meaning of the events and our corporate life together has been subject to such widely varying interpretations as to render constructive conversation impossible.

This book seeks to suggest ways that appropriate theological reflection might inform the Christian's presence and witness at the end of this century. The focus of the study is on developing a theology of culture for North America that is sensitive to global and cross-cultural issues. While recent discussion has focused either on God's present activity or on the mighty acts of God in the past, our argument is that God's active presence grows out of and expresses the inner reality of those acts. The key to this integration, we argue, is God's trinitarian character. Recent discussion of the Trinity helps us see that God's continuing project grows out of and reflects the triune character of the divine being. These discussions of the Trinity have underlined the way God's character has not only been revealed through what is called the divine economic order, but, from the human point of view, must come to be known in and through that order. If the incarnation shows us anything, it is that God comes to us and is known by us in and through the created order. This makes our embodied obedience—our face to face encounters with others, the practice of our work, and our stewardship of the goods of creation—either vehicles of praise or expressions of our indifference to God.

The first chapter argues that the inability to address our century's problems is, in part at least, the fault of the theological formulations that we have inherited. The language we have inherited to speak of God and the world has not been adequate to express this continuing relationship of God to the earth and its peoples. The rationalist insistence on theology as sure knowledge, for example, was not able to comprehend the biblical richness of God's mysterious presence and the project of the Kingdom which, like the mustard seed, is meant to grow into a great tree and a refuge for all the birds of the air. Even the more recent emphasis on understanding God's presence as "story," helpful in so many ways, reaches its limits when it comes to understanding our embodied stewardship of the created order. These inherited languages then must be complemented by normative categories that grow out of God's own trinitarian presence and reality. We seek to develop such categories in three ways: first, as God's nature is communal so our life in the world is invariably relational and communal; second, as God's presence is creative and active, so our human life in the world must be fundamentally understood in terms of the value of human agency; finally, as God has irrevocably identified with the created order both in his original creative purposes and in terms of the divine incarnation in that order, so the human and created order must be construed in terms of the value of embodiment.

The chapters on creation and culture are meant to fill out these claims in complementary ways. Creation is described not in terms of the processes of making, but in terms of the purposes and ends God embodied in that order. These processes express, indeed they embody, God's continuing and active presence in that creation, in spite of the rebellion and suffering that human sin has introduced. This presence takes the shape of a particular relationship between God and Israel, a community that is described in the Hebrew scriptures and that includes history and creation in a single project. The presence of God centering on God's incarnation in Christ and the pouring out of the Holy Spirit is described as an active and intimate governance of creation, cumulatively and non-coercively, which reaches to the smallest crevice of creation while it affirms and upholds the integrity of the creature. The visible and embodied dimension of God's work climaxes in the embodiment of God in the man Jesus Christ, which issues in the transformation of creation—what the Christian scriptures call the "New Creation"—as this is mediated by the pouring out of the Holy Spirit on "all flesh."

Culture, then, is described as the continuing human response to God's ongoing project of reconciliation and renewal. It is the communal, active, embodied engagement with God's purposes as these are both distorted by human rebellion and reflected in human institutions. Both in its pain and its glimpses of greatness human practices necessarily embody the human response to God's presence and the call of the Holy Spirit. Through discussions of contextualization and the so-called culture wars, we argue that God calls human culture to embody in its practices particular "forms of life" that can be called Christian. Though embedded in a great variety of cultural situations and spread widely over space the time, this Christian presence will bear a family resemblance both to other communities who seek to follow Christ and, more important, to the being of God, which is their living source.

The following three chapters—on ethnicity, ecology, and art—among many others that could be chosen, focus on areas where the Christian forms of life and God's presence appear particularly challenged today. Contemporary discussions of ethnicity, for example, have challenged our ideas of nationhood, of "brotherhood," even of the image of God in fundamental ways. We argue that in reflecting God the very nature of humanity is communal but must be enacted in practices which reflect that relationship—community is an ongoing project, it is something practiced and not simply a given. Indeed, this community is meant to be one day embodied in the multitude from every kindred and nation which sings praises before the throne of God, a reality that is enacted, however imperfectly, in the communities which meet and live in Jesus' name.

Ecology raises even more fundamental questions that involve the very survival of the human species in its earthly environment. These challenges themselves, we argue, must be understood in terms of God's own continuing presence and interest in the creation. Our hope and our challenge lie in the fact that our future and that of the earth are intricately bound up with God's continuing and trinitarian presence in creation. We are linked both to God and creation, and this linkage is not passive but an active call to responsible living. We are called to a form of life that responsibly and redemptively enacts God's purposes for the earth. But because God wishes the divine glory to be embodied, stewardship and species protection, however important, call for a larger perspective: God's final purposes in the New Heaven and New Earth.

Despite the secular detours of recent art history, we argue that of all human activity art can best point to this new order of things. Art raises issues of the uses of creation to a finer pitch, for what we do with creation, because of creation and the incarnation, can actually point people to God. Indeed, in the eucharist and baptism the very elements of creation can be means that, by faith, link people to God. And our songs, drawings, and dramas can either point people toward this relationship or they can stand in the way of such a vision of things. Art, in other words, raises in a unique way issues of idolatry and sacrament.

All of these arguments will lead us to suggest in the conclusion that human forms of life are meant to be embodied worship. In their communal and creative character they are meant to reflect the glory of the Creator and anticipate the final chorus of praise in the presence of God. Notice, however, that this enlarged vision of human life does not evacuate the earthly and bodily life of its incredible splendor; rather, it increases the canvas on which that splendor can be painted. Species protection, for example, and even the pursuit of human justice not only call for a larger perspective in God's purposes but are grounded in God's very trinitarian relationships. This framework will allow us to make some concluding proposals about the way social and political projects ought to be understood theologically. Christian forms of life, though they draw their nourishment from the experience of corporate praise and the celebration of God's redemptive work in Christ, like the presence of God itself, are fully present in the fabric of the world—so that the work of lawmakers and doctors can be seen, as Paul puts it, as *latreia*, the embodied worship of God's people.

1

God's Story and God's Presence

To the question *What has become of our world after the fall of the Berlin Wall?* many answers have been suggested. Some have postulated the end of history as we have known it[1]; others, more appropriately, have used the parable of Christ in which a woman freed from an evil spirit is invaded by seven others to describe our period of history.[2] Whatever answer is suggested, this question clearly dominates our thinking at the end of this millennium. Just when we felt there was a new opportunity for peace and security, little-known peoples from distant corners of the earth—Chechniyans, Hamas, Kurds, Hutus, Tutsis—have exploded into our consciousness. Meanwhile, the growing economic disparity between the so-called Western and non-Western peoples places increasing strain on the earth and its resources. While one civilization is barely keeping ahead of the technological curve, the other is struggling to feed its children. What is happening? What are we humans making of our world?

As Christians, even more striking than the urgency of these issues is the absence of serious and sustained Christian conversation on ways the church should respond to these crises—all of them related in various ways to what we humans have made of God's creation. More often than not reference to issues of our corporate life in the world degenerates into small-minded quarrels about the role of government or it recalls Chicken Little's lament that the sky is falling. Rarely do we ask what God is doing and how we might involve ourselves in ways that further God's purposes.

Of the many reasons, historical and sociological, that might be advanced for this failure of Christian nerve, I want to focus in this study on the particular area of recent theological reflection. This can only be done in a preliminary way because we are too close to these events and our perspective is skewed by our own limited experience. But I will argue that modern theological discussion has not provided us with the tools that make possible any creative response to issues of our human life in the world. We often lack even a vocabulary to think biblically about our relation to social and cultural realities, and so we are limited to reacting to what others—sometimes far more thoughtfully and carefully—are saying from their secular perspective.

A graphic example of this came to my attention through a nationally syndicated column by Cal Thomas that appeared in February 1996 in the *Los Angeles Times* under the title "God as an Endangered Species."[3] There Thomas refers to Interior Secretary Bruce Babbitt's efforts to protect endangered species. It is clear from the column that Babbitt's efforts are a result of his newly deepened Catholic faith. He is quoted as saying: "Outside the Church, I always had a nagging suspicion the vast landscape was somehow sacred and holy and connected to me in a sense that my catechism ignored." Then, through an encounter with the Hopi Indians from northern Arizona, Babbitt came to "believe, deeply and irrevocably, that the land . . . and all the plants and animals in the natural world are together a direct reflection of divinity, that creation is a plan of God." But this cautious and deeply felt reflection on the relation between God and creation does not impress Thomas. Indeed, the columnist fumes, Babbitt comes closer to animism than mainstream Catholic doctrine. If Babbitt would consult his Bible, Thomas insists, he would learn of the admonition to worship the Creator and not the things God created. Perhaps, in the environment, Thomas concludes, theological and political liberals have found a cause, "to substitute for their moral obtuseness on such issues as abortion and homosexual behavior."

Thomas's rhetoric shows how deep are the feelings associated with these issues. But this is all the more reason to reflect more deeply on our Christian presence in God's creation. Perhaps the matter is not as clear-cut as Thomas seems to think. One wonders, Can we not believe that the natural world is a "direct reflection of divinity" and that "creation is a plan of God" without worshiping creation? Indeed, might this not be a way of honoring the Creator?

But Thomas is right about one thing: Mainstream Christian doctrine, at least as recently expressed, does not give us the vocabulary that Babbitt found among the Hopi Indians to speak about the ways creation "reflects" God. But this is not the problem of the Christian tradition so much as what we have made of that tradition. Where Thomas is clearly misguided is in his reactionary stance to what is certainly one of the most pressing issues facing us: the wise stewardship of God's creation. And while we may not want to learn our theology from the indigenous Indian religions of America, we might, if we listen to them carefully, be reminded of something that our own tradition has forgotten.

Evangelicals generally have not been good at remembering the richness of their own tradition. As Mark Noll has pointed out, they have been too busy pursuing their missiological or, more recently, their political projects to spend the necessary time reflecting on their heritage. When they have engaged in conversation their work takes on a polemic edge, reflecting what Noll calls "intuitionism."[4] This all reflects a deeper and more serious weakness, which Noll calls their docetism or gnosticism. That is, Evangelicals have tended to feel that human life as embodied beings, and the created order generally, is somehow less important than the life of the spirit and soul, which, in the Gnostic view, came from God and was meant to be reunited with God. Since the realm of our bodily life is of lesser importance, the theological significance of the body is never subject to serious theological scrutiny. Worse yet, the presence and purposes of God in that world are not sufficiently articulated.

In a way it is unfair to single out Thomas and Evangelicals generally, for they are not alone in their failure to develop a theology of this world. Both conservatives and liberals have been unable to provide a theology of the earth. Conservatives continue a polemic against the social gospel of a previous generation and, more recently, against all forms of liberation (and environmental!) theology, without engaging theologically with the issues these movements have sought to address. Granted that our human projects, whether for reform or liberation, cannot simply reproduce God's own reforming or liberating work, they can draw on the cultural and political relevance of that divine activity. Christians cannot, indeed they must not, simply believe the gospel; they must practice it so that by God's grace they might embody its reality—what the Christian scripture calls the down payment of God's future glory.

With the collapse of the liberal project in the two world wars, theological liberals for their part have not been able to contribute much to an understanding of our life in the world. More recently, neo-liberals worry that the church may lose its distinctive voice if it should become overly involved in social change. Stanley Hauerwas and William Willimon, for example, cannot see much difference between the vision for social change of Jerry Falwell and that of mainline Protestantism. Both are busy trying to get society to uphold its ethics rather than seeking to be the church of Jesus Christ.[5] What Jesus' disciples are called to do cannot be made rational, they believe, from some neutral point of view, but only from the point of view of what God did for us in Jesus' life, death, and resurrection. But are there no theological implications of our Christian presence in the world or our responsibility toward that world outside of our life in the Christian colony? Is there not also a theology of the world alongside and related to our theology of the church? By this question we do not intend to ask whether there are some Christian things that we can say about our presence in the world, that we ought to do or refrain from doing certain things, but whether and in what respect God is present and active in that order and calls us to be co-workers there.

The weakness of both parties in this debate is the failure to engage theologically with issues of human corporate and bodily life. This in turn relates to the fundamental weakness of the theological language that we have inherited. The tradition of theology as sure knowledge, inwardly grasped, and, more recently, the understanding of theology as narrative, both leave critical areas of our corporate and embodied lives unillumined. Here too we have to remember some of the parts of our Christian heritage that we have forgotten. Theologians since the Reformation were insistent that we learn about God in two ways: first, by the "creation, preservation, and government of the universe, which is before our eyes as a most elegant book"; and second, more "clearly and fully" from God's written word.[6] Neither, they believed, was understandable apart from the other. Moreover, the reasons for this were related to God's own presence in both creation and scriptural revelation. In both, God by the Spirit has enlivened and continues to work for illumination of people and the renewal of the earth. Let us turn, then, to our work of developing a theological framework that we can apply to later discussions of various aspects of our corporate life in God's creation.

THE SHIFT FROM DOCTRINE TO THE ACTS OF GOD

Christianity as Doctrine

Thomas's reference to "mainstream Christian doctrine" itself calls attention to an important aspect of our problem. Up until quite recently most Christians have thought of theology as a set of doctrines that Christians believe and that must be applied to various issues that arise. Thomas probably has in mind teachings like God's transcendence over creation and the creation of the world *ex nihilo*, that is, out of no previously existing materials. Thus, Thomas believes, God cannot be "directly reflected in creation." But other teachings of Christianity hold that God *is* reflected in creation (Ps 19) and that God has actually become human, become "flesh," as John's gospel puts it. Moreover, in the events of Acts 2 God has poured out the Holy Spirit on "all flesh" (Acts 2:17, quoting Jl 2:28). Paul goes further and insists that "the creation waits with eager longing for the revealing of the children of God" for it too "will be set free from its bondage to decay" (Rom 8:19, 21). Creation, then, in some sense does reveal God and is implicated in God's purposes. How are these various strands of biblical teaching to be reconciled? Part of the problem lies with our conception of doctrine or teaching.

The understanding of Christianity as a set of doctrines has been influenced in the modern period—at least until the middle of this century—by the particular shape of developments of modern philosophy. These, in turn, were influenced by Augustine and the Reformation. We cannot go into this history in any detail here, but we can note its fundamental metaphor. In the eighteenth and nineteenth centuries the idea developed that theological reflection about God and the world was a kind of intellectual map in which all reality could be located. Most important, truth about God and the world was a matter of sure knowledge, inwardly grasped. Let us examine these two dimensions in some detail.

Theology as sure knowledge. A key figure here was René Descartes, the seventeenth-century French philosopher who sought to achieve knowledge that could not be doubted. As he looked around him at the final stages of the hundred years of religious wars, he was not impressed by the ability of religion to bring people to consensus. So, following the model of geometry—"I was astonished that nothing more noble had been built on so firm and solid a foundation," he notes[7]—he built his system of thought on what he could not doubt: the consciousness of his own thinking. This, he believed, provided him the means of achieving ideas that were both clear and distinct, and indubitable. Such clarity and distinctness after Descartes came to be identified with the scientific method of knowing that was based on the inalterable laws articulated by Isaac Newton. The thinkers of the Enlightenment continued this single-minded pursuit of pure rational truth, a preoccupation that would soon prove to be a jealous god indeed. From these roots our own century, defying its own social and political failures, maintained its unyielding commitment to what cannot be doubted.[8]

Theological knowledge inwardly grasped. Notice that though Descartes sought absolute certainty, his method was one of inward reflection. Following him, modern people came to believe that they reach truth about themselves and their world through introspection. This understanding of Christian truth as inward and primarily intellectual has roots deep in our Christian (and Greek) heritage,[9] and it would be wrong to give the impression that it is entirely mistaken. Emphasis on objective truth that is personally appropriated has provided important tools to describe Christianity with clarity and coherence, and it would be foolish to give this up entirely. These tools have given Christians the means to defend themselves in an environment where objective truth—especially as this has been understood in the scientific method—has been favored. But Christian thinkers have also become aware of the inadequacies of this intellectual heritage.

Christianity as the Acts of God

The most important challenge to this way of construing Christianity came in our own century in what has come to be called the Biblical Theology Movement. By mid-century, theologians, under the influence of Karl Barth, came to focus on God's acts in history—rather than ideas about God—as the primary locus of Christian truth. In 1952 George Ernest Wright published an enormously influential book called *The God Who Acts*.[10] Up to the present, he notes, we have thought about theology as "propositional dogmatics, stated as abstractly and universally as possible and arranged in accordance with a preconceived and coherent system" (11). This method, Wright believes, should be replaced with "a theology of recital or proclamation of the acts of God, together with inferences drawn therefrom" (11). This, he argues, is more appropriate to the way the Bible presents God's truth to us. The latter we usually refer to as the "word of God," but it is more accurately the "acts of God" (12). To confess the God of the Bible is to tell a story and only then to expound its meaning (85). What is known about humanity in the Bible is "inferred from the way he acts in response to the activity of God" (87). Wright believed that many of the current problems of theology stem from trying to use substantive categories (for example, the nature of the human or of sin) instead of following the biblical method. The Bible "does not seek to explain this situation [of human sin] as much as . . . describe it in narrative form" (94). Sin is an account of human inability to walk by faith with God in God's history with us.

Not everything in scripture is compatible with this conception of things, Wright admitted—a fact that will call for our attention further on. The Wisdom literature, for example, does not seem to fit well into this narrative scheme. This offers, Wright noted, "the chief difficulty because it does not fit into the type of faith exhibited in the historical and prophetic literatures" (103). But this focus on history does allow us to think in new and creative ways about God's relationship to the world, and it has had immense influence on subsequent theological reflection.

Indeed, from this has come the important focus on salvation in history,[11] in which creation, exodus, exile, the cross, and resurrection are all brought together in a single dramatic narrative. In the 1970s an important movement calling itself "narrative theology" emerged from soil that sought to use a narrative method in developing theological categories. An important and influential example of a theologian employing these categories is Stanley Hauerwas. He proposes, for example, that it is useless to argue over whether abortion is right or wrong. We should ask ourselves, rather, what kind of story we want to tell about ourselves. How does our story as disciples of Jesus Christ help us answer these issues as they arise in our personal narratives?[12] Whereas abstract statements of truth previously were favored, now history and narrative became privileged categories in working out our understanding of God's relation to the world. These found widespread application to contemporary theology as in, for example, liberation theology, or to biblical hermeneutics in the turn to literary and narrative structure, or even to the nature of God and the Trinity, as in Jürgen Moltmann's important work.[13]

Christianity as History

This way of thinking about theology has been so widely accepted on both sides of the theological spectrum—think, for example, of the way Evangelicals speak of history as "His story" or feminists speak of "herstory"—that we may fail to recognize the significance of this transformation of theological categories. History is not merely an objective context and support for Christian doctrine but truth that has been progressively realized in history and thus must be construed in historical categories. In biblical studies this has made possible a new recognition of the development of traditions within scripture as well as fresh ways of thinking about revelation as historically embedded. In particular, we might point out three areas in which this framework makes possible new ways of thinking about Christian truth: the logic of narrative, the nature of community, and new ways of understanding God's character.

First, the ways we understand rationality itself have been changed in crucial ways. As historical categories have replaced the abstract formulations which dominated previous theologies, we have come to think about logic in different ways. A contemporary of Wright's, Erich Auerbach, argued in a now classic book that the Christian story proved so powerful that it came to influence the whole subsequent development of Western literature.[14] Subsequent writers, often taking their cue from the narratives of scripture, speak of the "logic of the story" wherein a narrative is explained through the analogy of a musical score. In narrative, they point out, meaning emerges as an accumulation of events and speech by a process in which "character, verbal communications and circumstances are each determinative of the other and hence of the theme itself."[15] This way of thinking has had surprisingly large application. Studies of narrative have helped us understand ways in which stories draw hearers into their world, as Jesus' parables were able to do, and construct (or undermine) their assumptions about reality. Most important, historical understandings help us see the dramatic movement of God's program from the call of Abraham through the coming of Christ—which has introduced what Paul calls the "last days"—to the waiting in eager expectation for the final appearing of Christ to set up his Kingdom. In this view rationality itself has become historical.

The Christian understanding of community and the church is a second point at which narrative and history have provided important (and biblical) resources. It is easy to see that an introspective and intellectual approach inclined toward an individualistic approach to Christian experience, and this often made it difficult for Christians to conceptualize the church. One could argue that the statements of Vatican II which defined the church as the pilgrim people of God and picked up the theme of God's historical actions were the precursors for many subsequent treatments of God's people and the nature of the church—both among Protestants and Catholics.[16] Understanding God's self-revelation over time and the developing historical (and cultural) forms this took in Christian history has given Christians a new and important understanding of the role of tradition in theology.[17] Christians found new impetus to "remember" what God had done and thus to look forward to the fulfillment of God's purposes at the end of history. This movement again straddled the theological spectrum, issuing in the important theologies of hope, on the one hand; and an explosion of evangelical interest in eschatology, understood sometimes as a pre-written history, on the other.[18]

Third, historical categories also have helped us develop a more biblical understanding of God's attributes. Previously these attributes were expressed in timeless and abstract ways, some of which were internal to God and were said to be incommunicable, and others which God shared with creation, called communicable attributes. Both were thought to be proven by reference to various texts of scripture, often taken out of context. But the development of historical thinking gives us new ways of thinking about God's character. An example is the development of biblical treatments of the justice of God, which picture God's justice as the progressive realization of God's acts of righteousness in history and point to God's ultimate goal of creating a new heaven and earth "wherein dwelleth righteousness."[19]

GOD'S ACTS IN HISTORY AND IN CREATION

From History to Histories

These gains are obvious to even casual observers of the theological scene. Moreover, the historical and narrative methods, even when there is no consensus on what is meant by these things, are so widely accepted that we are not likely to see them eclipsed any time soon.[20] But certain developments, hinted at earlier in the chapter, have highlighted the limitation of these methods. These limitations suggest not so much an abandonment of the historical ways of thinking developed in the last generation as a more nuanced and careful use of them. There are many ways in which we might illustrate our situation, but let me use two of the most important issues which will occupy our attention in subsequent chapters: cultural pluralism, and the stewardship of our physical environment.

With the break up of the Cold War we have been met with a virtual explosion of claims of peoples for recognition and, often, for independence. After switching off the evening news, we are tempted to ask ourselves, Who are these people and where have they come from? The truth is they have been there all along, but, because of the machinations of the power blocs of the First and Second Worlds, their voices have not been heard. Now they are clamoring for attention by rebelling against various forms of colonial and neo-colonial authority and even by destroying peoples with whom they have lived for generations but whom they now perceive as a threat to their survival. How do these eruptions of violence fit into the history of the world we have known?

Nor is this a problem only in non-Western countries. The West is itself struggling with what is termed *new regionalism* and *multi-culturalism*. On every hand groups that previously have been excluded from cultural and political power are speaking out in novel and striking ways. Women, blacks, and more recently, Hispanic and Asian immigrant groups are making their presence felt in ways that can no longer be ignored. Picking up on the categories that have now become dominant, these people are all insisting on the dignity and importance of their own stories. They are not willing to accept a history that is written by someone else and that relegates them to the margins.

Just as history has been replaced by histories, theology now has been replaced by theologies. Each group, from its own perspective, is reading the biblical text and finding its own place in the story of scripture. Latin American theologians for example are insisting that scripture is heard differently when it is read from the point of view of the oppressed masses of Latin America. They have seen the Exodus as the major biblical paradigm for salvation, which is seen both as liberation from sin and from oppression. African theologians ask how the Good News relates to the ancestors and the perennial challenge of drought and desertification.[21] Women too have read scripture with new eyes and pointed out that women were the first witnesses to the resurrection and were actually commissioned by Jesus to tell the disciples about this great news. Their insistent questions focusing on gender roles and embodiment have also stretched the purely historical categories of the male theological establishment. The social and cultural questions of these theologians are straining the historical categories that Western theologians have been developing. Their bewildering diversity is often met with dismay if not outright hostility. What is happening to the unity of the body of Christ and the unified truth of scripture? I believe that the battles emerging are partly, though not solely, the result of our facing questions that we are not equipped to handle. They have stretched our ways of thinking about God and the world beyond the familiar ways of the past, and they call for new categories.

One symptom of our dilemma is the use these groups are making of history, or what they call their story. Having found their voice they are anxious that we hear what they have to say. More often than not their cries disrupt the narratives we have previously used in understanding our world. The traditional narrative of Columbus's voyages to the New World, for example, is now met with accounts of Native American presence on the continent. How does the diversity of these stories square with the Christian claim that the gospel is God's provision for the sins of the whole world? And when the narratives that have been constructed conflict, whose story is to be given priority? Of course, some are perfectly willing to allow all these stories to exist in a kind of grand cacophony of voices, cheerfully insisting that the whole idea of a *meta-narrative* (or a single overarching story that includes everyone) is no longer conceivable.[22] But this is not satisfying when it allows ethnic conflicts to explode into virtual genocide. Clearly some stories are better than others, but how do we decide?

Christianity as Story-Bound but not Story-Relative

As might be expected, some Christian theologians have been so troubled by this pluralism that they have questioned the whole drift of modern theology and its focus on story. In various ways they have sought to return to previous ways of thinking that seemed to allow more certainty about Christian truth and that use more traditional categories.[23] Many Christians appear more satisfied with what they feel are more stable and universal categories. But the risk here is that we cannot then profit from the more historical and culturally sensitive ways of thinking. The question facing Evangelicals seems inescapable: Can we account for this diversity in ways that are biblical and which allow us to escape the relativism that seems to threaten theological conversation these days? There are a growing number of voices that insist that we can.

Thomas Tracy, for example, has argued that Christian truth can be story-bound without being story-relative.[24] That is, truth must be bound to the biblical narrative and to the larger story of the Christian church. There is no way to escape the fact that biblical truth imposes a pattern of God's intervention on the events of human history and "weaves" these events together into a meaningful sequence, the central theme of which is the working out of God's purposes in relation to humankind (79). But it does not follow that this account is story-relative, that it is no better or worse than any other account or that it may be merely an elaborate fantasy. This is because, Tracy insists, it "purports to be the story of our lives and our history" and it connects God "to the events and individuals that populate our world" (79). The Christian story cannot be evaded because it "includes references to events that belong to our shared spatio-temporal frame of reference" (81). That is to say, the Christian story, in a unique way, makes claims about and implies connection with the shared spatial world that grounds our lives and cultures.

William Placher has made a similar case in arguing that the biblical narratives claim something about the shape of the world and depict the character of the God to whom we are called to respond. Moreover, the internal logic of the faith that results from this response, Placher insists, makes stronger claims for truth than relativism allows.[25] It has been characteristic of evangelical response to views of people like Tracy and Placher—which have come to be called *postliberalism*—to emphasize this connection with the external world. In a recent anthology of evangelical interaction with postliberals this is a recurring theme. David Clark, for example, argues that in the light of the proliferation of narratives and the assumption of relativism "faithful Christians should stress that although our knowledge of these matters is surely limited, the universe possesses a determinate structure and our grasp of truth should conform to that structure."[26]

These are helpful reminders, and we will want to return to this argument later. But if the distinction between story-bound and story-relative can be accepted in a preliminary way, it suggests that our theological work needs categories that history and narrative by themselves do not provide. We cannot avoid connecting Christian truth together into a coherent whole and making it fit together. But references to spatio-temporal reality and to public spheres remind us that this story must be fitted into our embodied and corporate world, with its teeming complexity of thought, activity, and emotion.[27] It must provide ways for us to understand cultural patterning (that is, the shared values and practices that constitute relations between our social life and our environment) in Christian ways. Here are areas that call out for theological articulation. The focus on the story line, the melody, of truth is helpful. But when we think about theology in this way, something seems to be missing. We can hear the story and sing it for ourselves. But how do we embody this story? How does it influence a whole culture? Better yet, how do we dance it and sing it together?

Christianity in Its Earthly Setting

A second area that has suggested limitations in our current theological vocabulary has been the challenge of stewarding our limited earthly resources. Here we need to start by the common-sense observation that our involvement with the world is not primarily intellectual but physical. We are always making something of our environment; for better or worse we are forever doing something with it. We have recently become aware of certain critical events which are the result of our human activity in the world. Scientists, while they debate the details and the implications, point out that the earth seems to be warming, that the protective ozone layer is disappearing, and that species are disappearing at an increasing (and, many believe, alarming) rate. Christians who believe that they are both of the earth—made of its soil and destined to return to it—and placed in a position of responsibility over it, cannot be indifferent to this deterioration. Moreover, if we believe that God is creator of this world and that Christ holds all things together through the ministry of the Holy Spirit, we can insist that God has a stake in what we are making of the world.

A related area is our aesthetic life in the world. Much of what we make of our environment cannot (and should not) be reduced to what we do to survive or prosper physically but to what we make for "fun." How we arrange our physical environment in ways that allow us to flourish as human beings and bring us joy is central to our human life on earth. How does this urge to shape our world relate to the story that we tell about God? A moment's reflection suggests there are important relationships. The sacraments and religious rituals remind us that our physical environment can become a vehicle of our worship and even of the presence of God. Artists for centuries have reflected both their praise of God and their rebellion against God in the works they create. Both Rembrandt and Picasso then have a religious dimension to their work. And given that every culture produces art (just as every culture displays a religious consciousness), Christians should be busy making this a part of their biblical discipleship.

But again we ask whether this does not imply that theological reflection must develop better ways of speaking about these things than our intellectual and historical orientations have allowed. Later we will argue that the Greek heritage lying behind previous ways of thinking about God tended to disparage the physical context of our discipleship as somehow unimportant to God. What went on in our hearts (which was really equivalent to Plato's cave) was what mattered. The scriptures, on the other hand, imply that, from God's perspective, all of life—what goes on in the work place or artist's studio no less than in the sanctuary—is meant to be brought under God's rule and reflect God's glory.

Story again reaches its limits here. We noted earlier that George Ernest Wright wondered how the Wisdom literature with its insistent focus on the whole of our social and physical lives, our eating and drinking, our playing and laughing, can be brought under the dominant rubric of narrative. But the prominence this literature is given in the canon is testimony to God's concern that all of life reflect the divine purposes. James Barr has gone even further in a recent book, arguing that the whole distinction between revelation and what we have called natural theology must be rethought. He says that much of what is included in scripture is not directly a revelation of God or implicit in God's creative purposes. Though what we call elements of natural theology were tied to creation indirectly, they "were not direct reflections of the structure of the created world. Rather, they were internal human constructions arising out of particular problems and controversies of religion in certain stages of its development."[28] In other words, they were ways in which people in the biblical period, for better or worse, made something of their world. And they were generously taken up into the redemptive program of God. All of this, apparently, is relevant to God's total purposes for humanity and the earth.

There is a wonderful image at the end of Revelation that underlines what we are saying. In chapter 21, after a graphic description of the new heaven and new earth that God will bring from heaven, John sees that all the nations will walk by the light of the Almighty and the kings "will bring their glory into [the heavenly city]" (v. 24). Then, in verse 26, the text insists that even the people "will bring into it the glory and the honor of the nations." This clearly involves the eschatological harvest of the goods of the earth and its cultures; and it implies that we need a theology of the earth and culture to supplement our theology of history, a theology that will ask: What are these goods? How can we see our hands are not empty when we enter the city on this final day?

Christianity and Space

A theology of history and narrative then needs a correction and a deepening. How can this be characterized? At the risk of oversimplification we might put matters in this way. History and story are categories that readily incorporate time but not *space*. They imply movement, as in a melody, but they cannot fully comprehend the soil—the complexity in which this movement is rooted. True, various details can be selected for mention, when it advances the narrative, but much is overlooked. It is also true that the created context can be made into a background for the drama, much as Wright needed to make the Wisdom literature into a background for the history. But then how do we make sense of these things theologically? How is God present there working out God's graceful purposes? How are background and foreground related?

It is in space that we encounter the other person, with all of the strangeness that not only does not fit into our story but may challenge it in fundamental ways. As John MacMurray points out, our relation to others is primarily tactile, we encounter them but we do not comprehend them.[29] So we must find ways to understand the physical nature of this encounter. For it is in space that our embodied practices are constructed, where we injure or heal the earth, where we shape objects and events that celebrate our deepest values.

Christianity and Sight

Another metaphor that might point us in the right direction is that of *sight*. Perhaps we need to find ways of incorporating the visual dimension of our human experience into our theology. Stories are born in oral cultures; we love to hear and tell stories. But notice that when the story has been very striking, we say "I see." Jesus finished his stories by always adding the enigmatic words: "Let anyone with ears listen" (for example, Mt 11:15, 13:15; Mk 4:9, 4:23; Lk 8:8, 14:35), which is really asking about the reception of what he had to say. For reception, and subsequent embodiment of what Jesus is saying, the better image is sight. This too is a metaphor that appears in Jesus' ministry. It is the man born blind who says after his encounter with Jesus: "Though I was blind, now I see" (Jn 9:25). And it is Paul who says of our life in the world, "now we see in a mirror dimly, but then we will see face to face" (1 Cor 13:12).

Jon Levenson, in an illuminating discussion of the biblical image of Zion, argues that for the people of Israel visual accounts were usually less important than verbal ones because the focus was on the word of God and not on the appearance of a person. Still, there are places where this rule is broken, such as the moving account of the nation's encounter with Zion in Psalm 48. There sight is the primary medium of revelation: "As soon as they saw it, they were astounded" (v. 5). In this instance the oral is fragmentary; the visual is more comprehensive. Clearly, this passage implies, in the Temple the usual dominance of the oral is reversed and the visual predominates. "Somehow," says Levenson, " . . . we cannot explicate in words [how] the sight of the Temple conveys a revelation about God."[30] Interestingly, he notes that both the rabbinic tradition and the subsequent Christian tradition "undermine appreciation of the nonverbal mode of revelation."[31] Perhaps part of the work that remains is to develop ways to reclaim this visual dimension of revelation, to elaborate ways to train our visual skills for the day when we will see God, who is the Truth, "face to face."

Is it possible to develop ways of thinking and acting that recover some of these lost dimensions of creation? The following section attempts to suggest a possible answer to this question.

THEOLOGY AS GOD'S ACTION IN CREATION

There is no better place to begin our constructive work than to speak of God and God's relation to creation. We will have a great deal more to say about this in the next chapter, but here we want to sketch out the ways reflection on *God's trinitarian relations* provides important clues for understanding our own life in the world. The starting point for our theological reflection is the personal being of God revealed to us in scriptures. But note that this theological starting point must be understood in terms of our human location: our embodied life in the world. God, we will see, not only brings about a series of actions that constitutes the story of salvation, but God also continuously upholds creation, and there, at the deepest level of reality, works out the divine purposes. But the great mystery of Christianity is that God's relationship to the world has been opened up in the very historical process that constitutes our human life. God has become a part of those processes in a way that uncovers the deepest reality of the divine being. So there is no need to escape our bodies or our cultural embeddedness to know God; rather, we in our human and bodily lives can be intimately related to God. Let us speak briefly of three ways this is so.

God made the world and continues to work in it. This would seem to be the most basic statement of Christian belief about God and the world and fitting starting point for reflection on our own life in the world. But, important as it is, it is not really the first word. For before this, indeed constitutive of this relationship, is God's own relatedness within God's own being. This mystery of God's own inner communion is grasped by us, writes Catherine LaCugna, precisely in the economy of salvation, that is, in the unfolding relationship of God with the world. And "vice versa, the economic self-revelation of God in Christ is grasped, albeit obliquely, as the mystery of [the Trinity] itself."[32] So when Christians cite the first article of the creed, we are confessing *a God who exists in relationship and as relationship*. But the point that will become critical in our discussion follows: this relationship is revealed by God's actions toward and in the world.[33]

This relationship has in view a genuine, if asymmetrical, mutuality.[34] That is, God gives to creation an integrity that allows it to have a life of its own, one that is rich in its interpenetration and that can "answer" God's loving call. Though God is sovereign over creation, this "other" is given a reality that can in the human form encounter God, and in both human and nonhuman forms can embody the glory of God. Scriptures say that on the seventh day God rested. This speaks of the mutuality in which, in this sabbath of creation, God waits for the response of creation. But it also refers to the last day, when the glory of the Lord will be revealed in the earth in what Moltmann has called the "sabbath feast of creation." On that day God will accept the perfected worship of the creature. Thus God gives to creation but also receives back from it.

Second, we note that God begins by acting. In the majestic words of scripture: "In the beginning . . . God created the heavens and the earth" (Gn 1:1). The world then is *God's act* rather than *God's thought*. Better, God's thoughts are expressed in and through God's work. So in addition to being constitutive of the divine story, these acts embody the free expression of God's loving and creative inner-trinitarian relationships. We might even say that the world can be called God's art work as well as God's story, and that God's thinking is inseparably linked to God's imagining. That is, something happened when the world was made that God declared "good" and to which God responded with loving attention. This goodness expresses the personal interest God took, and continues to take, in the complexity of creation. So we see that a critical dimension of God's relation to the world, and therefore constitutive of our own worldly life, is *agency*. In the New Testament Jesus speaks often, especially in John, of the work that he came to do, a process which culminates in the awful words from the cross: "It is finished." But note that the work the Father gave Jesus to do includes our response and embodiment of God's work. Jesus says to Nicodemus: "Those who do what is true come to the light, so that it may be clearly seen that their deeds have been done in God" (Jn 3:21), and later to his disciples: "This is the work of God, that you believe in him whom he has sent" (Jn 6:29). Once again, the work of God in the world does not alienate our human work but rather makes it possible (see Jn 14:12). The Holy Spirit, then, is given to continue the work of Christ. This Spirit will, Christ tells his disciples, "guide you into all the truth" (Jn 16:13).

Third, Christ reveals the ineffable mystery of God in human—that is, fleshly—form. *In Christ God becomes part of creation, God is embodied.* This statement makes two different though related claims. First, though God's being is a mystery and beyond understanding, God did not withdraw or remain in mystery. "Rather, the personal self-expression of God in Christ points to God's ineffable personhood."[35] This pointing takes place precisely in his form as the incarnate Son of God, which is, at the same time, an embodying and a fulfilling of God's interaction with people and creation from the beginning. Colin Gunton puts this nicely: "Jesus' lordship over the creation reveals his perfecting, his being the culmination, of patterns of divine human action begun in those who came before him."[36] Both creation and the work of redemption, then, are seen as from God through Jesus Christ (1 Cor 8:6).

We want to stress the significance not only of the story, that God sent Christ to bring about salvation, but the other side of this truth as well: that this sending was expressive of a previous commitment to creation that is inviolable. As Catherine LaCugna puts this: "That God should be intent on union with what is other than God is truly a mystery that defies explanation."[37] But as the life of Christ demonstrates, this union is such that the dignity and reality of the creature is affirmed rather than effaced.

If the distinctive work of Christ is to reveal the love of God for creation, that of the Holy Spirit is, through Christ, to perfect creation.[38] As Christ offers up to God the renewed life of God's human creation, so the Holy Spirit bears up the whole created order and moves it toward the perfection to which creation is directed. Resurrection, ascension, and Pentecost are the opening up of relations between God and the creation, and, at the same time, a reaffirmation of its value to God.

Just as these events become constitutive of creation's relationship with God, so they are constitutive of our own human way of being in the world. All three of these movements—God's own relationship and commitment to the creation; the work of God in making, sustaining, and renewing the creation; and the revelation of God's love and being in the human Jesus Christ, along with the continuing work of the Holy Spirit—are directed toward the perfection and glory of creation. In some fundamental way these three realities must become constitutive of our own relationship with each other and the created order. For not only is the only true account of God trinitarian, but the only true account of our life in the world is also trinitarian. Catherine LaCugna summarizes this: "We were created for the purpose of glorifying God by living in right relationship, by living as Jesus Christ did, by becoming holy through the power of the Spirit of God, by existing as persons in communion with God and every other creature."[39]

POINTERS TOWARD A THEOLOGY OF LIFE IN THE WORLD

If what we are saying is true to God's revelation in scripture, then we need to draw out the implications of this for our theological work. As we have implied, there is no need to supplant historical ways of thinking with categories which may then appear, once again, abstract and disconnected. Rather, we must find ways of enriching the story line of God's work with these other dimensions. One way of thinking about this is to point out that story theology is *diachronic*; that is, it carries us through time and does well in giving direction to our life in the world. Life in God has a *telos*, an end, that points to the final realization of God's glory in the new heaven and new earth. So far, so good. But it also has a texture, a complexity that we dare not overlook. So we must add to the diachronic method of narrative theology *synchronic* ways of thinking about our life in the world, ways that help us get a handle on our spatial and embodied lives in the here and now. For it is here in this complexity that we must seek to do the will of God, who called us out of darkness into light.

This is a good time to recognize that theologians have given a great deal of nuance to the historical method since the articulation of George Ernest Wright. These can be important guides to the future. The writing of history itself has come a long way since the 1950s. One movement called the French Annales school came to prominence about the time Wright's book was written and focused on *mentalités*, which include the broad cultural context and intellectual attitudes of particular periods. Consideration is given by these historians not only to the intellectual currents but to social, economic, and even the physical contexts for the development of people and movements.[40] Significantly, this movement represents a recognition by historians of the limitations of the generally accepted historical method. As Fernand Braudel expresses this challenge:

> It is possible somehow to convey simultaneously both that conspicuous history which holds our attention by its continual dramatic changes—and that other, submerged history, almost silent and always discreet, virtually unsuspected either by its observers or its participants, which is little touched by the obstinate erosion of time.[41]

We want to ask what it would take to conceive of a theology that takes account of this "submerged history," one that deals with God's interest in forests and mountains and not simply human thinking, with the sighs and laughter of people and not simply their written records.

A related development is a growing understanding of the way people are embedded in traditions that shape their corporate lives and therefore influence their view of things. Hans-Georg Gadamer was an important influence on hermeneutics with his book *Truth and Method*, which was edited and translated in 1975.[42] Gadamer argued that the "prejudices" which we bring to any act of interpretation, far from being a barrier to understanding, become the horizon against which that understanding must appear. Traditions coming to us from the past, on the other hand, can confront our own understanding and uncover truth. The goal is for the horizon of the past and our own to merge. Even more influential in the past decade has been the work of Alasdair MacIntyre, who states that moral argument implies a community in which these realities are embodied in what he calls "practices."[43] Charles Taylor has developed a historical and cultural argument for the development of the modern identity that is helpful. He says that this identity is an "ensemble of (largely unarticulated) understandings of what it is to be a human agent: the sense of inwardness, freedom, individuality, and being embedded in nature."[44] These thinkers have in different ways reminded us of the way our commitments reflect our corporate and even our cultural circumstances. MacIntyre and Taylor have been especially helpful in showing how moral truth must be embodied in the practices of a community and that, in the case of MacIntyre, confrontation is not so much between systems of truth as between moral communities. This is a helpful reminder of the complexity of our human life in a world that enriches our historical understanding. A major element of this complexity is the way human and natural evil interrupts (and corrupts) the stories of our lives. Theology must find ways to account for these "storyless" spaces in our corporate and individual lives.[45]

Our trinitarian starting point and these pointers lead us to suggest three normative categories to use in articulating the theological reality of our life in the world.[46]

Relationship and Commitment

From the way the world and our lives are constituted we have come to understand that the being of the world is in relationship. An individual creature exists in a series of relationships that are fundamental to its/his/her being.[47] Turning Descartes on his head we now know that the individual thinker is not able to construe reality on his or her own but is dependent on the history and culture that lie behind and around. Even psychologically we now understand that individuality is shaped out of the resources and contexts in which we are raised and what, with these resources, we make of our genetic makeup.

Taking our cue from the trinitarian basis we briefly reviewed, we understand that there are two sides to this relatedness. On the one hand, relationship implies the ongoing commitment of God to the world. There has been much difficulty in theology starting discussions about God with God's *immutability*, a term that has deeper roots in Greek philosophy than in scripture. We suggest, rather, that God's being must be construed in the personal categories that scripture uses: God loves the world. Love and commitment imply an active seeking and making contact with what is there. Nothing is done, no relationship is formed, without this activity of commitment. The basis of this is God, who not only expressed commitment in the act of creation but subsequently left heaven, and, as in Jesus' parable, went out to find the sheep that was lost. We humans, then, are created in relationships to which we are responsible—with God, the world, and each other. These relationships can be perverted by sin either by actively seeking to exploit or destroy the other or by withdrawing from the world in abrogation of our fundamental responsibility as God's image bearers. This latter has its central meaning in this responsibility (this "respond-ability," as Emil Brunner put it) toward relationship, both with God and the created other.

Emmanuel Levinas has insisted throughout his writing that "the face of the Other [is] the original site of the sensible."[48] That is to say, relationship with another human being, a bond that is meant to reflect (and facilitate) relationship with the living God, is meant to ground and energize our relations with the rest of creation. This does not mean that creation does not have an independent value apart from human creation, or that, contrary to the view of Cal Thomas, we cannot meet God in creation. But it does insist that all our dealings with creation are conditioned by a human and personal interest. As Michael Polanyi has reminded us, personal commitment is prior to and conditions our knowing. Knowing implies a commitment to what is to be known. Again in contrast to Descartes, who began with doubt, we insist with Polanyi that personal commitment, though it carries immense risk, is the way to discovery.[49] Knowledge is not reduced to commitment, but it is always conditioned by it; it is always, in Polanyi's term, personal.

The reference to risk reminds us of the other side of relationship, which is passive. To be in relation is to receive from another what is there. Knud

Løgstrup, the Danish philosopher, has recently provided much help in understanding this process:

> We know what we call things that happen in the world. In the attuned impression, on the other hand, we are open to a meaning in what we sense and meet with. . . . The mind does not exist without being in tune, without being a sounding board for everything that exists and occurs in the world and nature and in which human beings with their senses, eyes, and ears are embedded. And unless there is attunement, nourished by things in nature, there would be no zest and energy for a single life manifestation.[50]

Notice that reception cannot exist without this attunement, which reflects the created coherence of the world. Of course, we do not always properly appreciate this coherence—to do so we ultimately need to have our blind eyes opened through the ministry of the Holy Spirit. But the fundamental point of Løgstrup stands: this conscious and sustained openness to impression makes possible life together, it is the ground of worship and art. Iris Murdoch describes "attention," a word she borrows from Simone Weil, as "a just and loving gaze directed upon an individual reality."[51] Notice how this openness to what is there, ultimately to the creation and the other person, is founded on a certain confidence toward what is there. Because God is good and upholds the world by the presence of the Spirit of Christ, we can have the confidence that the world is a fit place for human life, and that our taste and our sight—especially our sight—are appropriate means to understanding and appropriating the world.[52]

The fact that relationship is both an active seeking and a no less active receiving indicates that the connection we enjoy with the world incorporates longing as well as calculation; it is a matter of our emotions as well as our intellect. Catherine LaCugna notes: "Desire—for God, for other persons, any kind of desire that seeks fulfillment and consummation, whether aesthetic, sexual, mystical or intellectual—lies at the foundation of what it means to be a person, human as well as divine."[53] So our relationship with another, rather than constraining us (though it can appear to do this) is potentially expressive of all the interests, purposes, and feelings that make us what we are, and, in their intentionality, echo God's own commitment to the world. Løgstrup describes these relations in this way: "It is characteristic of life manifestations such as frankness, sympathy and trust that they divert attention away from themselves . . . in order to direct attention instead out toward the individual's existence among other human beings."[54] Similarly, our relationship with creation provides a vehicle for us, when we take care and work carefully, to become something into which our spirit can pass, just as God's creative work was so "fitting" that it has been indwelt by the Spirit.

Agency

Relationship, as important as it is, cannot stand by itself. The mutual exchange of the ideal relationship, even the intimate fellowship with God, is realized and expressed by our life in the world. Life places a constant demand on us that something be done. Notice that the first request we make of God in the prayer Jesus taught his disciples to pray, after calling for the sanctification of God's name, is that the will of God be *done* on earth as it is in heaven. Relationships and projects are always incarnated in actions. Indeed, some action is often necessary to bring about a relationship—remember, commitment and reception are always active. And activity for its part is always carried on in the context of some relationship. The biblical term for the active bringing about of the divine-human relationship, which had been severed by sin, is redemption.[55]

We have seen earlier that in the Western philosophical tradition what happens, what is done, seems somehow less important than what we know (for sure).[56] But the Biblical Theology Movement pointed out that the acts of God are fundamental to our knowledge of God; indeed, they have a certain priority. Redemption is a series of acts that bring about human salvation. As God expresses the divine mind and will through acts, so must human activity express what it is to be human. John MacMurray argued during the height of the Biblical Theology Movement that thinking is primarily a practical activity—all knowledge is for the sake of action.[57] Perhaps it would be better, rather than to place knowing and acting in opposition to one another (MacMurray went so far as to argue that reflection was a negative moment in the practical program [p. 186]), to see that our knowing is realized and verified—is often catalyzed—in our physical and active life in the world. Thomas Tracy says that we do better to think of the human subject as a "psycho physical unit" rather than, as with Descartes, a mental substance. If this is so, then the intentional acts, what Tracy calls the "projects" of the person, have a certain logical priority.[58]

The reason for this priority is that life in the world always calls us to do something with what we have in our hands or with the person that stands before us. The question *What will you do now?* is urgent and inescapable. And the decline of religious certainties, even the eclipse of intellectual and scientific knowing, has not made this question any less urgent. As Charles Taylor notes, even if people are no longer able to base their lives on ideas or scientific truth, they still make claims to objectivity (that is, there are such things as human rights). So, he concludes, making sense of life must be related to deliberations of how to act.[59] Again the twin dangers of unthinking and possibly destructive activism and the failure to act are both present. But as human beings, agency, often grounded in restless longing and loneliness, is constitutive of our life in the world.

Here our being in the world must be understood in the light of the prior agency of God. While there is active communion in the being of God, this activity is prior to and independent of God's movement to create the world.

Again theology has often misled us by beginning conversation about God with the incommunicable attributes of the divine being. Rather we should begin discussion with the activity of God in God's word and work as this reflects the trinitarian nature. The very plenitude of God's own inter-personal being is the continuing basis for creation. "The God who is love does not remain locked up in the 'splendid isolation' of self-love but spills over into what is other than God, giving birth to creation and history."[60] So God chooses freely to act, and this acting becomes the basis of all human agency, which is always and inevitably contextual. And as God did not reside in isolation, so human agency is also directed outward toward another. Human agency was meant, as the Eastern Orthodox tradition emphasizes, to bring about an embodied mediation between creation and God. As Kallistos Ware puts it, "God's original plan [for] humanity was to act as a mediator and priest, to unify the creation and offer it back to God." But human response was destructive of this harmony within creation and between creation and God. So God's action again became necessary in Christ, who "has therefore come as true man to fulfill the task of mediation that we have left undone."[61] Human agency then is called to respond and to embody this mediation.

God's call comes to us through scripture, but the created context provides the moral context in which we respond. Our agency is meant to have a particular profile, which the scriptures often speak of as obedience. Indeed, it is very clear from the Bible that it is more important for us to *do* what is true than to *know* it. Christ says: "Blessed . . . are those who hear the word of God and obey it!" (Lk 11:28). Again, one would not want to put these in opposition; one must know something in order to do it. But biblical truth, indeed much truth we encounter in the world, must often be done in order to be fully understood. As Brian Walsh and Richard Middleton put it, biblical narrative is of such a nature that it requires enactment.[62] Both the active seeking love of God, as revealed in scripture, and the insistent call of our created context demand that human life be one of active response.

Embodiment

Reference to the enactment of truth and to our created context naturally suggests a third category that is necessary to our life before God: embodiment. Human life is necessarily a physical and bodily life. While this is becoming more widely accepted and understood, its significance for theology has yet to be fully appreciated. The reasons for this are not hard to identify. Our Greek heritage has tended to disparage bodily life as somehow secondary to the life of the mind. In Plato's famous dialogue *The Laws*, it was the mind that was meant to dominate the lower passions of the body. In Christian tradition since Augustine, this has translated itself into the superiority of "spiritual experience," the inward life of prayer and meditation in our heart, over our bodily life in the world. The latter is often considered—as in Luther, for example—the source of temptation and sin. As a result, it has been thought safer to begin theological conversation with abstractions from reality.

But the biblical account of God's work in creation and redemption surely makes this view of things impossible. In the first place, the account of the embodiment of God's purposes in Genesis 1, which is itself a kind of progressive incarnation leading to God's own image in the man and woman, is evaluated by God as "very good." Throughout the Old Testament God continues to indwell creation in various ways, supremely in the Temple of Zion—which is clearly intended to be a microcosm of the whole of creation—where God dwells in righteousness.[63] But now, because of the rebellion of the creature, God's presence must be intentionally directed toward atonement.

God's being at home in the world, a situation which even sin cannot efface, leads to God's full identification with creation in the incarnation of Jesus.[64] But notice how God's human presence in Christ is immediately directed toward the ordering (and reordering) of creation—when he rebukes the wind, they wonder, what sort of person is this? (Mk 4:41 and Mt 8:27). Just as his bodily presence becomes the vehicle of his saving work, so the Reign that he introduces makes no distinction between the spirit and matter. In his miracles and his teaching—especially in his parables—creation and bodily life become the sphere in which his lordship is carried out. Thus the work of reconciliation, which is put on display in the resurrection, involves a perfecting, not the denial, of bodily life in this world. "Do you not know?" Paul asks in dismay at the Corinthians' immorality, and with obvious reference to God's Old Testament presence among Israel, "that your body is a temple of the Holy Spirit within you, which you have from God, and that you are not your own? For you were bought with a price; therefore glorify God in your body" (1 Cor 6:19-20). Christ died not to make us angels, but to make us human.[65]

So, far from being a barrier to life with God, bodily life in scripture has become the privileged vehicle for that life. As the Temple in the Hebrew scriptures is the microcosm of creation, which in its entirety is meant to speak of God's glory, so God wills that the creation be filled with knowledge of the Lord. It is hard to imagine a place in which this theological reality is more important to affirm than contemporary America. On the one hand, fleshly life, as it was in the New Testament period, is belittled by the oppressive sensuality of modern life and its fruit, "recreational" sex or sexual harassment and abuse, which are in fact two sides of the same loss of human and bodily dignity. On the other hand, new supposed communities, called virtual communities, are being created in which bodily life is unnecessary. We are freed from the confines of bodily life to roam the world by computer, and, as we are discovering, to unleash our racist and sexist furies on a whole world of others. Herbert Dreyfus's argument is relevant here. He believes that the distinctive difference between human and computer intelligence is that human life is inevitably embodied and thus engaged with the physical world.[66]

Feminist theologians have done much to remind us of the reality of our embodied (and gendered) life in the world. Margaret Miles, for example, helps us understand human embodiment by her description of the Renaissance frescoes of the Italian painter Luca Signorelli in the San Brizio Chapel in the Orvieto Cathedral. They portray the Last Judgment at the point when the dead were being raised. There behind the altar worshipers are brought face to face with the reality of the Last Judgment in the context of their worship experience. But more than this, Miles points out, they are confronted with the reality of the resurrection of *flesh*. For, influenced by Augustine's *City of God* (Book XXII), Signorelli portrays a non-erotic, weightless, but very social and mutual bodily existence after the resurrection. So, for these worshipers the Eucharist can be seen to provide a proleptic experience of this heavenly and bodily existence.[67]

Signorelli's painting also makes a particularly emphatic statement about the nature of that salvation: it is bodily. Against the background of Savanarola's proscription of nudity and the experience believers frequently had of putrefying bodies during the plague, Signorelli reclaims Augustine's affirmation of the resurrection of the *flesh*. That is, life with God in heaven will not be disembodied but will involve a non-erotic and joyous bodily state. The tradition of "last things" is taken further by this visual statement, and its interpretation of both the Christian scriptures and Augustine. But, as Miles sadly notes, this kind of positive portrayal of the Christian bodily life was lost in the reaction of the Counter Reformation (especially in the restrictions put on imagery of the nude body by the Council of Trent) and has not been recovered.

Our bodily life, then, must be used as a means of orienting ourselves and understanding our world. This means that the senses as well as the emotions are facets of our knowing. Miles quotes Ruth Hubbard, who reminds us that "we cannot sort out biology from our social being."[68] Nor can we choose to ignore this; all our intentional and relational acts are invariably bodily. This enables us to have access to creation that is sympathetic and immediate; we indwell it as our spirit indwells our body. This image of indwelling provides rich resources for exploring and mapping our relations with each other and with our world. Helmut Kuhn describes this process:

> The comparison drawn between the scientist's dwelling in a framework of presuppositions and everyone's dwelling in his/her own body, far from being a mere metaphor, points to an analogy of immense scope. . . . The immediate but indirect awareness which we have not only of our hands but of the whole of our organic body prefigures the scholar's personal familiarity with his field of competence or the statesman's intuitive grasp of the complex situation within which he has to act.[69]

As Colin Gunton observes after quoting Kuhn, because there is continuity between our bodies and our world there is no need for a reason that is discontinuous with reality. This explains how artists think with their eyes and hands, or how skilled nurses intuit the needs of a situation when they enter a hospital room.[70] They exhibit practices that have been so carefully and lovingly learned that they are said to be intuitive—which is only a way of describing a form of life that the agent has come to embody. This is a form of life that issues in a quiet contemplation and enjoyment of the world, a sensitivity to its natural rhythms that is so often missing in our barren busyness.[71]

CONCLUSION

This discussion leads us to suggest that we can think about discipleship in terms of the concrete form of life that it implies. Discipleship is the art of being taught and led by the Lord Jesus, which, for Christians, is the goal of life and the end to which theological reflection is the means.

But this way of framing things may help us see that discipleship is less a matter of what we know, or of knowing all the right things, and more of being actively and rightly related to God, people, and creation. This relatedness has taken on a specific contour we might call a form of life. Pierre Hadot states that all ancient literature grew out of particular cultural and historical situations that sought to embody their ideal of wisdom. This setting he calls their "form of life," in terms of which their literature must be understood. What constituted the life of these ancient schools, Hadot notes, was a set of practices—meditation, exercise, and corporate rituals designed to ensure progress toward an ideal state.[72] The Christian life can well be described in terms of a form of life in which our practices of prayer and hospitality, our worship and our work, have been conformed to what Paul calls "the mind of Christ" (Phil 2:5).

This way of thinking about things also recalls that our life in God is a part of a larger context, which might be called God's project. For what God is doing is more than the "acts of God" and certainly more than the "process of God." To speak properly of God's agency we insist that it represents God's intention to carry through, most concretely and carefully, some pattern of performance, some project.[73] This project is specifically tied to the commitment God makes to creation that leads to the incarnation of Christ, and that is realized by the pouring out into the created order of the Holy Spirit, who works for its renewal and perfection as a fit vehicle of the Father's glory.

The argument then will rest both on the nature and work of God in history and on the categories which we have suggested flow out of this person and that work. It has become our conviction that this is the only appropriate way for Christians to make the argument needed at this juncture of history and to answer in Christian ways the questions with which we began this chapter. For it is now clear that the problem of our century is not secularism; rather, secularism in its problematic dimension is a difficulty that we Christians have made for ourselves. Recent historical work has suggested that when Christian philosophy has borrowed its methods from arguments not shaped out of biblical materials, it has left itself vulnerable to serious attack. Michael Buckley's discussion of the origins of modern atheism makes this point. He notes that in the eighteenth century Christians defended their Christian God without appeal to anything uniquely Christian. The result was they established a philosophy that little by little claimed its autonomy. Theology first generated a natural philosophy, which eventually became mechanics. And mechanics was easily able to deny any theological significance. Buckley concludes with words that we do well to heed:

> The Christian god cannot have a more fundamental witness than Jesus Christ. . . . Within the context of a Christology and a Pneumatology of both communal and personal religious experience, one can locate and give its own philosophical integrity to metaphysics, but Christology and Pneumatology are fundamental. If one abrogates this evidence, one abrogates this god.[74]

The arguments we make for the importance and theological meaning of our Christian form of life constitute a modest attempt to follow Buckley's advice.

2

Creation

God works within limits. Creation constitutes the limits that God has freely chosen. God works in and with creation in grace and judgment. The human creature is called to work with God on this project both with and on behalf of the rest of creation. For it is only in relation to God's presence and work in creation that the creature finds its meaning.

It is necessary to spend some time reflecting on this set of assertions, both because they have often been overlooked in modern theology and because they contain the key to understanding our own human life in the world. Discussion in this chapter prepares the way for reflection on culture in two ways. First, we will argue that it is God's continuing presence and activity that gives meaning to the created order. This activity is evident in the public acts of creation and deliverance but also in the active presence of God in all things. God works cumulatively and non-coercively from the deepest level of our natural life to bring about God's purposes. Second, we will argue that these purposes are both articulated and embodied in the human creature, which God has called to a special partnership. This partnership reflects—"imitates," as the Christian tradition has often put it—God's own communal and embodied being in the world. This theological vision of things prepares us for a fuller discussion of culture in the next chapter.

We noted in the last chapter some of the reasons for the eclipse of theological interest in creation and some of the indications that this interest is being recovered.[1] It is striking that this doctrine should ever have been eclipsed, for it was one of the early church's first contributions to theology, born in its struggle against the Gnostics. At the end of the first century Clement wrote this beautiful hymn:

> The winds from their different points perform their service at the proper time and without hindrance. Perennial springs, created for enjoyment and health, never fail to offer their life-giving breasts. . . . The tiniest creatures come together in harmony and peace. All these things the

great Creator and Master of the universe ordained to exist in peace and harmony. Thus he showed his benefits on them all, but most abundantly on us who have taken refuge in his compassion through our Lord Jesus Christ.[2]

Creation also figured large in the second century work of Irenaeus, who saw salvation as the recapitulation of God's creative work wherein true humanity is restored, a theme classically elaborated in Athanasius's *De Incarnatione Verbi Dei* two hundred years later. This emphasis was continued in the Eastern church, where worship and the liturgy are meant to anticipate the divinization of all creation in the heavenly kingdom.[3] Even in the Western church Thomas Aquinas elaborated his famous arguments for God in terms of God's relationship to the world.[4] And the Reformation placed great emphasis on God's creative work as the context for our human obedience. Luther argued that since creation itself implies God's presence (God's power not being a separable entity), "he himself must be present in every single creature in its innermost and outermost being, on all sides, through and through, below and above, before and behind, so that nothing can be more truly present and within all creatures than God himself with all his power."[5] Calvin similarly argued that creation is the theater for the display of God's glory, going so far in one place as to say, "I confess, of course, that it can be said reverently, provided that it proceeds from a reverent mind, that nature is God."[6] As Cal Thomas's remarks quoted in the last chapter illustrate, it is hard to imagine contemporary Christians, at least of the conservative variety, resorting to such language about God.

We saw in the last chapter that some of the reasons for this eclipse of creation lie in the way that theology has been approached since the Reformation: either as a system of true knowledge inwardly grasped, or, more recently, as a narrated story of God's acts in history. In the latter it is easy to see that creation might be relegated to the distant past as a point of origin, or a kind of backdrop to the "important stuff" of history. Gerhard von Rad, whose influence has been immense, argues that we can really begin our reading of the Hebrew scriptures at Deuteronomy 26:5, where Israel confesses its gratitude for God's deliverance from Egypt, which he believes is the theme of the first six books. To this, von Rad notes, the creation account can be seen as a minor later addition, a kind of theological afterthought. It is the confession in Deuteronomy that answers the question of what God is going to do about this marvelous world that is so scarred. Meanwhile, the creation accounts simply "undergird this faith by the testimony that this Yahweh, who made a covenant with Abraham and at Sinai, is also the creator of the world."[7]

But in our century there is another reason for reducing creation to the study of "beginnings." The scientific view of human origins, which today is understood in terms of evolution—often interpreted naturalistically—has achieved such cultural prominence that Christians have been put on the defensive. Since this secular discussion, given its scientific strictures, is limited to the question of process—How did the world come to be the way it is?—Christians have too often limited their response to answering this (rather narrowly defined) question: Why, of course, the world is the way it is because God made it that way.[8] This is true as far as it goes, but it does not take us very far. The larger theological issue remains to be answered: Why has God made the world this way? And what is to be done about it?

The biblical accounts of creation are clearly more interested in why God made the world and what the divine purposes are for its continued existence than in the process of creation. This, in large part, accounts for the difficulty of coming to a clear consensus on whether or not the Bible allows for belief in evolution. Clearly that is asking the text a question that it does not intend to answer. R. J. Clifford has shown us why this is the case. The ancient and modern worlds, he writes, come at the text with very different expectations about what is important. The Ancient Near Eastern person was convinced that the process of creation involved a conflict of powers in which the most powerful being finally achieved superiority. The modern person is likely to dismiss such accounts as mythological, preferring an impersonal and natural explanation (which in the end may be no less mythological). More important, the Ancient Near Eastern reader (or listener) would have been more interested in knowing how our human society came to be organized in a particular way; in Clifford's terms, how did the world get from chaos to a human home? They would have been puzzled by the modern fixation on the structure and development of the physical world.[9]

As we shall see, the biblical references have a much larger agenda in view than the composition and arrangement of the physical characteristics. The creation accounts are a beginning statement of an ongoing and dramatic involvement among God, creation, and the human creature, an involvement that culminates in a new heaven and new earth. As Clifford notes, the whole account from Genesis 2:4 to 11:21 is one long cosmogony; it recounts how the world—from the separation of the darkness from the light to the dispersal of the nations—relates to its creator and the purposes of that creator. The unity of the account, as with the unity of the scriptures as a whole, lies not in its quasi-scientific character or in its "myth of origins," but in the various ways in which God and the creation come to be related. As Colin Gunton puts this point: "The unity of Scripture is discovered . . . in terms of the limited number of ways in which it represents relations between God, the human race, and the world."[10]

We will return to this point presently, but first we need to say a word about that other modern reason for the eclipse of interest in creation: the preference for theology as sure knowledge. This led, as we noted in the last chapter, to the privileging of the oral over the visual and the abstract concept over image and metaphor. Colin Gunton points out that it was Hegel in the last century who crystallized the idea that comes ultimately from Plato, that concepts are alone reliable because they are purged from visual imagery which is inherently unreliable.[11] We will note below in our discussion of aesthetics what damage this way of thinking has done to our understanding and involvement in the arts. But here we need to acknowledge what a handicap it is in approaching a biblical perspective of creation and, in particular, God's involvement in it. Consider the two words most prominently used of God's relation to creation: *transcendence* and *immanence.* Now these are very useful words that have a long history in the Christian tradition.[12] They stress that God is both above and separate from creation and, at the same time, actively present in it. But while their cognitive weight is large, their affective and emotional impact is minimal. How has this happened? How can we speak of God's presence or distance without touching things closest to our hopes and fears as human beings? Scripture certainly does not do this (these words are nowhere to be found in the Bible). When Jacob awakens to the awareness that God was there with him at Bethel, his response was immediate: "How awesome is this place! This is none other than the house of God, and this is the gate [literally, the business district] of heaven" (Gn 28:17). When Moses asks to see the glory of God, God answers: "I will make all my goodness pass before you, and will proclaim before you the name, 'The Lord.' . . . But . . . you cannot see my face; for no one shall see me and live" (Ex 33:19–20). Is it any wonder that Moses' face shone when he came down from the presence of this God? Notice the way this reality—this awful presence and distance of God—is portrayed: dreams, a house of God, a gate to heaven, a "face," a name. These images portray God's presence in a way that strikes us deeply. Indeed, they remind us that this Presence is one that calls us to respond, even to change our life.

This comment illustrates the inevitable way in which biblical language is symbolic, or better, metaphorical. Obviously if truth is best grasped in the concept, this metaphorical dimension has to be overcome, as indeed it has been in most theological texts; in most theologies such fiery language is all but extinguished. But if God's commitment to the world is intractable, and we are inevitably creatures of space and time, then this language, so far from being expendable, must be the preferred means of communication. Happily, metaphor has come up recently for renewed discussion and appreciation—not least in the 1995 foreign film *The Postman,* where the poet Pablo Neruda gives the postman eyes to see his love reflected in the sea. Metaphor, by a transfer of contexts ("the application of an alien name by transference," in Aristotle's famous definition[13]), helps us "see" things that in their ordinary context are invisible to us. Of course, metaphors do not tell the whole truth, but the part they reveal turns out to be essential. The problem comes when we take metaphors for the whole truth. Descartes fell into this trap and carried Western history with him when he suggested: "I have described the Earth and the whole visible universe as if it were a machine. . . . "[14] Classical physics actually advanced with the help of this metaphor, but, alas, forgot it was a metaphor and took it for a literal description. Science, as well as art, continues to make fruitful use of metaphor, bringing together diverse corners of the world and "fixing a reference" that illumines a hidden part—as the contemporary use of "field" has done. But Colin Gunton's point will take us further. Metaphors help us because the world—as God has made it—is the kind of place, and we humans are the kind of creatures, that can interpret things this way. Gunton quotes S. J. Brown: "Imagery is a witness to the harmony between language and the world."[15] The causal structures and the inherent harmonies are such that certain parts of the world are "like" other parts, and we grope our way to understanding little by little, by holding to the handles that our imagination throws up for us. All of which testifies to the truth of the psalmist's praise:

> The heavens are telling the glory of God;
> and the firmament proclaims his handiwork.
> Day to day pours forth speech
> and night to night declares knowledge.
> There is no speech, nor are there words;
> their voice is not heard. (Ps 19:1–3)

Let us then see if we can come to a clearer view of God's creative work by using the handles that we have laid out in the first chapter. We will inquire into God's commitment to creation, into the role of agency in creation, and then finally the place of embodiment. Again we propose these as normative ways of approaching the ultimate reality that is God, who is in both self-communion and communion with creation.

GOD IS COMMITTED TO CREATION

In the beginning God created the heaven and the earth. With these majestic words scripture begins its account of God's relationship with the world. As often in the beginning of ancient books, this statement is less of an opening than a prologue, or a summary statement of what follows. The creation, as pictured in the Hebrew scriptures is less a matter of beginnings than a theological description of God's continuing commitment to the world. The intention that God has is certainly not exhausted in these first chapters; that does not become clear until we have reached the other end of the sixty-six books. That intention is to commit to a relationship of love and communion with creation, a relationship that will image God's own trinitarian communion. This is the project that God envisions.[16]

Though creation is grounded in the eternal communion of God's own being, we do not begin there. We must begin with creation, as that concrete manifestation of these eternal purposes. That these reflect God's trinitarian character is clear in the account. The first account of creation in Genesis 1, usually considered to be written after the second account and coming from the Priestly tradition, is clearly meant to be a liturgical representation of God's creative work used in Temple worship.[17] The recounting of this story was more likely to have been sung than told, as a hymn of praise to the creator. So the account is an instance of God's purpose of shaping creation into a vehicle of God's praise. Notice two further aspects of this movement of worship. First, the Spirit is intimately involved in lifting the creation from chaos to a human (and finally a divine) habitation (see Gn 1:2). Second, the movement from chaos is progressively, day by day, toward a concrete realization of God's own character and likeness, leading to the creation of the divine "image and likeness," the man and the woman.[18] God also exults in all this at the conclusion saying: "It is very good," that is, it reflects my divine character and purposes.

God's lordship over creation is stressed in various ways, both in the creation account and throughout scripture, a fact that theologians have referred to traditionally by speaking of creation *ex nihilo*; that is, God created out of no previously existing material. While this is an important notion, Jon Levenson, among others, has fundamentally challenged this formulation in ways that are important to our thesis. Levenson argues that the older idea of the battle of the gods with the forces of chaos has survived in the Hebrew scriptures and communicates a critical element of God's relationship to creation. While it may be strictly true to insist that God creates something out of nothing, what is intended in scripture—and what is called good—is "the emergence of a stable community in a benevolent and life sustaining order."[19] But this involved a conscious and determined action in which chaos—hinted at by reference to the "formless void" (Gn 1:2), to "darkness" (v. 4), and "sea monsters" (v. 21)—must be subdued.[20] Nor will the continued existence of this freedom from chaos be automatic. After the Fall, the event in which the evil of chaos spreads into and through the human (and creaturely) world, God must be called upon again and again to defeat the powers of evil. This God does supremely in the Exodus and in the settlement of Canaan:

> Your right hand, O LORD, glorious in power
> —your right hand, O LORD, shattered the enemy.
> (Ex 15:6)

This ever-threatening presence of evil accounts for the close association of Exodus and creation imagery in the worship book of Israel, the Psalms. There God's people in worship constantly ask, Can the creation of Israel, as the creation of the earth, be nullified?

See Psalm 44:23:

> Rouse yourself! Why do you sleep O Lord?
> Awake, do not cast us off forever!

Or Psalm 74 when enemies have invaded and defiled the Temple:

> Why do you hold back your hand? . . .
> Yet God my King is from old,
> working salvation in the earth.
> You divided the sea by your might;
> you broke the heads of the dragons in the waters.
> . . .
> Yours is the day, yours also the night;
> you established the luminaries and the sun.
> You have fixed all the bounds of the earth.
> (vv. 11, 12, 16, 17)

So creation confines but does not eliminate chaos. Moreover, creation's continued survival depends on God's active faithfulness, for signs of which God's people in their worship constantly cry out.[21] The account of deliverance (i.e., redemption) is told as a continuation of the creation story. God's lordship is finally victorious (Levenson prefers to say creation "without opposition" to creation "*ex nihilo*," see page 122), but the created order, through its appointed spokespersons—God's people in worship—has a continuing and critical responsibility to respond to God's loving work in faith and obedience. God works with creation; it has to be commanded, even coerced. The creature is constantly enlisted. This is true especially when the days again grow dark and God's presence seems most challenged—when God's enemies take the offensive. Notice that the relationship between God and creation is not an imaginary one, in which God actually does the work. God intends in creation to establish a communion of such depth and intimacy that God sees mirrored there the divine loving communion. Indeed, as we live out this relationship, that is by our worship and service of God (through Christ and by the power of the Spirit), we are brought into this trinitarian communion. While Christ's victory over evil is decisive, it is not the final one, for we still cry out with the souls of those slain beneath the altar (Rv 6:10): How long, Lord? While we will have occasion to modify it, Levenson's conclusion can stand at present: "As evil did not originate with history, neither will it disappear altogether in history, but rather beyond it, at the inauguration of the coming world" (50).

So the creation account in Genesis 1 (the second account we examine below) expresses both God's free decision to create and the fact that the creature is being introduced into a relationship with real, though asymmetrical, mutuality (expressed by the deliberation of 1:26, "Let us create . . . "). We need to consider this relationship further. We do so under two headings: first, the historical shape of this commitment of God, which we call the *covenant*; and second, the continuing (and intimate) care of God which extends this commitment to the whole of creation, usually called *governance* or *providence*.

Covenant

Biblical scholars and theologians have traditionally referred to God's commitment to the earth and God's people in terms of various covenants, beginning, it is supposed by some, with a covenant made with Adam and Eve at creation. In the past generation *covenant* came to be understood in terms of the various suzerainty treaties that were so common in the Ancient Near East.[22] While this helped us see elements of God's dealings that we had previously overlooked, it also forced Old Testament theology to see this relationship juridically (rather than personally).[23]

Covenant, moreover, as John Stek points out, is better understood as a means of kingdom administration, introduced especially into situations that were fraught with uncertainty, than as the dominant form of God's Reign. While covenants function with relationships, Stek notes, they do not constitute these relationships.[24] This is a helpful reminder. God's purposes made use of the covenant idea, but they went well beyond that idea, or any historical formulations thereof. Indeed, it seems preferable to think of the covenant as a metaphor that God uses to help us understand the relationship God wished to establish with the chosen people, rather than insisting that covenant defines the nature of that relationship. As with Jesus' parables, God may well be saying this relationship is "like" that of a lord with his vassal. But it is also *unlike* this—remember, it is a metaphor. Unlike the lord-vassal relationship, God's covenant is not unilateral, it is mutual. So both parties are accountable, complaints can go in either direction. Laments, prayers for justice, Job's dispute with God, were all entirely proper.[25] What kind of human covenant can account for this kind of mutuality and openness?

The relationship was not entirely mutual of course. In this way the covenant idea, with its suzerainty-like overtones, was helpful. God takes the initiative in relating to the earth, laying out the divine purposes through a progressive and developing series of promises: I will bless you and make your name great, God tells Abraham (Gn 12:1–3); I will establish your house forever, God promises David (2 Sm 7), and to Hosea, "I will make for you a covenant on that day with the wild animals, the birds of the air, and the creeping things on the ground" (Hos 2:18).[26] All of these elaborate and extend the commitment that God is making to what is created.

Scholars have recently argued that the placement of the creation account at the beginning of the Hebrew scriptures underlines God's intention that Israel understand itself in relationship both to the physical creation and to the nations of the world—just as God is related to these realities. Placing the creation account as the prologue of all God's work emphasizes these connections; it underlines the fact that history must be understood in terms of creation, time in terms of space. "What this canonical placing of creation does is decisively to reinterpret the Exodus-Sinai story in terms of a larger more comprehensive metanarrative."[27] God's deliverance of Israel from Egypt and planting it among the nations of Canaan places it decisively in the role of God's servant to the nations—indeed as a people existing for the world, just as God exists in and for creation.

None of this effaces, but rather establishes, the creature's reality before God. Consider two further illustrations. The famous word *hesed,* or "mercy," in the Hebrew scriptures has, since the rise of covenant studies, been understood almost entirely in a covenant context, as covenant duty, or covenant faithfulness. God is, in a sense, bound to the relationship that is represented by the covenant in which God and the creation share mutual accountability. This is clearly a misreading of the Hebrew scriptures and a case of a metaphor being taken for a literal truth. A better reading of *hesed* is "kindness," or indeed that which cannot be accounted for by any previous "contract." It is, as Francis I. Andersen has pointed out, that expression of God's loving kindness which spills over all expectations—it is personal and outside the rules. Mercy expresses that surprise love of God which comes unexpectedly and which is not "owed" the creature—if for some reason it were lacking, God could not be blamed.[28]

God's relationship with creation, at various points, is expressed in terms of God's kindness. But can God's relationship with creation be expressed in every way as an expression of *grace*? This seems to have been the position of Joseph Sittler, who claims that all creation must be seen as the sphere of God's grace. Grace, he argues, is "the most comprehensive term the scriptures use for the reality and presence of the acts of the triune God," and this reality is evident in relation to all that is not God.[29] Granted that the gift character of creation, its need-not-have-been quality, is a kind of echo of grace, God's mercy (both *hesed* and *chen*) is more properly related to God's intentional interaction with creation, which will move it toward the purposes God has envisioned. Psalm 136, for example, chronicles the work of God that displays divine mercy. Each verse lists an event—the wonders of creation, the Exodus, the defeat of enemies, God's rule over the creatures and, especially, God's rescuing activity—and responds "for his steadfast love [*hesed*] endures forever." All this expresses God's purposeful rule, which has introduced the creature into a real (and personal) relationship with God. "Grace," as Colin Gunton reminds us, "is a personal/relational concept, not a substantial or causal one, so that a sharp distinction must be made between grace and mechanical determination."[30] Another way of putting this, in terms of the argument we are making, is that mercy is not simply a fixed relationship but is expressed by God's free action. Mercy, then, is a character of God's project; it is not an attribute of creation.

A second example of the reality of the creature's standing before God is the famous *rîb* or legal charge that the prophets use to register God's complaint against Israel for its unfaithfulness. Hosea, for example, says,

> Hear the word of the LORD, O people of Israel;
> for the Lord has an indictment against the
> inhabitants of the land. (Hos 4:1)

and Micah charges,

> Hear what the LORD says:
> Rise, plead your case before the mountains.
> (Mi 6:1)

Through form-critical methods scholars have identified all the elements necessary to such a judicial proceeding: arraignment, indictment, evidence, verdict, sentence, and so on. But this metaphor hides as well as reveals. When we look closely at, for example, Micah 6, we see that God has been made vulnerable—negotiation is sought which will lead to reconciliation as the desired end (where mercy will triumph over justice).[31] When God asks: "In what way have I wearied you?" (v. 3), God becomes vulnerable—this is a real question by someone who wants to introduce Israel to a deep communion of mutuality.

GOVERNANCE

Clearly a rethinking of our understanding of *covenant* is in process, but much the same must be said for the traditional understanding of *governance*. This theological category seeks to convey the biblical teaching that God oversees all that comes to pass and works in all things for "good," as Paul puts it in Romans 8. The use of decrees in Reformation and post-Reformation theology provides an example of the misuse of metaphor in earlier theological reflection. Calvin speaks of decrees as that reality which God "had from eternity foreseen, approved, and decreed, [which] he pursues in uninterrupted tenor."[32] In a political structure where the sovereign ruled by decree, God's lordship could usefully be construed in terms of "decretal theology." But in a democratic world ruled by assemblies and common law, this metaphor has clearly lost its value. How then are we to understand this biblical teaching:

> [God] make[s] springs gush forth in the valleys;
> they flow between the hills,
> giving drink to every wild animal . . .
> [God] cause[s] the grass to grow for the cattle,
> and plants for people to use. (Ps 104:10, 11, 14)

In the Newtonian world view, the problems, if anything, increased. If, as Descartes saw, the world is something like a machine, then how do we think about God's continuing involvement, if indeed we need to do this at all? Newton's laws, which that scientist believed honored God by underlining creation's regularity, turned out to constrain God as clearly as they ordered creation. God's relationship in that context was primarily understood in terms of particular interventions, and so the problem of miracles dominated theological conversation. But if miracles are a kind of violation of God's ordinary activity—understood in terms of creation's regularity—they cannot be the only (or even the primary) way of understanding God's actions in creation. Miracles in scripture are integrated into God's larger purposes in creation. Let us seek to address this relationship between God and creation by making two claims. First, God expresses a commitment to creation by intimate and personal activity within the created order; and, second, this activity is such that it does not destroy but rather establishes the reality of the created entity.

First, God works from inside the created order. This assertion is based on the normative view that God's commitment to creation expresses God's eternal purposes. In this case God's commitment is a continuing personal activity that supports the created order. In a recent article Nancey Murphy states that there is a way of understanding God's presence and activity which avoids both deism (God created the world and left it to run on its own) and occasionalism (wherein God is the sole cause of all events).[33] Such a view must allow the law-like character of the world (so that science is possible at all) and be consistent with scriptural teaching about prayer and God's governance. Murphy stresses the "law-like" character because there is currently no consensus about the nature of causation among philosophers of science (337). At this stage scientists seem satisfied with saying that there are objective regularities in nature that can be measured and described. But in what are these grounded? Preference is currently given to what is called "bottom up" causality, that events are determined at the quantum level and cumulatively make the world what it is. But quantum events do not seem to obey deterministic laws, and thus there is a gap in our knowledge at this most fundamental level (338). Murphy's proposal is that God acts primarily in two levels in creation, on the quantum level and through human intelligence and action. Since the latter will concern us later, we consider here the former claim. God, Murphy argues, acts in and through the created structures of these subatomic entities to realize their potential, and, in the process, create a universe that, for all we know, is law-like. How do these events occur and determine all that exists at the macro level? God is the hidden variable, Murphy claims. "God's governance at the quantum level consists in activating or actualizing one or another of the quantum entity's innate powers at particular instants, and that these events are not possible without God's action" (342). Notice that this assumes these entities have inherent (that is, created) powers, which are "radically incomplete" without God's action (344). And God's actions realize the divine purposes through making a world that, in general, appears law-like. This is necessary, Murphy claims, not only to the practice of science, but also as a background for the responsible exercise of both our human free agency as well as God's own agency (348).

Notice two further implications of this argument. First, this account underlines the personal action of God throughout the created order, which ultimately constitutes, we have argued, God's intentional purposes (God's project). That is, only through God's active cooperation are the possibilities of these created entities actualized. This synergy, secondly, implies that God's governance is non-coercive. Though all events involve the specific intentional acts of God, this action is essentially cooperative; it liberates rather than impedes creatures' inherent powers.[34]

This continuing intimate relation to creation is consistent with the biblical teaching that God loves the world. Psalm 19 insists that in spite of the threat to creation that sin has introduced, the "heavens are telling the glory of God" (v. 1), indicating that creation's beauty continues to reflect God's presence in the created order. This goodness is bestowed on creation as God's free gift. Simone Weil articulates this in terms of the response it calls forth from the creature: "Every existing thing is equally upheld in its existence by God's creative love. The friends of God should love him to the point of merging their love into his with regard to all things here below."[35]

At the Reformation Calvin emphasized this personal presence of God in terms that almost echo the views we have developed in relation to quantum physics.

> The universe is ruled by God, not only because he watches over the order of nature set by himself, but because he exercises especial care over each of his works. It is indeed true that the several things are moved by a secret impulse of nature as if they obeyed God's eternal command, and what God once determined flows on by itself.[36]

Luther, too, understood the active personal character of God's presence in the creation. He insisted that "the agent who really works in all things is God, and not the personal and impersonal powers of this world which we think of as causes."[37] This faith in God's personal and intimate involvement with created order, we believe, can be integrated into contemporary readings of the character of this order.

But second, this cooperation respects the created natures of these (subatomic) entities—creation is not only a gift (*donum*), it is also a given (*datum*). This respect for the creation represents, as we noted at the beginning of this chapter, God's self-limitation. So there are things that God cannot do with creation. God cannot give an electron a positive charge or make one bacterium do the work of another. God could conceivably do these things, but the nature of the order is such that, as far as we know, God does not do them. This is to say that God has chosen to respect the integrity of what has been made. And as this order becomes the terms in which God works out the divine purposes, so we will see, it is also the material we humans use to shape our particular hymns of praise or our cries of despair and blasphemy.

In biblical terms, then, this presence of God at the center of things sets the terms of human accountability. Even, or especially, when we are most engrossed with our creaturely limitations, we can discover ourselves to be in a relationship with God. No one understands this better than African theologians, who have taught us to have new sensitivity toward this divine relationship. As Kwame Bediako says, the African has a sense of a unified cosmic system that is essentially spiritual, in which the "physical" is able to act as sacrament for "spiritual" power. Seeing things this way helps us understand that "at the heart of the universe and of religion is a divine-human relationship for the fulfillment of man's divine destiny."[38] This helps us keep in mind that the Bible knows nothing of a dichotomy between the spiritual and the physical.

CREATION AND AGENCY

Creation exists and continues to exist, says Julian of Norwich, the fourteenth-century mystic, because God loves it. As she meditates on a hazelnut in her hand, she reflects:

> It was round as a ball, as it seemed to me. I looked at it with the eyes of my understanding and thought, "what can this be?" My question was answered in general terms in this fashion: "It is everything that is made." I marveled how this could be, for it seemed to me that it might suddenly fall into nothingness, it was so small. An answer for this was given to my understanding: "It lasts, and ever shall last, because God loves it. And in the fashion all things have their being by the grace of God."[39]

This love, which issues in the commitment to creation we examined above, serves as a kind of continuo to the cantata of historical acts initiated with the creation of the earth. The relationship God initiates with the creation will be an active one. God surely takes the initiative with actions that have the character of call and promise, but the creature is no less active, called by the creation itself, and the voice of God in that creation, to respond. This call and response we examine here.[40] Remember that the possibility for genuine interaction between the human creation and the creature is dependent upon the order that is built in, which, we have seen, is dependent on God's continuing and active presence in that order. God has made the world in such a way that, for example, the exercise of reason in the form of science has a place and can therefore be appropriate and successful. Moreover, the biblical account implies that in interacting honestly with this order—if we have eyes to see—we ultimately have to do with God.

THE IMAGE OF GOD

But what is it, from the human side, that makes our human response to creation possible? Why is it that we are both at home in the world and, at the same time, restless for a home out of the world in God? The Genesis account seems emphatic that this has to do with God's special act of creation, on the sixth day, of the man and the woman. The special importance of this act is underlined by a three-step process: (1) God's careful deliberation: "Let us make humankind . . . " (Gn 1:26)[41]; (2) the act of creation itself: "So God created humankind in his image" (v. 27); and (3) the blessing: "Be fruitful and multiply, and fill the earth and subdue it; and have dominion . . . " (v. 28). This latter blessing, while not unique (see 1:22), does elaborate the human call in a more extensive way than any of the rest of creation. This creative act is special in its conception, its exercise, and in its end, which, notice, is directed toward the earth: the human creature "fills, subdues and has dominion over it." Clearly the image bearer is placed in a special relation with the Creator, but this relationship is expressed in the work that the creature is given to do in creation.

The *Imago Dei* has been the subject of intense debate throughout Christian history. Pre-modern comment centered around the human soul and rationality as the focal point of the image.[42] Modern discussion began to focus on relationship: with other humans (in Karl Barth's argument that it consists in our sexual differentiation); or with the created order (in Gerhard von Rad's use of image in the Ancient Near East as representative of the ruler); or with God as the covenant partner (in Reformed theology).[43] In a recent discussion James Barr notes that all of these elements may play a role but that essentially "the image of God is not something that can be defined, as if we could point to this or that characteristic. . . . It belongs to the confluence of a group of nodal theological issues: monotheism, creation, anthropomorphism and condemnation of idolatry."[44]

A proper understanding of the image, then, is contextual; it points to the place and role of the human partner in the ongoing creative purposes. This could be understood in three ways. The image, in the first place, clearly underlines the *relationships* into which the human creature is introduced. Barth is clearly not wrong to see a social dimension (in spite of Barr's scathing criticism of his argument), nor is it wrong to see a reflection of later covenantal responsibilities. Richard Mouw helpfully points out that a two-directional sociality is implied, toward God and toward one's neighbor.[45] But scriptures also emphasize the human relationship with the earth. Genesis 2 emphasizes that "the LORD God formed man from the dust" (v. 7), a fact reiterated in Psalm 139:13, when the psalmist testifies:

> For it was you who formed my inward parts;
> you knit me together in my mother's womb.

Since the context of this verse is God's creative work (and not just David's own birth) it seems clear the author intends to portray the earth as a womb in whose depths the human creature is made. This makes the divine commission given to Adam and Eve to fill, subdue, and have dominion over the earth all the more significant. They have been called out of the earth to exercise with God loving oversight of the creation.

This leads, in the second place, to the reference in the *Imago Dei* of God to the *agency* to which humanity is called. If the image does not consist in this work directly, as some have argued,[46] it is that work for which the image has uniquely suited the man and woman. As Harry Kuitert points out, we do not see the image of God in a person standing still: "To look like God has to do with the purpose God has for [the person]. The question, then, is: What is [the person] for? He or she is to reflect God."[47] Individuals realize their character in the active, concrete purposes to which they are called. They are called to work together with God on a common task of shaping the world into a vehicle that suits God's purposes of glorifying the divinity. The honor and glory with which they are crowned in Psalm 8, the psalmist says, lies in the fact that "you [God] have given them dominion over the works of your hands" (v. 6). God's work and ours are fully integrated.[48] In our work with each other and finally with God as experienced in Jesus Christ, we express and develop the character of the image. In the Hebrew scriptures the responsive nature of the image is expressed in the technical meaning that came to be associated with the word *to know*, especially in the context of the covenant. There, *to know* means to recognize the covenant relationships as binding and respond in appropriate ways. As Jeremiah explains to King Jehoahaz of his father Josiah:

> He judged the cause of the poor and needy;
> then it was well.
> Is this not to know me?
> says the LORD. (Jer 22:16)[49]

Finally, the image has to be seen in relation to the physical *embodiment* of the human creature. While for obvious reasons older theologians have shied away from tying the image in any way to the physical form, recently we have become aware that we cannot speak about spiritual capacities apart from their holistic interactions with our bodily life.[50] The Genesis account of chapter 2 goes out of its way to stress the continuity of human life with the (lowest part of) the physical creation. But even more directly, the end for which the image is given is related both to our human seed (which Genesis 5:1 specifically says carries on that image) and our physical interaction with the rest of creation (subduing and having dominion).

All of this is summed up by saying that the human vocation is to realize ourselves in the actual interaction with other people, with God, and creation. This relationship, moreover, is meant to reflect the character of God's own interaction, which we have described above. Our relationships are not only physical, though they are at least that. But they also flow from the depths of our heart, where our deepest emotions lie. This results not merely in a cooperation with God—as Barth argues—as though creation resulted in a kind of synergy. Rather, in faith and love one responds, corresponds, to what is simply the work of God. The image is in fact, participation in the being and life of God, a willing of what God wills and a doing of what God does.[51] In a word, the image realizes itself in response to the call of God.

SIN: VIOLATION OF THE LIMITS AND RELATIONSHIPS OF CREATION

The violence of our world and the distortion of our human relations are all too evident to us. They remind us that something has happened to these relationships. Order all too often has become disorder. In our worship we are moved to confess that we are guilty of doing what we ought not to have done, and of leaving undone those things we ought to have done. In the biblical account this disorder is called sin, and its nature is illustrated in two ways, which turn out to correspond to the different paths that theology has taken at the end of our century—in history and in creation.

The first way that sin is pictured in the Bible is its graphic portrayal in the second creation account beginning in Genesis 2:4. This account follows the typical pattern of movement from chaos to a settled human habitation.[52]

Here the human figure is introduced into an intimate relationship with the creator where they walked together in a garden during the cool of the evening. As we have seen, the close relation with the rest of creation is particularly emphasized in being formed from the dust, in the placing of the man in the garden "to till and to keep it" while avoiding the tree in the center (2:15-17), and finally in the intimate picture of God bringing the animals to the man "to see what he would call them"(2:19). The mutuality that is implied suggests that God really wanted to find out what Adam would do about what had been made. So the working relationships, the call to responsibility, and the setting are all in place for the work of bringing creation to its God-honoring ends.

But a figure intrudes and promises Adam and Eve that what God predicted would not happen, and, in fact, by exercising their human freedom they would actually "open their eyes." They believe the serpent rather than God, and it turns out, at least initially, that the creature's promises come true and God's do not. Where does this creature come from? What is happening here? We do not know the source of this temptation (except that it comes from within the created order), but we can say that the human creatures sin by violating the relationships into which they have been introduced and misusing the agency they have been given. They do not respect their assigned place in the created order[53] and disobey the word of God, by which they existed.

The result is that they are ashamed of their bodies and the earth is cursed "because you have done this" (3:14). As we will note further in our discussion of ecology, the good order is lost, weeds and pain intervene, and work now takes on the character of drudgery. But more than this the disorder spreads into the most intimate of relationships, that between the husband and wife (3:16) and (in chapter 4) between brother and brother, and into every part of created life. The institutions that follow bear the bitter fruit of this disorder, until even the imaginations of the human heart appear "only evil continually" (6:5). The situation reaches to the very heart of God, as the text says in some of the strongest words of the Hebrew language: "The LORD was sorry that he had made humankind . . . and it grieved him to his heart" (6:6). Though Noah and his family are preserved, the evil continues its relentless spread until it reaches the climax in chapter 11 where all the apostate human powers are engaged in an idolatrous project that is meant to challenge the God of heaven and earth.

This account then records the spread of sin in the historical (and created) order. The story, as it restarts in chapter 12, now is one of recovery and reconstruction, for sin has so invaded the created order that there is no hope apart from a new intervention of God. In traditional theology this origination of sin in history has been referred to as original sin. Because of a particular failure in history, in the situation of Adam and Eve, sin has been introduced into the human order and it spreads inevitably throughout all human projects.[54] Sin is something that occurred at a particular point in history and because of that event all the relationships of the created order have been fatally marred.

But sin is seen in the Hebrew scriptures not only as a historical process with a beginning in time, but also as a reality which, according to the account of Genesis 3, spreads throughout the whole of the created order. This corresponds with what the tradition has spoken of as total depravity. This is not to say that the world or humans are as bad as they can possibly be. The heavens, after all, continue to reflect God's glory; Adam and Eve still conceive children in the image of God; Noah can still find grace in the eyes of the Lord. But the evil that sin introduced has passed into every part of creation. We have noted already that family, work, and even the imagination and heart of humanity are fatally infected. But beyond this the curses on the serpent "among all animals" and on the earth eventually affects the man and woman in all the relationships of culture (and agriculture!). Finally, as if to underline the disorder that now reigns, the man and woman are put out of the garden; they become homeless on the earth. So while original sin stresses the origin, total depravity speaks of the extent of sin. The one stresses the historical beginning; the other indicates the extent in history and the created order. No part of God's creation has escaped. As the psalmist laments:

> The LORD looks down from heaven on humankind
> to see if there are any who are wise,
> who seek after God.

> They have all gone astray, they are all alike
> perverse;
> there is no one who does good,
> no, not one. (Ps 14:2, 3)

So we modify Levenson's point to note that evil, whatever its ultimate source, in the biblical view has come to be associated in a particular way with the disruption of the created and social order caused by human transgression and rebellion. All the stories of Genesis 3-11 together fill in this awful picture. While classical theologians have focused on Genesis 3 for the definition of sin, scripture clearly means us to see it in all its concrete twists and turns—the boasting of Lamech, the drunkenness of the righteous Noah, to the nameless and faceless builders of Babel. This is now the story of creation.

GOD IS KNOWN IN THE CULT AND IN CREATION

This interaction of the historical and creational will now continue in God's provision for human sin in the Hebrew scriptures. The historical we can treat more briefly, if only because it is so commonly appreciated. Beginning with Abraham in Genesis 12:1–3, God calls out a particular people that will become the bearers of God's blessing—which from the creation account we know was meant for the whole world. God "bares his mighty arm" and delivers a slave people from Egypt so that, God tells Moses, "you shall worship God on this mountain" (Ex 3:12). He leads them through the wilderness and into the land, as Levenson reminds us, in what is a typical pattern in the Hebrew scriptures (echoing the creation account): movement through the waters to the dry land, into a settled habitation, followed by the building of a sanctuary.[55]

But there are two aspects of this process that, for our purposes, call for special mention. These consist of the two primary elements of human agency, our work in worship and with the earth—representing the two poles that developed in Benedictine spirituality: *ora* and *labora*.[56] First we turn to the *meaning of worship* as it developed in the Hebrew scriptures. It used to be a commonplace among biblical scholars that the cultic ceremonies by which Israel is called to remember God's goodness are historical in their reference, rather than, as in the case of their neighbors, mythological. This came to be a kind of orthodoxy during the reign of the historical paradigm we considered in the first chapter. Ceremonies of Israel's Canaanite neighbors, it was said, celebrated the fertility of the earth; Israel remembered the historical act of God's deliverance from Egypt.[57] There is obvious truth in this, but a closer reading of the ceremonies that Israel celebrated makes clear that they had both a historical and creational reference. In the first place, the very language in which Israel celebrates this deliverance frequently recalls the original creation; both are remembered in cosmogonic terms (see the Song of Moses in Exodus 15 and Psalm 89). Establishing the covenant is like creation:

> [David's] line shall continue forever,
> and his throne endure before me like the sun.
> It shall be established forever like the moon,
> an enduring faithful witness in the skies. *Selah.*
> (Ps 89:36, 37)

A classic example of this interrelationship is found in the passage that von Rad used to support his thesis—that Israel's gratitude for God's deliverance is the theme of the Bible's first six books—Deuteronomy 26:5–10, where Israel is said to remember God's deliverance. As the context makes clear this confession of God's deliverance from Egypt is put in the context of bringing the firstfruits of their crops to the Lord (see v. 10). In other words it is in the context of celebrating the goodness of God as seen in the fertility of the earth that Israel was called to remember the historical deliverance from Egypt. As the confession says, since God has brought us out of Egypt into this good and fertile land, "so now I bring the first of the fruit of the ground that you, O LORD, have given me" (Dt 26:10). Similarly, consider what may be the most enigmatic of all the commands, "You shall not boil a kid in its mother's milk" (Ex 23:19 or Dt 14:21), which is also put in the context of bringing the firstfruits. This reference is now understood to be forbidding the sympathetic magic of the people of Canaan and urging them to celebrate God's goodness by the fact that God had taken the initiative both to deliver them from Egypt and to give the earth its fertility.[58] Finally, the sabbath day and year clearly have their setting in both the deliverance from Egypt and God's creative work. Not only was God said to rest on the seventh day after creating the world, but the land and the animals are clearly to be included in the purview of this celebration (see Lv 25:4–7 and Ex 23:10–12). So in the very celebration of God's deliverance Israel is called to remember the created context in which the people exercise their active obedience and which itself is meant to lend its voice of praise to God. It is the same God they honor by their firstfruits and by their thanksgiving for their deliverance from slavery.[59]

Further evidence for this conflation of creation and history is found in the instructions for the building and use of the tabernacle and eventually the Temple. Scholars have noticed, for example, that the instructions for the tabernacle are recounted in Exodus 25–31 in seven speeches that echo the creation account (cf. Ex 31:17). The order, the formula, the beginning and end of these instructions, and the vocabulary that is used all underline this parallel.[60] As the psalmist explicitly says,

> He built his sanctuary like the high heavens,
> like the earth, which he has founded forever.
> (Ps 78:69)

This has suggested to scholars that the Temple, beyond being the place where sacrifices are offered that recall the deliverance from Egypt, embodies in its shape and function a microcosm of creation itself.[61] The symbolism of the furniture has been found to have a cosmic dimension, from the basin representing the sea, to the lamp stand as a cosmic tree, and the altar itself as the center of the earth. Moreover, the priest in his elaborate vestments, which recall the splendor in which the first man and women were created, stands before God as a representative of all humanity. In his liturgical work he shares in God's cosmic reordering of creation that is intended by human worship.[62]

This same interaction between the historical and creational is seen in the law that God gives the people—instructions Moses says are to represent life for them (Dt 30:19). While the covenant law (particularly Ex 20–23) is given within the context of Israel's deliverance from Egypt and is peppered with reminders of that deliverance, keeping that law will issue in a blessing of the people in the land to which God is taking them (Ex 23:25, 26). We have already noticed that passage through the sea to dry land and the establishment of a sanctuary in the land itself reiterates God's creative work, so that instructions given for the land (see Dt 6:10–15) speak of the restored relationships—with the land, each other, and God—that God had intended in creation.

We have spoken of the interaction, relation, even the conflation of creation and history. But even this way of putting things does not make the case as strongly as it needs to be made. For here is yet another example of our theological analysis having separated out something that scripture presents as a single whole. Because of scholars having claimed the priority for a special sense of history—the acts of God—we are left with the impossible task of putting back together what should not have been separated in the first place. Jeremiah 31:35-37 portrays God grounding his very preservation of Israel on the stability and order of creation.

> If this fixed order were ever to cease
> from my presence, says the LORD,
> then also the offspring of Israel would cease
> to be a nation before me forever.
> (Jer 31:36)

The history of Israel is now the story of creation.

Second, we are called to express our human identity not only in our worship but also in our *work in creation*. When we turn from human work in worship to the direct relationship with creation that is portrayed in the Wisdom literature, we do not find ourselves in strange territory. In fact, James Barr posits that natural theology, which is itself so linked with the Wisdom tradition, in many cases cannot be separated out from what we usually think of as special revelation.[63] Even as the instructions found in the law have large areas of overlap with laws in the Ancient Near East, so the proverbial advice of the Wisdom literature reflects a broad international consensus. Both reflect God's continuing relationship with the natural order. As Al Wolters notes, "There is no essential difference between God's word of command to snow and ice and his command to his people. Whether laws of nature or norms, they belong to his universal law for all creation."[64] So in a wise and careful management of the created order we encounter God's purposes as surely as we do in keeping to Torah. Interestingly, even Gerhard von Rad later came to appreciate the role that creation plays in the Old Testament program, writing his own study of Wisdom literature. There he could go so far as to say, "Yahweh obviously delegated to creation so much truth, indeed he was present in it in such a way that man reaches ethical terra firma when he learns to read these orders and adjusts his behavior to the experiences gained."[65]

The Wisdom movement was spread widely over the Old Testament period and throughout the entire Ancient Near East. Its hallmark was careful observation and appreciation of life based on the order of creation. Life lived in accordance with what one learned by experience was both reliable and, in the mind of Israel's sages, connected with God. In learning how creation works, one is in fact taught by God. Take the farmers, Isaiah notes:

> Do they continually open and harrow their ground?
> When they have leveled its surface,
> do they not scatter dill, sow cummin
> and plant wheat in rows
> and barley in its proper place,
> and spelt as the border?
> For they are well instructed;
> their God teaches them. (Is 28:24–26)

How did God teach them? Certainly not from reading the scriptures (the Hebrew scriptures have surprisingly little to say about methods or principles of farming). No, they learned from watching the earth carefully in order to see how it works. Wolters puts it this way: "It is by listening to the voice of God in the work of his hands that the farmer finds the way of agricultural wisdom."[66]

This is all wonderfully pictured in Psalm 104 where God is shown to be intimately involved in keeping the earth "set . . . on its foundations, so that it shall never be shaken" (v. 5). Though chaos threatens, God is able to make the very winds his messenger—as Christ was to do at a later time. Indeed, all the wonders of earth are carefully described not so much to cause awe at their splendor, as to stimulate praise for the one who put it together. Jon Levenson says: "What it illustrates is the majesty, intelligence, and generosity of the God who authored and continually sustains this fascinating panorama of natural wonders."[67] As in the landscapes of Jacob van

Ruisdael, the seventeenth-century Dutch landscapist, the human figure occupies a minor place in this splendid scene, simply going out to "[their] work and to their labor until the evening" (Ps 104:23). Chaos is here kept under God's control, and even Leviathan, who strikes terror into the hearts of Ancient Near Eastern people, is here made by God to play in the sea (v. 26). But there is something that does threaten this order: "Let sinners be consumed from the earth, and let the wicked be no more" (v. 35). Sinners here are not necessarily those who disobey the covenant law, but those who run afoul of the created order, those who do not know their place in the scheme of things. This underlines once again the continuity between God's historical revelation and the revelation in creation, and that between the Wisdom literature and the rest of the Hebrew scriptures. The link is found in the "fear of the Lord," which is the way the Hebrew scriptures describe the proper sense a person has before God and before the created order (see Gn 22:12, Dt 4:10, Prv 1:7, et al.).[68]

This reference reminds us that a major function of our interaction with creation is to recall our creaturely dependence. We have come from the earth and will return to it; God sends his spirit and we are created and God "renew[s] the face of the ground" (Ps 104:30). Meditation on this fact has given us one of the most troublesome books in the Old Testament, Ecclesiastes or Qoheleth (the Preacher). In modern eyes the book appears to be an extended existentialist tract on the meaninglessness of life. While there is admonition to enjoy life, especially if one is young, the end of it all is weariness and finally death—that discontinuity in our story that results from sin. Because of this, life appears to be "vanity of vanities" (which is the usual translation for the Hebrew word *hebel*, which literally means "vapor" or "breath").[69] But recently scholars have come to feel that underneath the skepticism about life is an affirmation of the order of creation and the assigned "times" that God has placed in this order (see 3:1–8). While it first appears that life is lived within severe limits, it is possible to live life so as to recognize these limits as "proper and needful."[70] The universe as it exists is broken—perhaps "brokenness" is a better translation of *hebel* than "vanity." It does not operate the way we expect it to; good is not always rewarded or vice punished. A strictly rational approach is simply not up to the task. To one approaching it with these assumptions, life can only appear absurd or enigmatic.[71] But for one who understands that living in creation is an art, life can be understood to have meaning amid a fallen and broken order. There is a time to die, but also a time to give birth.

If this reading is accurate, it may be that artists will best understand what the Preacher means. Larry Kreitzer uses Ernest Hemingway as one witness. In his study of that writer's *Farewell to Arms* (1928) he points out the pervasive influence of Ecclesiastes. There Hemingway pictures a wartime love affair between Frederic Henry, an American ambulance driver, and an English nurse, Catherine Barkley. After they have fallen in love in a hospital in Italy, she becomes pregnant and they seek to escape the disasters of war, fleeing to Switzerland. Though they enjoy a brief time together, both the baby and Catherine die in childbirth The time to be born and the time to die turn out to be the same, but Frederic has not been properly prepared for either. Earlier, when she had become pregnant, he asks her if she feels trapped:

> "Maybe a little. But not by you."
> "I didn't mean by me. You mustn't be stupid. I meant trapped at all."
> "You always feel trapped biologically."

What is one to make of this situation in which life can be enjoyed and is threatening all at the same time? Where are the rules for such a life? At the end Frederic is sitting in a cafe across from the hospital after visiting Catherine as she weakens. He mutters:

> Now Catherine would die. That was what you did. You died. You did not know what it was all about. You never had time to learn. They threw you in and told you the rules, and the first time they catch you off base, they killed you. . . . You can count on that! Stay around and they would kill you.[72]

He goes back to the hospital as she is dying. Afterward he tells the nurses to leave:

> But after I had got them out and shut the door and turned off the light it wasn't any good. It was like saying goodby to a statue. After a while I went out and left the hospital and walked back to the hotel in the rain.[73]

It is through death, as the critics suggest, that Frederic comes to understand what it is to love. That there is a time to love and a time to die. As in Qoheleth, this is not a happy ending (unlike the movie version of the book), but neither is it pessimistic. It is about the life that we all know and are called upon to live: a life in which we find ourselves in relationships, in our actions toward each other, and embedded in creation, all limited by the bodily and broken character of life. Sometimes the hope is deep inside, and must be mined like gold,[74] but it is still there, because God is there.

To make these points is not to moralize about life but, the Preacher believes, to see it straight in the face (to "see" is important in Ecclesiastes.; the word appears forty-seven times[75]) and be moved by what we see. Another artist who understood this was Jacob van Ruisdael. His deep and rich depictions of nature refer often to *vanitas*.[76] There in the midst of the clouds and streams and verdant forest, are broken fences, trees that have died, even homes that are deserted. Still the human presence is there, small but determined, going forth to labor. Life is still rich, even beautiful. The sun is often seen breaking through the clouds. There is hope even in a world that is broken, because in the end we can still discover that our relationship to God pervades our human and earthly relationships. It is possible moreover to act out of that relationship. Brokenness is Ruisdael's own translation of the Preacher's "vanity," and it may in the end be the best reading of all. For we too are broken, seeking to make our way home at the end of the day. God has been there in the day, in the brokenness, and God will meet us when we reach home. But this is another part of the story to which we must now turn.

CREATION AND EMBODIMENT

Beyond relationship and agency, it is clearly God's purpose to see the divine glory embodied in the creature. We have noted that the creation account itself is a kind of progressive enfleshment of God's purposes—from the separation of light from darkness to the creation of God's image—until, at the end, God could say of this physical panorama: "It is very good." As Jürgen Moltmann notes, from creation it would seem we can conclude that "embodiment is the end of all God's works."[77] In scripture we might say that this purpose is expressed in four successive waves that incorporate creational and historical dimensions in a holistic way: God's people in the land, the incarnation of the Son, God's new covenant people, and finally a new heaven and new earth.

God's People in the Land

First, God's people in the land are to embody God's character. From the call of Abraham it is clear that God's people were to embody in their families, their corporate life, their institutions, even in their international relations, the justice and mercy of God. In the second iteration of the covenant with Abraham, God begins by saying: "I am God Almighty; walk before me ['in my sight'], and be blameless" (Gn 17:1). This is merely a continuation of God's purpose in the good (blameless) creation, which is summed up in Psalm 104:31: "May the glory of the Lord endure forever; may the Lord rejoice in his works."[78]

This embodiment of God's glory is graphically portrayed in the imagery of God planting Israel in the land. As the psalmist says:

> You brought a vine out of Egypt;
> you drove out the nations and planted it.
> You cleared the ground for it;
> it took deep root and filled the land.
> The mountains were covered with its shade,
> the mighty cedars with its branches.
> (Ps 80:8–10)

Once again the historical and creational imagery are intertwined. Israel is not only to work the land by keeping the law and capitalizing on the earthly fertility but by living in it as home. The land was always either an ally or an antagonist in efforts to glorify God. It would reward Israel's faithfulness by its abundance. The basic meaning of blessing, as Claus Westermann points out is "the power to be fertile."[79] So righteousness is correlated with the fertility of the earth: "All these blessings shall come upon you and overtake you, if you obey the LORD your God" (Dt 28:2). But the land can also punish Israel for its wickedness by its barrenness. If Israel did not listen, all the curses would come upon the people (Dt 28:16ff.). If they persisted in their unrighteousness, the land could even vomit them out as it had the Canaanites before them for their iniquities (Lv 18:25).

But the glory of God's creation came to focus in a special way on God's presence on Zion and in the Temple. The careful instructions for the Temple and its furnishings were all meant to underline the importance of the place where the glory of God's presence dwells. At the time of dedication God promises Solomon: "I have consecrated this house that you have built, and put my name there forever; my eyes and my heart will be there for all time" (1 Kgs 9:3). The Temple then became the central metaphor for Israel's life, bringing together as it did the language of God and heaven with the earthly language of the people's worship. It was the place where those two languages met and fused. Jon Levenson contrasts Sinai and Zion by the differing ways these metaphors functioned in the life of Israel. Sinai represented the possibility of a meaning in history, of God's descent, as it were, into Israel's life. Zion, on the other hand, "represents the possibility of meaning above, out of history, through an opening into the realm of the ideal."[80] So in climbing up to the Temple, singing the songs of ascent, the people were going up into the realm of God to be and dwell with him.

> The ascent of the Temple mount is a movement toward a higher degree of reality, one from the world as manifestation to the world as essence, the world as the palpable handiwork of God and his dominion. [81]

In the movement up to and into the Temple, what is earthly is taken up into what is heavenly (literally portrayed in the vision of Isaiah 6:3), but it is also the movement of God's glory into the world. This is also why the best of the earth is used in its construction and furnishing—from the cedars of Lebanon to the stones taken from the quarries of the hill country. And Solomon, when it is finished, brings into it "the things that his father David had dedicated, the silver, the gold, and the vessels, and stored them in the treasuries of the house of the LORD" (1 Kgs 7:51). The description of the Temple closes with the visit of the Queen of Sheba, representing the rulers of the earth, coming with her great retinue of camels bearing spices, gold, and precious stones. When she saw the house that Solomon had built "there was no more spirit in her" (1 Kgs 10:5).

All of this explains why the loss of the land and especially the destruction of the Temple struck such a blow to Israel's spirit. Was this not the place where God's heart would be "for all time"? As is often the case in biblical revelation, just at the time when their loss was felt most keenly God's promises appear most striking. God promised to bring the people back to the land and assured them that the Temple would be rebuilt. But the terms of these promises were so extravagant as to stretch not only Israel's credulity but even its imagination. They seemed to imply nothing less than a new creation. "Do not remember the former things" Isaiah says,

> Or consider the things of old.
> I am about to do a new thing;
> now it springs forth, do you not perceive it?
> I will make a way in the wilderness
> and rivers in the desert.
> The wild animals will honor me,
> the jackals and ostriches;
> for I give water in the wilderness,
> rivers in the desert,
> to give drink to my chosen people,
> the people whom I formed for myself
> so that they might declare my praise.
> (Is 43:18–21)

Ezekiel sees a rebuilt Temple that included this vision: At the gate facing east "the glory of the God of Israel was coming from the east; the sound was like the sound of mighty waters; and the earth shone with his glory" (Ez 43:2). Clearly, even at the greatest extent of Solomon's kingdom, the Temple and the people were not capable of embodying God's glory to this extent. In fact, God tells Jeremiah that God's people too, and not only the land and the temple, must be "rebuilt" to be capable of properly honoring their creator. He tells the prophet: I will make a new covenant, unlike the one I made in bringing them out of Egypt.

> I will put my law within them, and I will write it on their hearts; and I will be their God, and they shall be my people. . . . I will remember their sin no more. (Jer 31:33, 34)

The Incarnation of the Son

These intimations bring us to the central way that God embodied his glory in creation: the incarnation of God. From the beginning of Jesus' ministry the sense that God was present in creation in a new and more intimate way was palpable. From his name, Immanuel, which means "God with us," to his uncontested authority over creation, Christ represented the presence of the Creator. "Who then is this?" the people wanted to know, "that even the wind and the sea obey him?" (Mk 4:41; cf. Mt 8:27). It is clear from their contexts that this question was meant to be academic. In his nature miracles, his healing ministry, the Wisdom materials in his parables, even in the prayer he taught his disciples, Christ embodied and promoted God's created purposes. In the Lord's Prayer, James McClendon points out, Jesus' interest in creation is underlined in all six petitions. "The petitions declare the divine creative purpose: a creation at peace (shalom) with its creator, a creation that fulfills the divine rule, a creation that blesses God who is its blessing."[82]

Here patterns of thought formed by historical (and forensic) categories have sometimes obscured our vision of scripture. Christ came not only (or perhaps not primarily) to pay the debt that our sin had incurred, to unravel, as it were, the historical situation that we humans had gotten ourselves into. That is part of it, but the larger and more inclusive framework is God's creative purposes. H. Berkhof insists that "the world was created in view of Jesus Christ; God would not have created the world if not in connection with his coming and exaltation."[83] As J. G. Gibbs's study makes clear, the linking of Christ's work with creation was an early and dominant motif in the New Testament understanding of Christ's work. It is important to remember that Colossians 1:15–20 and Ephesians 1:10ff. were probably written while the gospels were still in oral form; they represent the view that God's creation purposes provide the broad horizon against which the intricate pattern of human salvation was silhouetted.[84] Already in the second century, Irenaeus, in his battle with the Gnostics, saw that Christ's work had to be described in the categories of creation:

> So the Lord now manifestly came to his own, and, born by his own created order which he himself bears, he by his obedience on the tree renewed and reversed what was done by disobedience in connection with a tree. . . . There he renews these things in himself uniting man to the Spirit; and placing the Spirit in man, he himself is made the head of the Spirit; and gives to the Spirit to be the head of man, for by him, we see and hear and speak. He therefore completely renewed all things.[85]

And in the fourth century the classical statement of the Eastern perspective of Christ's work is given in Athanasius's *De Incarnatione Verbi Dei*. This description of the incarnation begins with the creation and the fall. Pointedly, Athanasius says that if it had been a matter of trespass only, repentance would have done well enough. But that is to misconstrue the nature of the offense. For once transgressions began we "came under the power of corruption proper to their nature and were bereft of the grace which belonged to them as creatures in the Image of God." Repentance would not meet this case. Who could deal with this corruption of creation, but the One who made all things out of nothing? Jesus alone could "bring again the corruptible to incorruption and to maintain for the Father His consistency of character with all. For He alone, being word of the Father and above all, was in consequence both able to recreate all and to suffer on behalf of all and to be an ambassador for all with the Father."[86] So, in the classical summary, God became human so that we might become divine. And this is done by dealing with the fundamental problem that eats at its heart: the corruption of God's good creation.

Colin Gunton in his recent study of the atonement has argued that the forensic and sacrificial themes that have dominated in the West both need to be rethought in terms of their setting in creation. Even in the case of Anselm, satisfaction has a broader meaning than a simple payment of a debt. As Gunton says: "If injustice goes unpunished, the universe is shown to be an unjust and so irrational place and the God responsible for its order no longer worthy of the name God."[87] Justice, in other words, has to do with cosmic order and not simply with historical offenses. Indeed the latter are significant because they threaten the former, as Psalm 104 shows. These were addressed together in the death of Christ. God's righteousness as expressed in Jesus Christ is not an alien righteousness, as Luther argued. It is constitutive of our very created being—indeed it characterizes the cosmic order. Similar things can be said about the imagery of sacrifice, Gunton points out. Sacrifices have to do with keeping order and removing the uncleanness that has polluted the creation. Christ's life and death then restores the proper direction to human life and to creation as a whole.[88]

It is clear even from these brief observations that this view of Christ's work does nothing to belittle the nature or effects of sin; rather, it expands the canvas on which that reality works. Moreover it expands the focus of that work from the death and resurrection to the whole event of the incarnation, especially as this is seen in its trinitarian context. When God became flesh and perfected that flesh, this view insists, something definitive happened for the healing and restoration of the creation—a fact underlined by the darkness and earthquake said to have accompanied the death of Christ. Although as the eternal Son of God Christ did not have his origin in this created order, he entered fully into it and—empowered by the Spirit—his life "took shape in patterns of horizontal relatedness with others and with the world."[89] Moreover, at Pentecost God sends the Holy Spirit in Christ's name to continue the sanctifying work Christ had embodied.

God's New Covenant People

But this brief survey brings us to the third way in which this principle of embodiment characterizes biblical revelation. It is clear from the New Testament that the reality of Christ's incarnation extends into the life of the people of God who live in Christ by the power of the Holy Spirit. God's people are meant to embody God in a quite literal manner. Consider first the events surrounding the resurrection and ascension of Christ and the pouring out of the Holy Spirit at Pentecost, a collection of events that the New Testament intends us to understand together. Here perhaps is the key to that enigmatic saying of Jesus, recorded in John, that if you "destroy this temple . . . in three days I will raise it up." John tells us he is "speaking of the temple of his body" (Jn 2:19, 21), but the two (body and Temple)—in the biblical scheme of things—are clearly not mutually exclusive. For Christ's body was destroyed only to be reconstituted in the resurrection as the Temple in which believers would dwell—a reality that was constituted by the Holy Spirit on the Day of Pentecost. Jürgen Moltmann calls these events the New Testament doctrine of creation,[90] for in them the creation is being remade. Once again, as in the Hebrew scriptures, the Temple becomes the microcosm of the larger creation. Paul says to the believers, "Do you not know your body is a temple of the Holy Spirit within you, which you have from God, and that you are not your own?" The logical extension of this follows: "Therefore glorify God in your body" (1 Cor 6:19-20).

Notice here the import of our larger argument: This reality—God's people as the embodiment of God's glory—reflects the trinitarian work of God in creation. First, the incarnation of Christ, through his life, death, and resurrection, is that redoing of creation; "the true light which enlightens everyone," John says, "is coming into the world" (Jn 1). Next, in the ascension Christ sits at the place of authority at God's right hand and becomes the source of salvation. But notice that he performs this role "as one who is still on the side of creation."[91] Christ thus realizes the glorified state that perfects God's creation. Finally, and coming from this, the Holy Spirit is poured out (not simply given!) into our hearts as a bearer of this new created nature. Remember, it is the distinctive work of the Holy Spirit through Christ to perfect creation.[92] And so in calling out "Abba" to the Father, the Holy Spirit is expressing the down payment on the renewal of all things for which all creation longs (Rom 8:15-22). This Spirit, Paul goes on to say, actually brings about our status as children of God (and joint heirs with Christ) so that—this seems to be the point to which Paul's argument is heading—"we may also be glorified with him" (v. 17). Another way of putting this is that the Holy Spirit moves in God's people to join Christ in offering his perfected humanity to God to the praise of God's glory.

This corporate body of Christ, Paul calls in another place "a new creation" (2 Cor 5:17), which is being renewed in righteousness so that it may one day become a perfect embodiment of God's original purposes in creation. Meanwhile it is the place in which those purposes are inaugurated. This point bears special emphasis in the light of our following discussions. Robert Wuthnow has criticized both the liberal and Marxist theories of cultural innovation for placing too much emphasis on beliefs and attitudes, rather than stressing the symbolic expressive acts which embody those beliefs, and, equally important, the actual economic and cultural situation in which these were formed.[93] If this criticism characterizes our understanding of recent history, it is even more true of our understanding of the Christian scriptures. For Paul expressed his understanding of the new creation within the constraints and opportunities of a particular cultural situation.

Consider, for example, the apostle's instructions to the Christians at Colossae. After establishing both Christ's link with creation and his lordship over it (Col 1) and the believers' fullness of life in Christ (Col 2), he moves in chapter 3 to the specific form of life that this implies. "So if you have been raised with Christ, seek the things that are above, where Christ is, seated at the right hand of God" (3:1). "Seeking things that are above," he goes on to say, is a matter of setting your mind (v. 2): putting certain practices to death (v. 5), and "clothing yourself" with certain other practices (v. 12ff.). This means, Paul says, exchanging one form of life—"These are the ways you also once followed" (v. 7)—for another, which is embodied in Christ who is seated in the place of divine authority—as creator and sustainer. This involves very concretely certain practices which Paul lists: humility and kindness, forgiveness and love, enjoying the peace and thanksgiving of Christ, even engaging in new marriage and family practices (3:18–4:1). In a word, Paul summarizes, "whatever you do, in word and deed, do everything in the name of the Lord Jesus" (3:17).

A second example is to be found in 2 Corinthians. In a recent study Frances Young and David Ford argue that Paul is making his argument in the specific terms of a particular economic arrangement, that he is using the metaphor of "economy" (*oikonomia*) to underline the new situation in which believers find themselves.[94] The economic situation of that day was of the "limited good," in which equilibrium and sustainability, exercised through prudence and reciprocity, were the only reasonable economic goals. The 2 percent comprising the elite controlled the economy, which left very little opportunity for social mobility. Scholars have recently pointed out that this was the reason Paul continued to practice his vocation as a leather worker. He wanted not only to support his ministry but also to keep from becoming entangled in the patron-client relationships that were common in the Roman Empire.[95] Against this background Paul pictured the "new creation" of reconciliation (2 Cor 5:17, 18). In this new economy abundance and fullness are the rule. Even when we suffer abuse and experience decay, our inner nature is being renewed, grace is being extended yet more and more (2 Cor 4:15-16).

This fundamental transaction of exchange, what Paul refers to as fellowship, is presented in 2 Corinthians through an extended comment on the collection among the saints for the poor brothers and sisters in Jerusalem.[96] This collection features in important places in Paul's ministry (see Rom 15:25–27) and is clearly meant to be a centerpiece in God's new economic order. The believers in Jerusalem were suffering under a series of economic misfortunes, and Paul began, first among the Macedonians (who were by no means wealthy themselves), to make a collection that would illustrate the mutual sharing and dependency that the Christian "form of life" implied. What is the meaning of this? The primary precedent, Keith Nickle argues, is the Temple tax. By this tax Jewish people in the diaspora (outside of Palestine) were asked to contribute annually to the upkeep of the Temple in Jerusalem. In asking for the Christians in Greece to contribute to the needs of Christians in Jerusalem Paul was saying, in effect: Here is a new kind of Temple tax. Here is the new Temple, the body of Christ, sharing its resources for the sake of its needy members, and thus embodying the glory of God. Through this ministry, Paul says, "you glorify God by your obedience to the confession of the gospel of Christ and by the generosity of your sharing with them and with all others" (2 Cor 9:13). And in case the readers miss the theological grounding for this, Paul goes on to say, "Thanks be to God for his indescribable gift!" (v. 15).

Notice what is implied here. In the Hebrew scriptures believers went up to the Temple to encounter the glory of God and experience, through worship, the reality of what Jon Levenson has called the transcendent. In the Christian scriptures the glory of heaven has invaded and begun to perfect the creation in Jesus Christ, the revelation of the Temple in time and space. By our baptism and through the ministry of the Holy Spirit we are made to share in this reality. And this sharing issues in a new set of practices whereby the generosity of mutual sharing replaces prudence and caution. The Temple reality has been embodied, and by the gospel, its reality is extended into all nations and the whole creation. But even this is imperfectly seen, because the one who is our life has yet to come from heaven. As Paul says, "When Christ who is your life is revealed, then you also will be revealed with him in glory" (Col 3:4; cf. 1 Jn 3:2).

Notice that there is a grand "cosmic cycle" at work here—what Irenaeus called "recapitulation." God has given gracious gifts to us in creation. In our fellowship in the gospel these are mutually shared and multiplied with an ever expanding circle of God's people (as in the feeding of the five thousand). These gifts then are returned to God in the form of praise which reflects back to God the splendor of God's creative work—the whole cycle glorifies God.[97]

A New Heaven and New Earth

This leads to the final wave in which God's glory is revealed in scripture: the new heaven and new earth. The work of making the earth a suitable vehicle for God's glory, while it has been begun in Christ's resurrection and in the Pentecost, awaits a final revelation. And though we know little about the details of this event, we do know that it will be an embodied event. Centering in what the Christian scriptures insist will be a bodily return of Jesus Christ—what John calls the revelation of Christ (see Acts 1:11 and Rv 1:1)—it will involve nothing less than a reconstitution of created reality. This event is clearly the end toward which creation moves and represents the fulfillment of all God's purposes with reference to creation. Here Jürgen Moltmann has been a helpful guide. He notes that while creation is the beginning—the first act, as it were, of salvation history—the latter exists for the sake of the new heaven and new earth.[98] This new creation John sees coming down out of heaven from God "prepared as a bride adorned for her husband" (Rv 21:2). That John should apply this language, which elsewhere in the New Testament is used of the body of Christ (see 2 Cor 11:2), to the new creation is significant. For it implies that the creation itself will share in the feast of the marriage supper of the lamb, which is prepared for the body of Christ.

This final celebration also fulfills all that the metaphor of the Temple expressed throughout scripture. John pointedly notes that he sees no temple, as he might have been expecting, for its temple "is the Lord God the Almighty and the Lamb" (Rv 21:22). Nor is there sun; God provides the light by which all the nations walk. That this embodiment of God's purposes involves the complete reconciliation of God and creation is clear from the imagery involved. First, all the honor and glory of the nations will be brought into the heavenly city (Rv 21:24, 26), though nothing unclean will enter (v. 27). But the dominating creation imagery—the trees for the healing of the nations, the river of the water of life, and the complete provision of human needs (no hunger, thirst or homelessness; see Rv 22:1, 2 and 7:15–17)—indicates that at last the shalom of God's rule will be finally and perfectly realized. "See," John says, "the home of God is among mortals" (21:3). Notice that the direction of movement is not upward toward heaven and the transcendent "place" of God but downward toward the human creation. It is as though the incarnation itself foreshadows this final created revelation of God's work, where God's very dwelling is with the creature. There together in a perfected pattern of life all things will be made new.

God's relationship and commitment to creation; God's action in creation, which calls for the response of the creature; and the embodiment of God's glory in creation and new creation; these comprise the theological categories that express God's reality both as we have witnessed it in creation and as it has been revealed to us in scripture. If we are right, they may well provide important clues to our own human responsibility toward the earth and its creatures. We now turn to exploring these implications.

3

Culture

Culture is what we make of creation. Our making is a response to—indeed it engages with—who God is and what God has done and continues to do in creation. Most important, human culture is directed toward God's future, what the New Testament calls the revelation of Jesus Christ. In the meantime, culture is both the vehicle for expressing our human values—where, to use modern language, we "find ourselves"—and, at the same time, the limits we make for ourselves. We focus in this chapter on the theological meaning of patterned human practices—family, worship, work—for it is precisely in these practices that we respond to and encounter God's continuing and active presence in the creation. It is in this human and physical context that God has made himself known in Christ, and it is this human world that God seeks to renew by the pouring out of the Holy Spirit. So we encounter God and do God's will not by transcending culture or by feeling its unconditioned depths—as Schleiermacher and Tillich have argued—but by working alongside God in bringing people and the earth to the place where they reflect the divine glory.

From the beginning Christians, even when they did not have our modern idea of culture, have understood both the possibilities and the constraints of this human activity. Augustine, for example, understood well both the beauty and the sorrow of human striving.

> Neither the charm of countryside nor the sweet scents of a garden would soothe (my soul). It found no peace in song or laughter, none in company of friends at table or in the pleasures of love, none even in books and poetry. . . . These things of beauty would not exist at all unless they come from you. Like the sun, they rise and set. . . . Not all reach old age, but all alike must die. . . . Let my soul praise you for these things, O God, Creator of them all; but the love of them, which we feel through the senses of the body, must not be like glue to bind my soul to them. For they continue on the course that is set for them and leads to their end, and if the soul loves them and wishes to be with

> them and find its rest in them, it is torn by desires that can destroy it. In these things there is no place to rest, because they do not last.[1]

At the Reformation Calvin understood the human instinct to promote and preserve society in terms of people's unvarying consent to what he called "seeds," which have been implanted in everyone.[2] The excellencies of this order Calvin—like Augustine—believed were a reflection of God's presence.

> Some men excel in keenness; others are superior in judgment; still others have a readier wit to learn this or that art. In this variety God commends his grace to us, lest anyone should claim as his own what flowed from the sheer bounty of God.[3]

These brief quotes, which could be multiplied, make clear some basic assumptions about how human life in this world is to be understood. For Augustine and Calvin life was lived in the fullness both of God's creation—flawed though it was by sin—and of God's continuing presence; this set of relationships constituted the basis for all that human effort was able to achieve by its own wisdom. This point bears emphasis because it has become so foreign to our modern way of thinking. We have come to take for granted that the world must be understood, and therefore life must be lived, on its own terms. We no longer believe these things exist for God. Rather, if we believe there is a God, we assume God exists to promote our happiness.

The decisive change in perspective came during the seventeenth and eighteenth centuries. During this period the rise both of scientific thinking and of philosophical speculation tended to see human life in terms of this physical world and its processes. The significance of the transformation can hardly be overestimated. Previously believers, and even nonbelievers for that matter, understood human life in terms of a larger pattern of things, ultimately in terms of God's eternal purposes—what Owen Lovejoy called the Great Chain of Being. The reevaluation began, Charles Taylor argues, with Francis Bacon, who believed that the highest human dignity comes from a transformation of nature for the sake of human progress. In the *Novum Organum* (1620) Bacon proposed a disciplined and orderly management of God's creation, concluding: "Now the true and lawful goal of the sciences is none other than this: that human life be endowed with new discoveries and powers."[4] Goodness now has a human and earthly focus. Rather than raising humanity to participate in God's program, God is shrunk to concern for the "common good."[5]

Christians, rather than holding to the biblical perspective that had undergirded thinking about human activity in the world, changed the way they defended their faith. They adopted the practice of "proving" God from observing effects of God's activities in the world. The universal mechanics that were derived from Newton's laws, for example, were now understood to ground religion. The problem was that though the effects of God were everywhere, God was nowhere to be seen. Newton and Descartes both sought to base their careful procedures on the causality of God. But while the world accepted their procedures, it gave up their cause. As Michael Buckley puts this critical step, "Newton was denied his theology, but his mechanics were admitted as universal; Descartes was denied his first philosophy, but the mechanical character of his principles eliminated the contradiction inherent in Newton."[6] If all God needs to do is guarantee the order of mechanics, it did not take thinking people long to realize that what passed for religion was expendable. One by one the sciences declared their independence from first causes, and, in Buckley's apt words, "the theologians who had deposited all their coin with them found themselves bankrupt."[7]

James Turner notices a similar process in nineteenth-century America, a process that will serve as the starting point for modern reflection on culture, and, not coincidentally, Christian reactions to the idea. The scientific method and allied rationalities had achieved such cultural prominence in the nineteenth century that the temptation to use these methods to assess religious claims was overwhelming. Turner traces the failure of this strategy, which sought to assess religious truth claims by using "standards of judgment structured to assess secular truths."[8] Not only did many educated people come to dismiss the reality of religion, but church leaders, for their part, came to see the task of coming to terms with modernity as primarily an intellectual one.[9] But the God who formed the world and upholds it through Jesus Christ and works to bring it to completion by the Holy Spirit could not be comprehended by the methods that were being used.

This is not to say that Christianity did not have an influence in nineteenth-century America. The second great awakening at the beginning of the century and the mid-century revivals, especially in their social concern and their voluntarism, made a lasting impact on the developing American ethos.[10] But their interaction with culture, rather than embodying a world-shaping view of God's involvement (as their Puritan forebears had done), was often limited to appropriating various cultural strategies in evangelism.[11] And while higher education was still largely in the hands of Christians, the intellectual initiative was being given up. The defensive posture of apologetics that we have noted became symptomatic of a faith losing its cultural initiative.

In the twentieth century the story becomes still more complicated.[12] Fundamentalism continued the older apologetic strategy on an even more narrowly defined front—first defined in terms of the few basic doctrines called the *fundamentals*, later reduced further to the inerrancy of scripture and the resurrection.[13] Consistent with their view that the modern challenge was primarily an intellectual one and placed increasingly on the defensive by the Social Gospel Movement and the moral dislocation of the 1920s, fundamentalists adopted a distinctly anti-modern stance toward culture.[14]

A faith could prosper, as it did in the bible colleges and the bible conferences that grew up between the wars, but it was a disembodied faith, which did not interact with or affect the surrounding culture. Christians came to focus unblinkingly on a few good things (who can quarrel with the fundamentals?), but they no longer had a larger vision of God's creative and redemptive activity—past, present, and future—in the world. Dr. Martin Lloyd-Jones put this well in his reference to the Keswick Higher Life Conferences:

> No Christian in his right mind will desire anything other than true holiness and righteousness in the church of God. But Keswick isolated one doctrine, holiness, and altered it by the false simplicity in the slogan "Give up, let go and let God." . . . You asked me to diagnose the reasons for the present weakness (of Christian intellectual life) and I am doing it. . . . If you teach that sanctification consists of "letting go" and letting the Holy Spirit do all the work, then don't blame me if you have no scholars.[15]

For most of this century, as a result, Evangelicals have not had the cultural influence that their numbers would lead one to expect. But recently an interesting transformation has occurred. Evangelicals have aggressively entered the political and social arenas to promote their understanding of biblical values. They have also been busy finding ways to use modern culture and technology in their missions and evangelism. But because this activism does not rest on any consensus about the meaning of culture and its role in God's purposes, much Christian practice still reflects an uncritical acceptance (or rejection!) of reigning cultural values.

All of this raises a question that will bring to focus the issues we mean to address: How can conservative Christians, who entered the century determined to oppose modernism and all it stood for, end up being so influenced by the culture this modernism produced? We have noted that Marsden stressed the anti-modern character of twentieth-century fundamentalism, which led to its consistent opposition to theological modernism. But scholars taking a closer look at this period of fundamentalism have recently questioned this supposed opposition and the cultural polemics it engendered. In his history of Wheaton College during this period (1921-65), for example, Michael Hamilton argues that Wheaton demonstrates the ability of fundamentalism, like its evangelical forebears, to adapt modern technology and appropriate (especially) the youth culture in its evangelistic and mission institutions.[16]

What is happening here? How did a movement nourished by the separatism of the holiness movement become so enamored of cultural innovation? The answer, I believe, lies in the inability of conservative Christians to understand the nature of the cultural challenge and their tendency to conceive of its problems in strictly intellectual terms. So, while they were able to oppose intellectual modernism, they did not understand the challenge of social modernism. This led to what John Seel calls an "inconsistent anti-modernism."[17] Modernity, indeed the challenge of culture generally, is not simply one of ideas but a social reality that impinges on Christian living at every point. So one can resist theological modernism while overlooking the challenge of social modernism.[18] Even in this brief summary of the issues it is clear that mistaken habits of thought and behavior has muddied the discussion. An emphasis on separation from what is evil has blinded Christians to the ways they are inevitably related to the world God has made (and for which Christ died and rose again); a focus on intellectualist challenges has allowed Christians to overlook ways in which they are implicated in the problems that pervade their culture; and all of this has obscured the Christian call to see God's glory embodied in the social and cultural life of God's people.

THE DEVELOPMENT OF IDEAS ABOUT CULTURE

Culture is itself a metaphor that has come to stand for what humans have made of their particular corner of the earth. *Culture* comes from the Latin *cultura*, which means "to cultivate," and which probably for medieval believers recalled Adam's cultivation of the Garden of Eden.[19] So this figurative language relates, not accidentally, to cultivating or rearing a plant or crop or even certain animals. Like all metaphors, however, it has its limits. It illumines the intimate relationship between human activity and the earth, but because of the unique historical context out of which it has arisen, it has also been used to restrict that understanding to human and social processes. To see this we pick up the story of culture where we left it a moment ago.

In the nineteenth century the scientific method in its evolutionary form raised questions about the nature of race, which became the first business of what we now call anthropology (originally a branch of history). As we will note in the next chapter, ideas of race grew both from the evolutionary notion of progress and from the philosophical idea of a unitary notion of "a people" (coming from J. G. Herder and Wilhelm von Humboldt). This idea of a people with a particular pattern of life began a tradition that stretched from Humboldt through Hegel and Spengler to Ruth Benedict in our own century. The founder of modern notions of culture is generally recognized to be the American Franz Boas, who opposed this notion of an ideational pattern at the root of culture and insisted on the historical interconnections among peoples. In the 1920s he attacked the Nazi version of a "Volk" tradition by similarly discrediting any attempt to explain a people on purely biological grounds. He understood that cultures needed to be studied in all their pluralism, in their particular historicity, and especially in their interconnections. Earlier he had written that the two fundamental questions which must be answered are: Why are the tribes and nations of the world different? And how have the present differences developed?[20]

Because of the continuing influence of the idealistic tradition, anthropologists did not immediately pick up on the questions that Boas posed, though they did begin to develop his emphasis on the diversity of cultures. Bronislaw Malinowski, for example, in the 1940s underlined the multiple dimensions of culture. He recognized that culture integrated meaning and practices in terms of "the community of blood through procreation; the contiguity in space related to cooperation; the specialization in activities; and last but not least, the use of power in political organization."[21] While this implies a fuller view of the variety of life forms, notice that it conspicuously leaves religion out of account.

Finally, in the 1950s, anthropologists began to address Boas's questions, especially in terms of the symbolic and cognitive dimensions of culture.[22] These anthropologists, represented most famously by Clifford Geertz, wanted to explain culture not in terms of some typology, but as constitutive processes. These processes are facilitated by the symbols that cultures devise, which do not provide windows on those cultures so much as act as "operators" in the social process. Geertz claims to be looking for webs of significance, articulated in cultural forms by flows of behavior, and written down in ethnographies.[23] His work has helped us see how practices and ideas are brought together in culture, thus addressing Boas's second question. As Sherry Ortner puts it, Geertz has helped us see the "pragmatics" of culture.[24] But subsequent developments have suggested two areas of weakness in the symbolic and cognitive interpretation of culture, both of which prove important for any Christian evaluation. On the one hand, how do we respond to the first of Boas's questions? How do we account for "difference" in the cultures we find, especially for the asymmetrical power relations in which they exist? On the other hand, how does this difference come to be embodied and practiced by actual actors in the real world?

The first question was raised initially in the late 1960s and early 1970s by Marxist theorists, and later by critical feminists. Marxists asked what power relations are "disguised" by the social relations of the world we take for granted? In theological circles this cry was raised by liberation theologians, who argued that the symbolic interpretation of culture, while claiming to be neutral and scientific, was actually supportive of a whole range of power differentials. In studying how symbols worked in a given cultural situation—how, for example, the church in Latin America had become a socially oppressive reality—this functionalist view of culture appeared to favor the status quo. These thinkers wanted to raise a further question: How can social change take place?[25] Notice that these questions not only ask about the role of power in cultural practices (Malinowski and others had understood this very well), but they inquire into ways moral judgments might be made about a given social arrangement, something social scientists had been reluctant to address. Anthropologists who were sensitive to these questions had to ask themselves: Were the tools of scientific objectivity that anthropology had inherited sufficient to deal with these larger human questions?

A second criticism of the symbolic and cognitive anthropology has come from the direction of the French developments that we referred to briefly in the introduction. There historians, called the French Annales school, focused on the actors in real life situations. They stimulated theorists in the 1980s to focus on the other side of the patterns of culture—the actors who made use of, and often subverted, the patterns that they inherited. This school, represented by people like Pierre Bourdieu and Michel de Certeau, was interested in what people actually do with the resources of their culture and with the practices that develop, seen from an individual and political angle.[26] The most trenchant criticism of Geertz has come from this perspective. Talal Asad argues that Geertz is simply representing the Enlightenment view that belief is individual and privatized.[27] Geertz assumes the priority of belief as a state of mind rather than as constituting a set of activities in the world. But, asks Asad, can the meanings of the symbols be constituted, like language, independently of the forms of life in which they are used (53)? Is it not better to understand belief as a mental state, surely, but also as a "grounded disposition . . . confined to people who have certain social institutions and practices"? (48).[28]

This development has also proven troubling for anthropologists. As the grid becomes finer and tools more precise, the larger questions become more distant and unreal. No one any longer dares to speak of what it means to be human—this is dismissed as an Enlightenment abstraction, but anthropologists have come to the point where they find it difficult even to make comparative judgments about two contexts. For the radical exponents of this view—now called post-modernism—this is merely the necessary constraint of the human situation. Those who have followed Jean François Lyotard[29] argue that what we used to call meta-narratives, those stories that hold people together, have irrevocably split into micro-narratives, those scraps and pieces of narration that people use to get along. But what do we make of this situation if we still intend to practice anthropology? What do we do with these threads and patches of cultures we are left with? Lyotard proposes that we leap out of existing paradigms through "performativity."[30] Others celebrate the diversity by exploring transcultural social processes, "social constellations."[31] It is clear that the older ways of understanding culture individualistically—what Eric Wolf calls the "grammatological approach"—have been given up. This leaves practitioners with a dilemma: On the one hand there is a growing consensus that we are all interconnected—culture has been "creolized" for all of us, as Eric Wolf puts it.[32] Still, with this new awareness of plurality and interconnection, and since we have given up the idea that we share a common story, we do not know how we should relate to the "other."[33] What language do we use to speak of our differences?

A recent exchange in *Current Anthropology* gives a sense of the bind in which anthropologists find themselves. After a brief overview of anthropology since Boas, Eric Wolf notes the advances that have been made—a richer and more evocative sense of how culture works. But, he confesses, in spite of working with a number of different models—personalist, cultural-ecological, Marxist—the *whys* still elude us.[34] All of our models seem to privilege either the zigzags of the mind or the earthbound material processes. How do we bring the two together? Nor do we properly understand how power works in ordering cultures—power wielding in the symbolic sphere is poorly theorized and usually isolated from questions of cultural meaning (6).

Immanuel Wallerstein in his response to Wolf suggests why we cannot answer these questions. Up until 1989, he notes, there was a general consensus that it is possible to ameliorate material conditions and "move in the direction of greater material equality" (9). In 1989 this ideology of liberal reformism (whose roots are in ideas of progress from the nineteenth century), whether of the Marxist or capitalist variety, collapsed. People no longer believe any system (or any alliance of states) can help them, and they are now forced to look for their "salvation" (Wallerstein's word) elsewhere than in the state. As we will see in the next chapter, people increasingly are placing their hopes in their own local groups. As though frightened by the growing encounters with strange cultural practices, people are retreating into cultural enclaves. What can be done? Wallerstein wonders. We can, he notes, demystify the hopes people place in these groups, but this is not enough. "We must also engage in the utopistics of inventing the alternative order into which we wish to enter at the end of this crisis." But as he readily admits, "Classical anthropology, along with all the other social sciences, has . . . demurred at grappling directly with such enterprises" (10).

However hampered by the naturalistic assumptions that have shaped their disciplines, anthropologists, like the rest of us, have trouble leaving things the way they find them. Even the so-called new ethnography has trouble keeping its hands off the practices it so carefully describes. Consider Alma Gottlieb and Philip Graham in their *Parallel Worlds*, which fastidiously places their ethnography alongside their own reactions as Westerners in order to avoid any pretense of a homogenizing interpretation. But while describing marriage practices Alma Gottlieb cannot resist making this comment:

> I was disturbed by the inequities in the arranged marriage system. Women were not allowed to spurn the men who were offered to them, though in the case of strong, independent women such as Afwe . . . they often tried to. In contrast, men rarely rejected the women who were offered to them as arranged brides. But they were legally permitted to do so.[35]

But where does one go to find the moral leverage to suggest so unequivocally that there ought to be gender equality? On the other hand, if we make no judgments of this kind, is it human culture we are describing? Moral discrimination, after all, is part of what makes human culture unique.[36] Could it be that the tools that their history has bequeathed to them, however valuable they are in so many ways, are not up to the job that anthropologists are setting out to do? Putting this more positively, can we suggest there is a more comprehensive framework in which cultural processes can come to focus?

A THEOLOGICAL FRAMEWORK FOR UNDERSTANDING CULTURE

In assessing contemporary ideas about culture, then, we are left with an apparent contradiction. On the one hand, our intellectual history, at least since the eighteenth century, has convinced us that all theological or religious truth can be accounted for by the social and historical conditions that give rise to it. As Emile Durkheim put it early in this century: "Religious phenomena are the consequence of the social conditions within which they are found."[37] Notice the implications that have been drawn from the history we have traced. Religion does not help us account for social life; rather, the reverse is true: society determines religion. From this has sprung the orthodox view that one cannot make moral judgments about a given cultural practice because each culture embodies its own particular cultural logic. But on the other hand, in actual practice, anthropologists cannot help but make comparative judgments about the cultures they study. Indeed, there is a growing recognition that global and intercultural processes are dominating our human situation, so that even descriptive work is necessarily cross-cultural and comparative. True, many anthropologists try to carve out a more modest role for their work. Clifford Geertz, for example, concludes the description of his interpretive approach by saying: "The essential vocation of interpretive anthropology is not to answer our deepest questions, but to make available to us answers that others . . . have given, and thus to include them in the consultative record of what [humans] have said."[38] But while this positivism is still the goal, it is a goal honored as often in the breach as in the observance.

One solution would be to suggest that the basic assumption under which we are operating is false and that culture cannot be adequately described with such parochial assumptions. As Benjamin Nelson has noted, all the major issues facing the human race at the end of this century—social, scientific, technological—relate to civilizational complexes and even intercivilizational encounters. These complex processes, he writes, cannot be gotten at by reference to narrow perspectives.[39] Is it possible our assumptions reflect a rather provincial (that is, Western) way of seeing things?

The Western tradition, of course, has bequeathed us many valuable tools for the study of culture. But the normative implications of those tools have not been adequately faced. How do we gain a perspective that allows us to evaluate our own tradition? What mirror do we hold up in front of our own face? The problem is not to have a perspective on another culture; we all naturally form opinions and make judgments on others. Our problem is to find a way of seeing the weaknesses of our own culture—to take the beam out of our own eye before we address the speck in our neighbor's. Nothing in our "social conditions" gives us material for this kind of objectivity. This fact suggests to Gil Baillie that the apostle Paul may have been the originator of what we call anthropology.

> [Paul's] anthropological insights began when he discovered, with a moral shudder, how murderous he had become in the name of his own culture. Anthropology is simply the study of culture by people who are no longer entirely contained within one, and Paul, along with the Hebrew prophets before him, is its originator.[40]

For Paul, the encounter with the risen Christ and the revelation that this Christ had identified himself with a particular group of Palestinian peasants gave him this insight into his own "particularity." The implications of this alternative assumption we will seek to elaborate in what follows.

Culture as Patterned Relationships

To begin with, we might reiterate the gains that contemporary anthropologists have made in their efforts to understand and describe culture. For our purposes we might define culture as that changing set of communal practices and assumptions that serve as a repertoire of a people's actions and by which they express their identity. Notice that culture is changing, under the influence of unavoidable and increasingly widespread outside influences and relationships; that it includes practices (pilgrimages, games, and rituals) as well as assumptions about the world; and that it is communal, the possession of a people who have a sense of their (separate) identity and express this in patterned action.

Let us begin with the last of these claims. The notion of a "people" will occupy us at length in the chapter that follows. Here we notice that we start our observations and reflections as people situated within a particular cultural situation. Much conversation about Christianity and culture would be helped by the initial recognition that we don't start with two things, something called Christianity (or as Niebuhr put it even more narrowly, "Christ"[41]) and something called culture, which we then need to bring together. This way of putting things seems to assume that Christianity is something "pure" that either will become contaminated by culture or will enter it as a cleansing agent. This approach is simply a version of the purity that Descartes sought in his darkened room, when he sought to locate fundamental reality in certain indubitable ideas. Neither Christianity nor culture can be adequately approached in this way.

Christianity, we have argued, is constituted as the project of God: the work of forming the world at creation, involving a continuing commitment to the creation, in spite of the rebellion of that part made like God; the entrance into its history (and its physicality) of Jesus Christ to suffer from and heal its corruption; and the continuing divine presence expressed both through the historical body of Christ, the church, and by God's general providential work, as God through the ministry of the Holy Spirit seeks to bring creation to its created purpose as a vehicle for God's glory. This patterned relationship is a given for the world (and for God). For my part, I stand in a particular cultural situation, that of being a middle-aged, white male, raised in Midwestern America in the generation after World War II, and committed to being a disciple of Jesus Christ. This set of patterned relationships is a given for me and informs any discussion that will follow. But notice that my relationships are already embraced by the set of relationships that God sustains with the world. This is true whether I acknowledge that relationship or not. I may deny this, just as I often try to deny the fact that I am part of the physical and organic order, but this does not keep me from being formed by these relationships.

It is well to remember these limiting relationships because, as we noted at the beginning of the chapter, they both restrict and make possible our life in the world. Modern people harbor the idea that they can do anything they like with their world. But this is an illusion. We can make something of our world but not anything we like. We are introduced—before our efforts begin—into a set of patterned relationships that become the setting and raw material of our lives.[42]

These relationships are something that I can enjoy; the patterns include spaces for celebration and games as well as for work and prayer. This reflects the fact that God has made the order and its potential good and continues to sustain it by the divine presence in its processes—that is because of the goodness of creation and common grace. But these relationships also cause pain. According to scripture, this is because the patterns have been distorted by human rebellion against God's purposes. We cannot read God's original purposes from the present state of human cultures; indeed, we often cannot make any sense at all of things we come across.

So the understanding of our culture and Christianity's relationship to it can only be approached from inside our particular lived situation. Our challenge is not a theoretical one, how to reconcile the idea of Christianity with some theory of culture, but a practical one, how to respond to our particular situation in a way that is consistent with what we know about God's purposes. We must discover how in practice God's presence "works" in our cultural situation.

For Christians, this response is made in terms of two sets of relationships in which they exist: one represented by their cultural location, and the other by their relationship with God and with those who gather in the name of Jesus, the church. Christians never live their cultural lives outside of these relationships. Notice that because of God's presence and action, our involvement in culture has real theological significance. Its practices will reflect either obedience or rebellion. This is because we are called to reflect God's own commitment to the world in the way we commit to our culture. For Christians, this means both acceptance of its patterns and, at points, rejection of them, when they have been diverted from God's purposes. We might, of course, choose to escape our particular cultural situation altogether, feeling it is either harmful or irrelevant to our Christian faith, but to do this is to deny the reality of the relationships in which we exist and also to deny God's own presence in, with, and under those relations.

The most helpful way of speaking about Christians' relation to their culture, then, is to say Christians live out what has been called an internal difference with that culture. As Miroslav Volf expresses this idea:

> Christians should neither abandon nor dominate their cultural environments. Rather, we should live differently *in* them, and that difference should be *internal*, not simply to a given cultural space, but to cultural forms.[43]

This is because, as he goes on to point out, Christians live simultaneously in God and in Corinth (or Los Angeles or Nairobi). To spell this out we move to a second related claim.

Culture as a Call to Service (Agency)

We saw earlier that creation was not made to stand still but to allow something to happen between God and the creature. In a sense the goodness that was built in was a *potential* good, what it could become. But what it would become was dependent on the human image of God, who was given the special role of articulating and embodying the various relationships of creation. Nor was the human creation given an option in this regard, as though they might choose to do nothing with what was in their hands. As we will explore in greater detail in the chapter on ecology, the human relationship with creation is an intrinsically moral one. We must do something with the patterned relationships in which we find ourselves, and what we do is a moral act because creation is good and because God is there. We are called before God to responsible stewardship, and the call cannot be evaded—we will simply answer it poorly or well.

The forum and terms in which this stewardship is exercised is a particular culture, the human and social world which humanity shapes for itself. As Clifford Geertz puts this: "We are, in sum, incomplete or unfinished animals who complete or finish ourselves through culture—and not through culture in general but through highly particular forms of it."[44] We become human through a set of practices in specific social settings, as an African-American from Indianapolis or a Cantonese-speaking Chinese from Hong Kong. For Christians, these practices will be, as Miroslav Volf reminds us, internally different from those of the culture around us. An illustration of this is found in the so-called haustafel (household codes) found in the New Testament (see, for example, Col 3). Making a list of virtues was a common practice in the Roman world, and, as with the Wisdom movement in the Old Testament, the apostles felt free to borrow this cultural practice. But Paul saw these lists from a unique perspective and thus placed them in a set of relationships that reached beyond his particular culture.

We noted in the last chapter that Paul reminds his readers in Colossians 3 that they have been raised with Christ and therefore they are to "seek those things that are above, where Christ is, seated at the right hand of God" (v. 1). For the Christian, life in a culture is lived in response to the Reign of Christ. The rule of Christ, in turn, is exercised through his people and it is to be realized through a specific set of practices that Paul describes in the following verses. But even where there is overlap with other Greco-Roman household lists, there is an internal difference. Paul here draws on the dominant social unit of Greco-Roman culture, the household, which was made up of an extended family in which each member was responsible to the others and ultimately to the householder. Within this setting the so-called household codes called each member to behavior appropriate to his or her role in the household. Paul adopts the form but infuses it with the mutuality and love that is to characterize relationships in the church.[45] These practices then, as Paul describes them, while retaining their social setting, reflect a new situation: a renewed relationship with the Creator, what Paul calls "the new self, which is being renewed in knowledge according to the image of its creator" (Col 3:10), and a rejection of "the old self with its practices" (v. 9). The new reflection of the image is manifested in new interpersonal relationships (vv. 12-15), a new family ordering (vv. 18-21), new master-slave relationships (v. 22; 4:1), a new attitude toward "outsiders" (4:5; see 3:11), and a new attitude toward work (3:17, 23). In the latter, Paul underlines the future orientation of the Christian's responsibility. "Whatever your task, put yourselves into it, as done for the Lord and not for your masters, since you know that from the Lord you will receive the inheritance as your reward; you serve the Lord Christ" (Col 3:23, 24). Work, family, friends, and strangers were all bound up in a particular set of patterned relations that reflected Paul's Greco-Roman setting. These are not done away with, but they are now pressed into a higher calling—into another set of relations, and so serve the risen Christ who rules his creation. Believers are raised with him, find their life in him (Col 3:1, 3), are ruled by his peace (v. 15), and are indwelt by his word (v. 16). These practices, then, reflect the cultural realities of the day, but they will also subvert them.[46] The believing communities' assignment in culture, John Howard Yoder notes, is to represent a "real judgment upon the rebelliousness of culture and a real possibility of reconciliation for all."[47]

Notice that this new orientation corresponds to an inner renewal of the human heart, but one that is a "grounded disposition . . . confined to people who have certain social institutions and practices."[48] It contains beliefs about the world that issue in a highly specific set of embodied responses—responses, we might point out, of ordinary people living everyday lives. Robert Wuthnow believes that classical theories of social change—both functional or developmental and conflict models—have stressed the more subjective features of culture rather than particular expressive acts. We must, he insists in a reference that has much relevance for the way we interpret the Christian scriptures, pay more attention to actual speakers and audiences and concrete ritual activities. This is because change occurs in terms of what he calls specific communities of discourse, what we are calling particular "forms of life."[49] The social realities are not "expressions" or "symbols" of some hidden values; rather, because of the nature of the created order and God's calling and presence within it, they are instances of that goodness. As Miroslav Volf puts this, referring to Ernst Troeltsch: "The beliefs and practices of a Christian community are inextricably bound to its character as a social reality; when you change one you will change the other too, sooner or later."[50]

Let us seek to put this "form of life" in its larger theological context. Culture, we have argued, is a reflection of the call that God has put in creation, especially as this comes to expression in the commission given to the human creation: be fruitful, have dominion. In the Reformed tradition two views of this call have been developed. On the one hand are those, represented by Klaas Schilder, who argue that humanity works to develop potencies that are inherent in the created order. This view has put emphasis on God's self-limitation, which gives the creation a certain amount of autonomy. The human creature works in this realm of inner potencies, discovering the laws and processes that God originally placed there.[51] On the other side, theologians following Abraham Kuyper have placed more stress on God's continuing activity in creation in the form of what is called common grace. Kuyper acknowledges that God has placed potential for growth and meaning in the creation but points out that we discover and develop those potencies in the presence of God. This presence, what he calls (after Calvin) common grace, especially functions in relaxing the curse on the world—which he believes is not directed toward the world itself but toward what is sinful in it.[52] As William Berends helpfully describes the difference between the two, Kuyper stresses the already of what we have been able to do (with God's help) in culture; Schilder stresses the not yet, what is left to do.[53] The danger inherent in Kuyper's view is the temptation to view the structures that existed in his time as grounded in creation and common grace, and thus as sanctified. This danger was famously evident among Kuyper's followers in South Africa, who used this view to validate the apartheid system. But Schilder's views carry their own difficulties in seeming to cut off human work from the continuing presence of God in creation.

A way forward, it seems to me, is to ground the human mandate in creation both in the history of salvation and in God's self-revelation there. That is, human culture develops in terms of the particular callings that have been given humanity in creation and the new creation, and in the presence of the trinitarian life of God in that process.[54] In situating the human call within salvation history, the terms of "already" and "not yet"—ordinarily used of New Testament eschatology—might provide a valuable handle. The original call to have dominion is further spelled out in the important instructions given in Genesis 2:15: "The LORD God took the man and put him in the garden of Eden to till it and keep it." That this instruction comprehends both human and earthly relationships becomes clear in the chapters which follow where human culture develops—the human responsibility is both to "develop" earthly relations and to "guard" them. Notice that Cain responds to the Lord: "Am I my brother's keeper?" The careful reader will recall 2:15 (the Hebrew "to keep" is the same word in both) and know that the question is academic, but he or she will also notice how closely God is watching over these developments—how closely God's interests now merge with human culture. So the "already" of culture is the necessary human response both to the relationships of creation and to the presence of God. Human culture develops before the face of God. The "not yet" is represented both by the distortions of our patterns, which result from the fall, and by the fact that cultures are allowed to develop, for the moment, outside the sphere of God's particular presence in Israel.[55]

In the incarnation God's presence becomes even more intimately related to the cultural processes as God expresses the divine vocation as a first-century Palestinian peasant. The further call of God, issued by Christ, is represented by the statement "You are the salt of the earth. . . . You are the light of the world" (Mt 5:13-14). Salt and light are further permutations of tilling and keeping and must be understood in the light of these. But they represent a further stage in the development of human responsibility toward culture and the earth that is based on the work of Christ: they represent both a "yeast-like" presence, which is more intimate, and also a renewing and correcting presence. The cultural calling for the Christian, then, is more intimate, expressed through the most personal values. But, more than this, because of the work of Christ, the Christian's impact may also be "redemptive" in a broad sense. It seeks to transform and enlighten the cultural practices it finds—as Paul and Peter do in the New Testament. In the light of the full New Testament message this clearly is related to our status as God's children, who are "in Christ."[56] Our vocation as dominion-havers is now reinterpreted in terms of Christ's Reign in heaven, in whose image the believer is remade. Our work is now to reflect (and embody) his; our lives and communities, as nearly as possible, are to reflect the good news that we are commissioned to announce.

Notice that the principle of cultural renewal is now identified with the gospel: the announcement and enactment of the new creation. Christ has been victorious over the forces of evil and has renewed the creature in the resurrection. Thus culture, like the gospel, has its larger context in God's creative purposes. Culture is in creation. But both are comprehended in God's project, which has been made visible in creation. Human life can now reflect this.

This new situation is made manifest in creation by the Pentecost event, in which the Holy Spirit is poured out on the church. That Luke intends us to understand the "salt and light" impact of this event is clear from the way he describes the results: "With great power the apostles gave their testimony to the resurrection of the Lord Jesus, and great grace was upon them all. There was not a needy person among them . . . for they distributed to each as any had need" (Acts 4:33-35). This was their natural and spirit-filled response to the call to "repent and be baptized" that Peter gave in chapter 2; it is also the realization of Christ's announcement that they are salt and light. But—and this is the critical element—both their repentance and their changed lives were part of the fall-out of the renewing presence of the Holy Spirit.[57]

As the human calling to be salt and light rests on and further elucidates the calling to till and to keep, so the work of the Holy Spirit rests on and elucidates the work of God in creation, and the Son in the incarnation. The Holy Spirit in the Christian scriptures is always linked with the presence of the age to come (the Spirit is called variously the down payment and the firstfruits of this), and thus the Spirit plays the further role of calling creatures toward their fulfillment in the heavenly kingdom. As we sigh inwardly, "too deep for words," the Spirit, interceding for the believer, elicits the groan of the creature who waits for the final revelation, which involves both the redemption of the bodies and freedom from the bondage to decay (Rom 8).

The Spirit then directs the creature toward the revelation of the new heaven and new earth wherein dwells righteousness (Rv 21-22). Here is where the final realization of culture as a vehicle for God's glory occurs. This city will perfectly embody God's presence with God's people in the midst of creation. For this reason the Temple is done away with: "I saw no temple in the city, for its temple is the Lord God the Almighty and the Lamb" (Rv 21:22). Nor is there need of sun for the Lord God is its light and "the nations will walk by its light" (v. 24). That is to say, both the work of salt and light will be complete. Then the kings and the people will bring all their treasures into it to signify the tribute that all the cultures of the earth will one day pay to the living God when culture will have become a sanctuary—that final goal of creation. So the vocation of the believing community to be salt and light, expressed as internal difference with their culture, has finally a future reference, even as it rests on God's previous creating and redeeming work. There is a "not yet" aspect to our work, still a groaning and sometimes a suffering, that points to the unfinished character of God's work. But there is also an "already" to our work. We can already show in actual practice, as Peter put it, the glorious deeds of him who called us out of darkness into his glorious light. We are able to accomplish even this because we have given the firstfruits of that heavenly realm in the Holy Spirit. And, if the Revelation account is any indication, even this work will not be lost but will be taken up into that new cultural setting when God will be all in all. For this we wait, we work, and we do not lose heart.

As in any cooperative project, it is impossible to sort out what is our own human work and what God does through us. This is why it is helpful to think of our relationship as both call and response. We are called to stewardship in creation by God's grace, and this makes us responsible. As we respond, God's Spirit bears witness that we are the children of God. In a similar way it is impossible to say where God's sustaining work ends and the material structures of creation begin. We know that God exists eternally in the communion of Father, Son, and Holy Spirit, but it is often difficult for us to separate out their various activities. But we dare not lose sight of the fact that just as we are fully immersed in the processes of creation so we are being brought fully into the life of God as we worship the Father, through the work of the Son, by the power of the Holy Spirit. There is no incompatibility between these projects.

Culture as Sanctuary (Embodiment)

This last point brings us to the final assertion about culture: the promises of God imply that human cultures themselves—in their practices and their artifacts—are to be arenas in which God's glory is made manifest. We have seen in our discussion of creation that there is a clear pattern in the development of creation: first, there is the defeat of the powers tending to chaos; and then there is the establishment of dry ground and the building of a sanctuary. That this is the pattern of the history that God intends for creation is clear from the first and last books in the Bible: the account begins in a garden specially prepared for human occupancy and ends in a city into which the honor and glory of the nations are brought and which incorporates a garden in its center. Christians, especially under the influence of our Western Greek heritage, have not seen their bodily and cultural lives as having very much importance for their Christian discipleship. They have sought to escape from these either by creating an apparently Christian alternative (which as we have seen may turn out to reflect some of the worst aspects of the culture they sought to flee), or they have been content to bide their time until the Lord comes to take them home to heaven, feeling no sense of responsibility for the world in which God has placed them.

Stanley Hauerwas and William Willimon have given us a fresh and lively reading of Peter's description of Christians as aliens and exiles.[58] Our job as Christians, they argue, is not to respond to the questions the world poses, but as citizens of the heavenly kingdom to be the community of the faithful in the midst of a wicked generation. The overriding political task of the church is to be the community of the cross rather than developing particular social or political strategies to influence the world (47). They worry that Christian strategies designed to affect the world are more effective in transforming the gospel than the world (22). There is much that we might learn from this argument, especially in the affirmation of the central role of the body of Christ. And, as we have seen, their fears of Christians being coopted are not ungrounded. But it is impossible either for the Christian or for the church not to play some role in the culture where it resides. Because of the relationships within creation and with God in which we exist, religion cannot be reduced to the private sphere. It exists, in fact, on a continuum from the private to the public spheres.[59] In a way Hauerwas and Willimon are right in what they affirm, then, but mistaken in what they deny. We are called to be the community of the cross in the broken and fallen world, but we are also called to make our culturally embedded presence constructive and considered. While helpful in many respects, it is tempting to read their argument as a sophisticated version of our Western tendency to flee the world.[60]

While a superficial reading of 1 Peter (that most apocalyptic of all the New Testament books) might suggest that our responsibility to our culture is limited to being God's people, a closer look gives a different picture. Rather than simply being a compliant presence accepting "the authority of every human situation" (2:13), even taking persecution when it is unjustly administered, Christians, in Peter's view, have a particular purpose for existing fully as members of a given culture. They are called distinctly to be a "people," a "holy nation" (2:9-10), so as to "proclaim the mighty acts of him who called you out of darkness into his marvelous light" (2:9). Though fully embedded in the culture—Peter urges them to honor the emperor, be members of a family, accept authority, and honor everyone—the Christian works from a different frame of reference. Peter says that God the Father "has given us a new birth into a living hope through the resurrection of Jesus Christ from the dead" (1:3). That hope invigorates all that we do as members of a given culture. In Peter, the new set of relationships represented by this hope issues in a wide range of honorable works (2:12), which will call forth a variety of responses: some will "blaspheme" (4:4), others will glorify God (2:12), still others will be silenced by good behavior (2:15) or even won over (2:12). But in every case, even with our "alien" perspective, we fully share the culture, and our good works, in their internal difference, have a clear political and social impact on those around us. This is because in our solidarity with our neighbors our believing community exists not only in front of them but, in an important sense, among them and for their sake.[61]

We have been arguing that God's creative and redemptive project calls for a response that is inevitably physical and embodied. Religion throughout history has had its material dimension. The tendency of recent Protestants to disparage this aspect of their faith has not kept them from displaying their faith in concrete and material forms. Colleen McDannell has recently studied these material forms, from the pictures that hang on people's walls to the objects and symbols they wear on their clothes. She maintains that "people create and maintain spiritual ideals through the exchange of goods and the construction of spaces."[62] Popular art and Christian artifacts serve as important means not only for symbolizing faith but deepening (or cheapening) it in various ways. Again, the issue is not whether our faith will be embodied in material forms, but how faithfully and constructively this dimension will reflect God's presence in our human communities.

The body of Christ exists as a part of a cultural and political situation because God is interested in these spheres. God's good creation and what humans have made of it, although painfully distorted by human sin, exists in hope. As Paul says, it waits for human redemption because its subjection to futility is "in hope that the creation itself will be set free from its bondage to decay and will obtain the glorious liberty of the children of God" (Rom 8:20-21). We will note later the implication of this for our responsibility toward the earth, but here we notice the interconnection of the goal of creation and that of humanity—one will not reach its end apart from the other. This has clear implication for human culture, which is the place where these streams of God's work flow together. We wait as we work, in hope.

Meanwhile, as God's special creation we humans, especially those in touch with the Creator and Sustainer of things, ought to pay attention to the value of living embodied and located lives. The rootlessness of modern life, exacerbated by the communication and transportation revolution, has created profound and widespread anomie, that cultural (even cosmic) sense of disintegration. Relationships with the earth and with others are treated like interchangeable and disposable parts. We are moving away from our natural rhythms. As Sven Birkherts puts this, "We are becoming shallower. . . . We have turned from depth, from the Judeo-Christian premise of unfathomable mystery, and are adapting ourselves to the ersatz security of a vast lateral connectedness."[63] But we are created for God, and that means for each other and even for the earth. There is much talk these days about virtual communities in cyberspace. Clearly these opportunities are not going to go away and can be taken up and critically used by Christians. But our argument so far has made it clear that any value the Internet might have works off the spiritual capital of actual communities and relations between embodied persons. It cannot replace these. It means further that we are called to cultivate a sense of physical place that contributes to human well-being, because such a place exhibits our created relations with the earth. Place, as poet Kathleen Norris puts it, is the crucible for a people. This process of making a people takes time; roots must be allowed to go deeply into the soil, both literally and figuratively. And this process is ultimately a spiritual one. "You have only to let the place happen to you . . . the loneliness, the silence, the poverty, the futility, indeed the silliness of your life."[64]

But we remember also that it is not some New Age view of the earth that gives us this sensitivity to our cultural and earthly setting. As in the case of Norris, we honor the earth and our place on it because God made it good, Christ sustains it, and the Holy Spirit's presence broods over it. This is why I am attracted to J. H. Bavinck's notion of "possessio" as the clearest imagery for the Christian attitude toward culture. The Christian life does not accommodate, or contextualize itself to "pagan" culture, in the process of translation it takes culture in possession and thereby makes it into something new, transforms it. For

> Christ takes the life a people in his hands, he renews and re-establishes the distorted and the deteriorated; he fills each thing, each word, and each practice with a new meaning and gives it a new direction. Such is . . . the legitimate taking possession of something by him to whom all power is given in heaven and on earth.[65]

This possession takes place in terms of a form of life that Christians display in and through the cultural patterns of their own culture. Their differences will not be in using another language or another set of practices but in employing their mother tongue and their familiar habits in the service of the Reign of Christ as energized by the Spirit. They will live in houses and go to work every day like everyone else, but their houses will be centers of prayer and hospitality, places where the peace of Christ can be felt; their presence in the work place will be humanizing and hopeful. As our references to the New Testament show, Christians have had this sense of Christlike cultured presence from the beginning. In the second century *Letter to Diognetus* Christians are described this way:

> They dwell in their own countries, but only as sojourners; they bear their share in all things as citizens, and they endure all hardships as strangers. Every foreign country is a fatherland to them, and every fatherland is foreign. They marry like all other(s); but do not cast away their offspring. They have meals in common but not their wives. They find themselves in the flesh, and yet they live not after the flesh. Their existence is on earth, but their citizenship is in heaven.[66]

In order to test these claims we refer to two important discussions of culture that have recently occupied the attention of Evangelicals: the contextualization discussion of the 1970s and 1980s, and the more recent debates that have come to be called the culture wars.

Contextualization or Rereading of Scripture?

The contextualization discussions began largely in missiological circles and concerned the use of cultural forms in the presentation of the gospel. Missionary leaders seized on the term *contextualization* as an apt description of the dynamic process of cultural change that was missing in the older term *indigenization*. Many felt it better suited the dynamic way that scripture was interpreted in the cultures where the gospel was proclaimed. In 1979 a conference was sponsored by the Lausanne Committee to explore these issues. In the preface to the collected papers from this conference John Stott noted two questions that concerned participants. One had to do with how a person from one culture "takes truth out of the Bible which was addressed to people in a second culture, and communicates to people who belong to a third culture, without either falsifying the message or rendering it unintelligible." The second question asks how hearers of the message relate it to their own culture in their corporate lives.[67]

Among Roman Catholic missiologists a similar discussion, begun during the Second Vatican Council (1961-65), led to the widespread use of the term *inculturation* for a similar process. Hervé Carrier has recently defined this as "the effort to inject Christ's message into a given socio-cultural milieu, thereby summoning that milieu to grow in accordance with its own values, so long as they can be reconciled with the Gospel message."[68] These discussions have learned much from recent anthropology and represent an important advance in Christian understanding of culture—missionaries trained since this time, whether Protestant or Catholic, have become thoroughly conversant in the issues involved in cross-cultural communication. But a closer examination of the discussion leads one to conclude that—at least in evangelical circles—it has not led to consensus on the use of culture in mission or even to any Christian understanding of culture itself. While the conversation did much to help missionaries in training understand the cultures to which they were sent, too much was covered by the term *contextualization*; participants have not come to consensus about either the process or its terms.[69]

The reasons for the weakness of these discussions lie in two related directions. First both *inculturation* and *contextualization* imply that there is some entity—called either the gospel or Christ's message—that is not already inculturated and that needs to be introduced into a given culture. We have now seen that this mistake has a long history in the way that Western theology has been conceived as sure knowledge. This "sure knowledge" is not encumbered with any social or cultural trappings, which are understood to be less important, if not positively harmful. But whenever the question is asked as to what exactly Christ's message includes, the debate begins. For the answer given will surely reflect a previously inculturated understanding of what the "really important" elements of the gospel are. Of course, having persuaded themselves that their version of "sure knowledge" is the right one, most missionary agents have been blind to their own social and cultural conditioning.

This is bad enough, but the second effect is even worse. Since this "sure knowledge" must be introduced from outside the culture—in recent history largely from the West—the implication is given that this "outside" form is normative. Christianity is thus immediately perceived as a foreign religion, one that stands in judgment on all the religious and moral impulses already present in a given culture.[70] Of course, as we have argued, the gospel will judge (and redeem) elements of culture, but not in terms of some other inculturated form of the faith. Here is where the contextualization debate proved unhelpful, for it was not able to define either what was contextualized or who was doing the work. Is there another way to conceive of the relationship between Christianity and cultures?

The most helpful recent treatment of these issues is that of Lamin Sanneh in *Translating the Message: The Missionary Impact on Culture.*[71] Sanneh proposes that we speak about the *translatability* of the gospel rather than *contextualization* or some other term. He argues that it is the process of translation of scriptures into vernacular languages that has unleashed the dynamic of the gospel. In his frontispiece Sanneh notes: "The issue that frequently escapes the dragnet of the historian is the cumulative capital Christianity has derived from the common language of ordinary people" (vi). How does this capital develop? Sanneh concludes, "Translatability is the source of the success of Christianity across cultures" (51). His is a complex and illuminating argument, but we note that Sanneh stresses two aspects of the process of translation.

> One was the resolve to relativize its Judaic roots, with the consequence that it promoted significant aspects of those roots. The other was to destigmatize Gentile culture and adopt that culture as a natural extension of the life of the new religion. (1)

Let us explore briefly these two movements. In the first place, the process of translation relativizes the culture from which the gospel comes. Of course, missionaries have been consistently criticized for bringing their own Western interpretations with them, and Sanneh is not blind to this problem. But the process of translation into the vernacular is such that "in time Africans could complain about the unacceptable degree of Westernization in the church, believing, with justice, that they have support for their position in the highest quarters of scriptural Christianity itself" (174). As we have argued, cultural understanding begins by seeing the weaknesses of our own culture—the beam in our own eye. As Christianity takes on a new (vernacular) form, it carries on the critique of the Hebrew prophets and of Paul—it becomes, in other words, critical of the very forms of life in which it is conveyed. Just as there are no cultural barriers to the transmission of God's word, the process of translation shows that there is no cultural "center" to

God's work of creation and redemption. Cultural innovations are now subject to vernacular (and ultimately) scriptural vetting. "In this way, the Gospel is potentially capable of transcending the cultural inhibitions of the translator and taking root in fresh soil, a piece of transplanting that will in time come to challenge the presuppositions of the translator" (53).

In the second place, the process of translating scripture into the vernacular "destigmatizes" and "energizes" the culture in which it takes root. Sanneh's discussion ranges widely throughout Christian history and the modern mission movement to demonstrate the correlation between the reception of the scripture in the vernacular and the renewal of those cultures. In the regions of Africa where traditional religions were widespread, for example, translation was able to find ready to hand ideas and practices that could be used to express the reality of God's love for the world:

> It was by such a natural congruence with the vernacular that the Christian impact sent sound waves reverberating throughout the land, and there were numerous communities of people for whom the message of the new prophets came as confirmation of old dreams. (184)[72]

The importance of this argument lies in the unique role it gives to scripture in the cultural reception of the gospel. There is no uncertainty about what is being inserted into a culture: it is what Christians call the word of God. In the Protestant view scripture is the authoritative witness to God's purposes in creation and the new creation. Moreover, as all interpreters of scripture understand, the truth of scripture comes to us in a form that is already inculturated in Hebrew and Greco-Roman culture, so the process of translation always involves finding equivalent patterns and structures in scripture and in the receiving culture. In this way the process of translation is a part of the larger process of our human interpretation of God's truth in the real life setting of our family, work, and school.

Notice we have answers for both of John Stott's original questions. First, the Bible is translated into another culture as it is reread (and reenacted) in that culture. *Rereading* is a better term than *contextualization* because it underlines the larger process by which scriptures are received and understood in every setting—a process that judges the missionaries no less than their audience. The term *rereading* comes from liberation theologians who emphasized the impact of a fresh reading of scripture from the perspective of the powerless, but it can be applied more generally to any new situated reading. And all readings are situated—the missionaries' no less than their audience's. As fresh readings (and new "enactments") take place in new churches, more than once missionaries have, in their own rereading of scripture, begun to see things they had previously overlooked.

The answer to Stott's second question is implicit in what we are saying: in every case the learners relate scripture to their corporate lives by reenacting the truth they understand. Notice the agents of this work are always those who are receiving and applying God's word in their own setting. The richness of the vernacular interpretations of God's truth adds substance to Paul's observation in Ephesians 4. There he insists that coming to clarity in the body is a matter of making use of all the gifts the risen Christ has poured out on his people. The goal of this process is "to equip the saints for the work of ministry, for building up the body of Christ, until all of us come to the unity of the faith and of the knowledge of the Son of God, to maturity, to the measure of the full stature of Christ" (Eph 4:12, 13).

This passage is very important to the argument that we are making. Notice that the gifts themselves, which are poured out by the Holy Spirit, reflect the Reign (and victory) of Christ. They reflect the relations and actions of the triune God and issue in a corporate growth that includes works of ministry, understanding, and unity—a process that Paul summarizes as maturity, "the full stature of Christ" (v. 13). Christ then is the source and the goal (cf. v. 15) of a process that is carried out corporately by the growing and properly working body of Christ.[73] Translation and rereading underline, in a way that contextualization is unable to do, the mutuality by which the parts of the body of Christ learn from each other as they come to maturity together. So Christians do not seek merely to make available the answers that others have given to the deep human questions[74]; rather, they seek to incorporate those myriad, Spirit-inspired responses to the gospel into their corporate growth toward the likeness of Christ.

Culture Wars or Cultured Witness?

A second and more recent example of conversation on the relation between Christianity and culture is the so-called culture wars that have been raging in America during the early 1990s. The terms of these wars have been laid out by sociologist James D. Hunter, especially in *Culture Wars: The Struggle to Define America*.[75] Hunter believes that in America there are two competing notions about the nature of social reality and that these notions are deeply embedded in American history. They ultimately have to do with different ways of defining the sacred (131). One group, which Hunter calls the orthodox party, is committed to an external and definable transcendent authority; the other, the progressives, are committed to a process of resymbolizing historic faiths according to prevailing assumptions of contemporary life (43, 108). These underlying assumptions about the nature of reality provide the moral energy for the struggle, which involves nothing less than a battle for domination in private and public spheres (52). Hunter closes his book with a plea for the development of a "language of public morality" that rejects quiescence, that recognizes the sacred within different communities, and that is self-critical (322).

There is no lack of evidence for the fissure in American life that Hunter points out—struggles between the Christian Coalition and People of the American Way, between the Pro-Life Movement and the Family Planning Association are all too evident. The questions we want to ask are: What is the definition of culture that is implicit in this discussion? What might be wrong with this polemic way of putting things? Then, in the light of our argument, how might this situation be construed in a more constructive fashion? Culture, in terms of Hunter's discussion, consists of a competing set of values that express themselves in various forms of political (and social) practices. "The divisions," Hunter notes, "are . . . the result of differing worldviews. [They] revolve around our most cherished assumptions about how to order our lives" (42). But describing things this way seems to run two serious risks.[76] One, it implies that at the center of culture there is (or ought to be) a group of ideas which should then be put into practice (contextualized). But we have seen that this intellectualist notion of culture is inadequate both to the rich social and cultural patterns of a culture and to the way individual actors use (or misuse) those patterns. Two, it ignores the fact that both sides of this debate share deeply held convictions about reality, which neither of them, to my knowledge, has held up for discussion or critique. Both sides, for example, interpret the debate in terms of their own version of the American project, which is meant to be somehow privileged—a light to the nations. The debate for both is framed as one of extremists *vs.* guardians of some particular version of the American Dream. Then, too, both sides express their values in terms of the freedom (or worth) of the individual person and his or her development, and both groups are all too willing pragmatically to use the political tactics that may win them advantage.[77] It may be that what troubles these warring factions has more to do with values that both sides share than with what separates them. So matters may not be as simple as either side of the debate would have us believe.

In terms of the theological perspective we are developing, how might these issues be recast? We have been arguing that, for better or worse, we are situated within a given cultural situation. This suggests that Christians can never be self-righteous about their perspective on culture, as though they dwell in some special (and more pure) cultural territory. Christians have no special cultural space, or, to put it more accurately "our own proper territory has always already been inhabited by others."[78] This means further that Christians exist in an important solidarity with their unbelieving neighbors. Ultimately, what troubles them is also what troubles us. This is true, we have argued, for theological reasons. We share the same created space and together we seek to work out God's purposes for creation. Moreover, God has invaded this cultural space, incarnating in it the very righteousness of God. The Holy Spirit has subsequently been poured out to invade our social beings (including, potentially, all of our cultural spaces) in order to bring all this to perfection—to the praise of God's glory. So what we Christians share as cultural beings with our neighbors—our language, our holidays, our workspace as well as our being fallen and being loved and sought by God—is in some ways more important than what separates us. At least that is the attitude that Jesus consistently asks us to take: we are to love our neighbors as ourselves.[79]

Further, this situation of cultural solidarity suggests, as we pointed out, that we share with them the fallenness that all cultures exhibit. This should lead us to mutual repentance and understanding rather than recrimination. I am often impressed with how each side of these debates is starting from premises that can be affirmed. Who would quarrel with the value of the lives of unborn children? Or the value of a woman to choose what happens to her body? The problem is that these values sometimes conflict, but they conflict not because one value is right and the other wrong, but because we all seek to pursue these values in a fallen order—where women are raped and unborn children are killed for no good reason. But none of us is immune from this situation, and it should bring us closer together rather than drive us apart.[80] Moreover, we both share a world where Christ continues to rule through the Holy Spirit so that culture as well as creation is upheld by his presence. This says to me that my political activity might as likely be allied with unbelievers as occasionally opposed to them.

All of this suggests that the Christian internal difference in a given culture is to the end of embodying Christ's reconciling work. Our faithfulness to Christ, our insistence on holding up his life and work as the only way to reorder our fallen human situation, may sometimes bring us the wrath of our neighbors, sometimes even their violence. But we do so because we believe this is the only thing that will allow us to reorder our corporate lives. We hold up Jesus as the only way to break down the barriers and to bring people together so that they might share together the gifts God has given them. Something has gone wrong when the church becomes known as a battle station rather than a center of hospitality,[81] or a place of self-righteous judgment rather than a community of moral reasoning and of reconciliation.[82]

Both of these discussions reflect a Christian conversation that goes back to the New Testament. There has always been a struggle between those who felt their pagan past had to be rejected and those who felt the gospel affirmed much of that past; between those who felt that the brilliance of the gospel put all of culture in the shade, and those who saw the light of Christ illuminating the treasures of culture. In the early church Tertullian felt the gospel put an end to human speculation, while Justin Martyr saw all of Greek philosophy in the light of the gospel. In modern Africa early missionaries often felt African culture needed to be supplanted by Christian civilization, while the African Independent Churches believe Christ calls people to celebrate their African heritage.

Our argument leads us to the view that God's actions and continuing presence call Christians to build actively on the cultural situation that is present. Every culture, because of the divine connections, embodies glimmers of a light that God's word can bring to full view. The gospel is always a principle of renewal, not a destructive power. It is fire that purifies as it burns. Christian presence in culture is shaped by ordinary believers who seek in any way open to them to fill the cracks in their cultural space and even permeate the centers with practices that reflect their Lord—in this work more than in any other the ordinary believers are often the "experts." This form of life has a unique set of values, expressed in scripture but grounded in a particular community that meets in Jesus' name and then scatters to exercise its function as salt and light—a community we examine in more detail in the next chapter.

We have spoken about hope, and it is fitting to end this chapter with a final word about the role of hope in human cultures. People who work with development recognize that without hope a people will not develop, even when they have everything else that might be necessary. Hope is what gives us the energy to respond to the relationships in which we are created, to enjoy and develop their potential. Christians believe that hope is best found in responding to that call which comes to all people: "Come to me, all you that are weary and are carrying heavy burdens, and I will give you rest. . . . For my yoke is easy, and my burden is light" (Mt 11:28, 30).

CONCLUSION

We conclude this brief study by making some summary statements about the Christians' understanding and use of culture. The first point we have stressed is that, at any given point, and with any question Christians face, their culture provides the terms and structures in which they can proceed. That is, culture, initially at least, constitutes the limits of the possible. This is neither a prescriptive statement nor is it a result of the fall, but a description of what it means to be embodied social creatures made in God's image.

We have noted that this cultural reality is the human response to God's creative work, which continues to set the limits and the terms for human culture. Because of human rebellion, the patterns of human relationship in culture and creation are distorted to various degrees. God, of course, opposes this distortion, but God does not stand against cultural activity in itself—indeed insofar as God continues to uphold creation through sustaining work, God may also be described as involved in the making of culture. The absolute qualitative distinction is not between God and the world, as Kierkegaard supposed, but between God and human sin.

The dynamic factor in cultural change, from a Christian perspective, is the word of God as this presents the good news of God's creating and reconciling work—our model here is the critique of the Hebrew prophets and the apostles. We have argued that in the process of translation and rereading of scripture the vernacular factor in a given culture is energized and the culture is (potentially) renewed. The Holy Spirit has a special role to play in this hearing of God's word, which always comes from outside as a word of judgment and of comfort—what we call its "transcendence" is not its heavenly shape but its character as *news* that liberates by creating unheard-of options within our setting. The call of God articulated through scripture creates a situation in our own context to which we must respond. Christians ultimately believe cultural involvement and creativity that are just and righteous are a response to the call of God in that situation.

Hearing this word of God in our own situation ordinarily involves stepping out into an unknown future. Discerning the direction of this path will often involve, in John Yoder's term, a communal hermeneutics, wherein the fellowship is allowed, by the Holy Spirit, to dream dreams. Stepping out in this way may well involve creating cultural possibilities that have not previously existed, but it will always involve an actual embodying, a doing of the word—what the Bible calls obedience.

In this hermeneutical process of presenting and translating the word into the pattern of our cultural reality, our situation is necessarily transformed. It is judged, and it is also redeemed. After the analogy of our personal transformation, which Paul speaks of in 2 Corinthians 4:16—"Our inner nature is being renewed day by day"—our corporate life may also progressively reflect the character of Christ as produced by the Holy Spirit. Patterns of creative efficiency in the work place will be more sensitive to the disadvantaged; habits of hospitality will become more inclusive; and relationships will be more caring and less discriminatory. Spaces will be made for people's creativity to flourish, and times will be set aside for celebration. In all, pain will be lessened by a mutual bearing of burdens, so that joy may abound to the glory of God.

4

Ethnicity

If culture is what we make of God's creation, our ethnicity is the identity that we derive from what we have made. Since it is clear that God intended a wonderful diversity in creation, the diversity of peoples, tongues, and nations must figure in God's good purposes. Yet ethnicity immediately raises issues that the discussion of cultures can overlook: the differential of power that exists among the cultures of the world, and the resulting oppression and violence that are all too evident in our post–Cold War world. In many respects, since the 1960s discussions of culture have come to center almost entirely on what we call—without a great deal of clarity—*ethnicity*, and since 1989, claims for ethnic recognition have become our most burning political issue.[1] What is to be made of these strident voices?

The problem has become especially acute for Americans, because the 1990s have raised issues of race and ethnicity in particularly painful ways. Not only have issues of racism surfaced in debates about affirmative action and educational policies, but our identity as an immigrant nation is being challenged in fundamental ways. Americans are proud of their heritage of welcoming oppressed strangers from all over the world. "Give me your tired, your poor, / Your huddled masses yearning to breathe free, / . . . / Send these, the homeless, tempest-tossed to me" inscribed on our Statue of Liberty defines our national ethos, or at least Americans would like to think it does. That this statue was a gift of the people of France is significant because that country, like America, has seen itself as founding a new kind of society based on ideas of brotherhood and freedom rather than on ethnic or racial solidarity. Both countries have assumed, at least until recently, that immigrants would trade in their cultural patterns for new ones more nearly reflective of these modern ideas of unity and tolerance—that America would become a "melting pot" of the peoples of the world. Needless to say, not all those who arrived felt it necessary to give up their old ways. And the resulting diversity of dress and manners has troubled Americans from the beginning. A recently discovered letter from a student at Williams College, written in 1798, articulates sentiments many today would share:

> The prevalence of foreign manners in America, is certainly an evil. But how is that to be remedied? . . . The diversity of dress, manners, & customs is greater in America than in any other country in the world, the reason of which, is very obvious. It is considered as a country where people enjoy liberty and independence; of course persons from almost every nation in the world come here as to an asylum from oppression; Each brings with him prejudices in favor of the habits of his own countrymen. And we, monkey like, imitate them all. The consequence of which is, we have no national character. And until we throw off this servility of imitation, unite with zeal, and form an original, distinct one for ourselves, we shall be without any.[2]

Arthur M. Schlesinger, Jr., recently reiterated a similar argument.[3] He sees what he calls a "cult of ethnicity" threatening the American creed, which brings people together around a set of common ideals (42). The American creed, he argues, envisions a nation of individuals, not inviolable communities, all ruled by law, speaking a common language, and enjoying common institutions (121). This common culture, he admits, has Anglo-Saxon roots, but this need not dominate our cultural patterns. Once this cultural heritage has been learned by the people in America, he argues, we can all be open to other cultural values without giving up our own identity as Americans. At present, however, this common identity is being seriously threatened by this "cult of ethnicity" that "challenges the concept of 'one people,' and protects, promotes, and perpetuates separate ethnic and racial communities" (15). Schlesinger's views have struck a chord with many people who are troubled by the growing diversity and the disunity that seems to result. These feelings have fueled movements to scale back public services to (especially illegal) immigrants, to limit affirmative action programs in government agencies, and to lower immigration quotas.

But at the same time other voices are being raised that take exception to this mono-cultural version of the American project. They insist that the supposed tolerance and freedom that are central to the American ideal have allowed the free expression of certain ideas and cultural values but have excluded others. Some argue that insistence on assimilation to one set of cultural traditions, as Schlesinger seems to do, amounts to cultural aggression, even, some argue, to cultural genocide. It is clear that deeply felt values—many of them amounting to religious convictions—are at stake. Moreover, it is obvious that these values are tied to issues of cultural identity, which is felt to be threatened either by the influx of foreign groups or by the oppressive character of the host culture. There are clearly some goods to be preserved—and some evils to be avoided—here. But how are these to be sorted out? More important, what theological issues are at stake?

FROM RACE TO ETHNICITY: THE EVOLUTION OF AN IDEA

While the Greek word *ethnos* originally referred simply to a "bunch," without reference to descent or cohesion, it soon came to be associated with the differences between peoples. During the Greco-Roman period a twofold distinction grew up about inhabitants outside the core of civilization (which constituted the obviously "superior" people): first were those who were rude in their manners and, because they seemed to be inarticulate in language, were called barbarians (Bar-bar speakers); and beyond these, on the edges of the world, were creatures who were even more monstrous than the Barbarians, whose "heads grow beneath their shoulders" (Shakespeare) or who have one eye in the middle of their heads.[4] This division of peoples was accepted as common knowledge even into the Middle Ages, and beyond. For Christians, the debate often settled on whether a people belonged to the barbarians, and were thus redeemable, or whether they were somehow less than human and thus unredeemable. Bartolomé de las Casas in Central America carried on a long and bitter debate over the humanity of the Indios with the Catholic church in the sixteenth century.[5]

Although the Swedish taxonomist Linnaeus divided people into racial groupings in 1735, in Europe Christian views of creation and Enlightenment notions of humanity converged to underplay the significance of the differences well into the nineteenth century. In the middle of that century supposedly scientific attitudes emerged that challenged these universalist notions.[6] With Darwin, the various types appeared to be fixed, and thus anatomy became destiny (14, 121). Ernest Renan, who was hugely influential on Matthew Arnold, insisted that science proved the Indo-European races were superior, and that inferior races were destined to give way before the superior ones (68-70). Race as it came to be defined was, as Robert Young points out, a "summation of historically accumulated moral differences sustained and slowly modified from generation to generation" (45). What we now call culture was invented, Young argues, to account for these differences (49). What is particularly interesting for our purposes is the way scientific and academic leadership championed the idea of permanent racial differences, which became, especially in France, the major principle of historical explanation (119). In fact the Anthropological Society in Britain was founded in 1863 to pursue science and "facts without deference to assumptions derived from biblical or theological beliefs" (134). These "facts" soon led to the widespread view—especially among academics—that certain races were meant to rule. Young concludes: "The close connection between the development of the concepts of culture and race in the nineteenth century means that an implicit racism lies powerfully hidden but repeatedly propagated within western notions of culture" (91).

In our century scientists have reached a virtual consensus that any simplistic division of people on racial grounds is questionable. Human migration and contact stretching back millennia have mixed up the human gene pool to such an extent that most scientists believe no clear human taxonomy can ever be achieved. As Michael D. Lieber of the University of Illinois (Chicago) put it in an interview: "The problem with human populations is that they are all mongrel."[7] Modern genetic research has made it possible to draw international genetic maps of human populations. These show that popular indicators of race—hair texture, skin color, or facial features—"are superficial traits that were caused by recent evolution in response to climate and perhaps sexual selection"(A9). Older, more reliable genetic traits do not divide people into groups that correspond to what we call races. Michael Crawford of the University of Kansas, who compared DNA taken from samples of hair and blood of people living in a region of Mongolia, has found that this area, like many others, is a crossroads of human migration. He notes: "There's no dividing line where on one side you can say it is Asia and on the other side it's Europe" (A9).

Immediately after World War II, alongside of this growing scientific consensus, a larger public consensus developed about the unity of the human race. In the 1940s and 1950s, in the face of Nazi racism and other forms of chauvinism and bigotry, many people began to speak on behalf of "one world" and "the family of man."[8] Over against the German assertion of blood and the Soviet claim for class, thinking people reasserted Enlightenment notions of reason and rights that were enshrined in the United Nations Declaration on Human Rights.

But it did not take long for such universalistic ideas to fall into disfavor. Though Martin Luther King, Jr., wanted his children to be judged by the content of their character rather than the color of their skin, his more radical brothers were soon insisting that black is beautiful. At the same time, revised immigration quotas passed in 1965 greatly expanded the Asian and Latin American population. These new arrivals, unlike previous waves of immigrants, held out for a more particularistic version of the American project and gave rise to a celebration of "multi-culturalism" in the 1970s and 1980s. The melting pot imagery gave way to the tossed salad image.

While there was much to celebrate in this era of cultural liberation and the rediscovery of roots, the problems associated with earlier forms of particularism reappeared in the 1990s. Public discussions and feelings about racial diversity grew more intense—indeed, it is not an exaggeration to say that race has become one of the most pressing public issues in America. In 1994 Richard Herrnstein and Charles Murray caused a great deal of consternation with their book *The Bell Curve,* which tried to correlate intelligence with certain races.[9] It was this argument that finally stimulated the American Anthropological Association in its annual meeting in Atlanta in late 1994 to declare that "differentiating species into biologically defined 'races' has proven meaningless and unscientific."[10]

Nevertheless, the debate about the influence of "race" in American society continues. On the one side are those who belittle the importance of race.

Dinesh D'Souza, for example, follows the line of Schlesinger. He does not deny the existence of racism, but argues that "racism cannot explain most of the contemporary hardships faced by African-Americans."[11] These hardships can be properly addressed only through colorblind public policies and by encouraging African-Americans themselves to address their cultural problems. Equally strong arguments are raised from the other side, which insists that, while race may have little biological basis, it is still very much alive as a cultural construct. Stephen Steinberg, for example, argues that race must be addressed as a cultural force because of the injustices that are perpetrated in racial terms. The kind of colorblind policies D'Souza endorses, Steinberg believes, "absolves the nation of responsibility for coming to terms with its racist legacy, and takes race off the national agenda."[12]

In general, while physical anthropologists have decided race is not a "natural" category, behavioral (and political) scientists now regularly use the term *ethnicity* to describe social groupings.[13] They agree that ethnic labels are socially constructed as well as being historically defined. *Tribes* in Africa, for example, while once denoting independent societies, are better described today as "the historical products of constant flux, with segments breaking away and reforming according to modified regional, socio-economic, and political criteria."[14] Terms applied to groups have such ambiguity that they sometimes mean simply "the people," or they have been applied arbitrarily by foreign traders or missionaries. Modern study of such supposedly fixed orders as castes in India have shown them also to be "fluid, changing dynamic social groups."[15]

Whatever scientists may feel about the natural status of *ethnicity*, the term carries enormous emotional freight, and perceptions associated with it are causing some of today's most bitter geopolitical struggles. This fact is not without its ironies, for what are now accepted as "national" cultures were often imposed by hegemonic groups—English culture supplanted the Welsh and Celtic, and French and German culture similarly displaced or incorporated tribal groups. In many cases of nation building, people "set out to rediscover and create a cultural repertoire, consciously selecting cultural items, often from rural folk culture," which were then identified as "German" or "Czech."[16] Note that what later was accepted as natural was often originally collected and, at times, constructed to confirm and promote the solidarity of the group (as has happened with the recent introduction of Kwanza among the African-American community). While artifacts and rituals of a culture are in some ways conventional, they often become so identified with the identity of a people as to become almost sacred, as debates over the flag in America demonstrate. Whatever their history, these symbols and the solidarity they represent have become major reasons for tensions among peoples. In fact, historian Samuel P. Huntington asserts that reasons for warfare have evolved from struggles between nation states, through an era of ideological conflict, to the present situation in which the battles are almost exclusively cultural and ethnic.[17] Whatever their source and origin, it is clear that ethnic identities have turned out to be a persistent factor of our international and our American situations. By cultural adaptation and mutual influence these ethnic identities have developed in ways that have fundamentally marked this period of history.

In spite of the fact that group identity and ethnic violence have obvious theological significance, sustained Christian discussion of these issues is all but nonexistent. There are exceptions, of course; African-Americans have given long and thorough consideration to these questions, as we will note below. But among white Evangelicals only missionaries and some cross-cultural evangelists have given any consideration to a theology of ethnicity. In the latter case, missionaries of the Church Growth school of missiology have made extensive use of ethnic categories—in a way that parallels the discussion of culture in the service of evangelism that we examined in the last chapter. Missiologist Donald McGavran and his disciple Peter Wagner have written some of the few Christian discussions of ethnicity.[18] Their discussion can serve as an instructive case study of the current state of the question among many Evangelicals.

Clearly McGavran deserves credit for being one of the first to incorporate contemporary social-science methods into the work of cross-cultural evangelism. He insisted that we study the cultural realities in the places where we work. For "when we comprehend the social structure of a particular segment of the total population, we know better how churches are likely to increase and ramify through it."[19] Whatever else can be said about churches, McGavran says, they can also be described in ethnic and in socio-economic terms. Now McGavran understands that all true members of the Christian church are one in Christ, but, in their actual setting, he points out, Christians also exist as Tamil or Akamba churches. In reality, then, churches "have many faces, and each is a true face."[20] But is each face really true? What about churches that adopt a caste system? Is this adopting a true face? McGavran faces this question and admits that there are arguments on both sides. After a brief discussion he concludes that it is right for members of churches in these castes to practice endogamy (only marrying their own members), for, after all, McGavran notes, that is what a Japanese, Scottish, or American Christian will do. But it is wrong for them not to practice evangelism outside their caste, as they too often fail to do (57-59).

What is the theological grounding for this use of culture? McGavran is careful to state at the outset of his study that "church growth begins in and is required by Christian theology" (11). What is that theology? His answer is straightforward: "God wants the Church to grow."[21] Apparently for McGavran the purposes of God in creation and redemption have been reduced to this single goal: the growth of the church. Later he reiterates this point. The central purpose of the Christian mission is "to propagate the Christian faith" (88). This theological grounding then gives guidance to the use of culture. McGavran repeatedly insists that becoming a Christian cannot look like a traitorous act. "Christians must not betray and abandon their ethnic units in becoming Christian" (12). So even though he does encourage evangelism across cultural boundaries, he is hesitant to support table fellowship across these boundaries. This is because, as nearly as I can see, it would *appear* to be traitorous to one's culture to act in this way, and this would then become a barrier to becoming Christians for others in that group. "To keep the door of salvation open to your relatives, our actual degree of fellowship [with other groups] will remain small for years, even decades"(60). But whatever the appearances (and Christ often had trouble here), does not the Bible encourage table fellowship, indeed all kinds of hospitality, across ethnic boundaries? Here another aspect of McGavran's theological assumptions seems to be at work. He laments that educated Indians often return from the West with liberal ideas of scripture and "supra racial views of society" (192). Apparently these leaders try to form multiethnic churches, which, as often as not, to McGavran's mind, arrest the growth of people movements (80). Are such supra racial views simply wrong in themselves, or are they wrong because they seem to impede growth? One is not sure. But a clue is to be found in a statement in McGavran's concluding chapter. "Since the heart of the Christian religion is an inner righteousness and not obedience to external rules, congregations . . . obviously had to assume the shape of the society in which people came to belief and salvation" (211). But is this so obvious to a missionary in Rwanda today, or in Croatia? Is there no relation between the inner righteousness and the external conduct between races?

The ethical issues connected with this view became so widely discussed that in 1979 one of McGavran's students, Peter Wagner, addressed them in *Our Kind of People.* Wagner describes an ethnic group as "those who conceive of themselves as being alike by virtue of their common ancestry, real or fictitious, and who are so regarded by others" (39). People's identification with their birth community is a natural and positive dimension of their created reality. The impetus in American Christianity toward what used to be called integration owes more to assimilationist civil religion than to scripture (54-55). In fact, Wagner goes on to state that "the heart of the Gospel is that God . . . sent his son Jesus to free, to save, to liberate" (81) and that at the root of the oppression that Christ's death addresses is the "policy of cultural assimilation" in America and elsewhere. So that not only does scripture allow for separate ethnic churches to develop, but to deny people such ethnic freedom is a violation of the gospel.[22] Since God first liberates and then reconciles, God intends each group to express its freedom in Christ by worshiping in its own way (82-83, 94). The New Testament shows that though "the Christian movement was ultimately to transcend racial . . . barriers . . . its spread continued along homogeneous unit lines" (124).

Wagner's discussion is clearly an important addition to the missionary literature on ethnicity and makes a real contribution to our understanding of how groups form. But justification of the use of ethnicity by appeal to Christ's work of liberation without reference to God's larger purposes for creation raises questions. Are ethnic solidarities always to be accepted as they exist? What other relationships or responsibilities impinge on these solidarities? Clearly, these categories must be used with great care. As with culture, the moral questions that ethnicity raises call for a larger and more comprehensive framework than either contemporary social science or current theological reflection has been able to provide. Let us turn, then, to a sketch of some elements of such a framework.

A THEOLOGICAL GROUNDING OF ETHNICITY

Relationship, Identity and Difference

Two issues that surface regularly in contemporary discussions of ethnicity call for comment because of their importance for our theological discussion below. In the first place, the power (and volatility) of ethnicity relates to its ability to give identity to a people—or, when it is denied, to deprive people of their proper identity. Eric Wolf concludes his discussion of the topic by noting that while there may or may not be genetic (and thus racial) components, ethnicity more accurately relates to "a common descent as a transgenerational vehicle for the transmission of an authentically rooted culture"[23]; that is—while complex, sometimes unstable, and often changing—ethnicity grounds identity in a group's consciousness of itself as separate and identifiable. It thus enables people to work together on common cultural projects that contribute to (or sometimes disrupt) the common good. The historical rootedness of ethnicity enables groups to share a (sometimes painful) common story and gives them resources to survive and even prosper in situations in which they are marginalized. So ethnicity is a given, a starting point for human activity. But that is not the whole story. A group identity is sometimes formed by constructing the "other" as inferior so as to compensate for some alleged injustice. Recent studies of what it means to be "white" in America, for example, have shown that white identity arose in the nineteenth century among white laborers to compensate for their feeling of exploitation. In spite of their difficulties, they were still "white" which is to say not as bad as the blacks who were slaves.[24]

This suggests that ethnicity is not only a category of identity but a moral category. That is to say, in asserting our identity as a particular member of a tribe or ethnic group, we are often making a value judgment: I am a member of this group, and that is a good thing. All too often this also means: This is not only who I am, but it defines you as well. You are not of this group, and therefore you are less valuable. Examples of identity that are established over against the "inferior other" are all too common at the end of our century, and the problem is certainly alive and well in America.

Perhaps the most poignant example of ethnicity used as a category of identity—as a historical given that relates to a person's history and culture—and as a moral category is the current struggle between the Hutu and Tutsi in central Africa. Interestingly, commentators on the situation tend to emphasize either one or another of these categories, sometimes in a simplistic fashion. Alex de Waal, for example, stresses the arbitrary and moral factors. While these groups had different cultures during the last century, de Waal argues that they cannot be distinguished strictly on the basis of historical or biological grounds. Indeed, they "speak the same language, share the same territory and traditional political institutions and . . . it is often impossible to tell which [group] an individual belongs to on the basis of physical appearance."[25] In the nineteenth century Tutsi herders granted the use of cattle to their Hutu clients, agriculturalists, who in return shared pastoral and agricultural products.[26] While these groups were largely endogamous, social mobility across categories was common in the nineteenth century. In this century, however, the Colonial powers "seized upon the occupational categorization imbuing it with a hierarchical racial classification"—the Tutsi were Hamitic aristocrats (even, the early missionaries believed, with an Aryan strain); the Hutu were Bantu peasants, categories that have no real historical or biological grounding.[27]

In the 1930s, de Waal points out, when the Belgians issued identity cards because the groups were so difficult to tell apart, officials were obliged to count the cows a family owned: nine or more cows designated the Tutsi, fewer than nine the Hutu. On the evidence of one cow hung destinies that determined life and death when, after a Hutu republic was installed in 1959, political conflict and communal violence ensued. More recently, one can claim the very identities of these people are being kept alive by the violence that has spiraled out of control, especially since 1990. In a study of a different East African group, the Mursi and their neighbors, David Turton argues that their political identities are kept alive by conflict. He writes: "I suggest that for the Mursi and their neighbors, warfare is not a means by which an already constituted political group seeks to defend or extend its territory, but a means by which the very idea of it as an independent political unit, free from the normative claims of outsiders, is created and kept alive."[28] Similarly, de Waal argues that mutual violence "has created distinct and mutually opposed Hutu and Tutsi identities."[29] At the seminary in Nairobi where I am writing this, when the violence first erupted in Rwanda, Christian students from different groups could not meet to pray together, so deep was the mistrust and alienation. When asked to join a group for prayer, one Tutsi staff member responded, "I will pray only if we pray for the RPF [Rwandese Patriotic Front, the Tutsi rebel movement]."

While evidence is not lacking to support this view of things, it is clearly not the whole story. Ethnicity *is* a legitimate grounding for a people's identity, one which cannot be dismissed as a modern rationalization. Jean-Luc Vellut, for example, has disputed de Waal's characterization of the differences. The rationalizing Colonial powers may have shaped these differences, but they did not call them into existence. Group consciousness based on the culture of the spear and the culture of the hoe had existed for generations.[30] My African friends insist that these groups are physically distinguishable.

Identity grounded in a shared culture and common descent is a part of our created nature. Though it plays a critical role in the current violence in central Africa, it cannot be blamed for that tragedy. What, then, are the theological categories that make sense of our ethnic differences?

The fact that ethnic relationships are the ground for human identity expresses something very important about human existence: it is invariably corporate and communal. Relationship is a given for humanity as created by God. The particular intellectual history that Americans share has sometimes served to obscure this fact, for, at least since the time of Thomas Hobbes and John Locke, Americans have conceived of humanity in individualistic terms. One starts forming culture as an individual and then, by a process that is called a social contract, one joins a group or partnership that appears to serve the individual's interests, which are always perceived to be primary. Many have come to believe this individualism is at the root of many of America's social problems.[31] Being confronted with issues of ethnicity, and thus with the necessarily corporate component of human life, however difficult, may prove to be an important means of growth for American Christians.

In the Christian view human existence is from the beginning a being-in-relationship. This is grounded in the fact that God exists from eternity in a community of love among the persons of the Trinity. Jesus says, "The Father is in me and I am in the Father" (Jn 10:38), and he goes on to tell his disciples that when the Holy Spirit comes, "he will glorify me, because he will take what is mine and declare it to you. All that the Father has is mine. For this reason I said that he will take what is mine and declare it to you" (Jn 16:14-15). Jesus exists in God and works through the Holy Spirit, who speaks from the Father and from the Son. Notice that these relationships define their existence but they do not undermine their threefold reality; they have individual existence but a corporate identity. This identity is expressed through what they do and say in the world, which, we learn later in the New Testament, focuses centrally on reconciliation. Peter Wagner argued that God liberates, then reconciles; for Paul, by contrast, reconciliation *is* liberation. "In Christ God was reconciling the world to himself, not counting their trespasses against them, and entrusting the message of reconciliation to us" (2 Cor 5:19).

In creating human persons in the divine image, then, God intends that they reflect in their human and created way this relational existence. They are created in actual relationship with other persons, with God, and with the rest of the created order. This is an actual and substantial relationship, not one that is optional or theoretically possible. Moreover, it is a relationship that is expressed—but not formed—in and through our activity in the world. These relations must ground our individual and corporate understanding of our identities if they are to be authentic to our created reality. As Colin Gunton puts it: "People and things, in dependence on God understood substantially and not abstractly, are also to be understood as substantial beings, having their own distinct and particular existence, *by virtue of and not in the face of their relationship to the other.*"[32]

Relationship is a given of our created reality. As we noted, this "giveriness" implies both its gift character and also its limiting function. We can enjoy and celebrate these relationships, as we do in marriage and communion; we can also injure and destroy them, insisting, with Cain, that we are not our "brother's keeper." Thus the relationships into which we are born are invariably moral, and our responses are necessarily praise- or blameworthy. It is clear that these relationships were all injured with the disobedience of Adam and Eve. At the Fall our first parents lost their easy fellowship with God (and with each other). They then struggle over their connection with the earth, and immediately jealousy, hatred, and even murder intrude into the intimacy of the family. As these ideas are developed in scripture it becomes clear that human flourishing is tied to the process of reordering these relationships, and that most of society's struggles relate to their absence or distortion. Colin Gunton expresses this dimension well, in words particularly relevant to our American context: "When individual self-contemplation becomes the basis of the self, rather than the relation to the divine and human others on which our reality actually depends, the self begins to disappear."[33]

Our ethnic diversity depends on our natural relationships with the earth and its diversity, and with each other—all of this must be part of God's original and good purposes. But the actual existence of this diversity reflects the distortions that sin has introduced. In the Tower of Babel account human audacity reached such a point that it sought to realize the empty promise of the tempter in Genesis 3: "You shall be as gods." Their project is to build a tower to "make a name for ourselves; otherwise we shall be scattered abroad upon the face of the whole earth" (Gn 11:4). Apparently denying the diversity that God intended, they joined efforts in an idolatrous project that reflected distorted relations—certainly with God, and probably with their neighbors. So God intervened in what must be seen as an act of mercy—perhaps a reflection of the covenant God made with Noah—to "scatter them . . . over the face of the earth" and "confuse their language" (Gn 11:8,7).[34] There is a melancholy aspect to the end result of this. True, because of this scattering, sin will not threaten the continuance of the race. But something is lost too; people are no longer together, and they struggle to understand one another. In Karl Barth's words:

> The time of man's existence as one people of one language, as he was first created, has now come to an end. Men will no longer understand one another self-evidently. . . . Their being as humanity must now be one in the antithesis of near and distant neighbors, who can neither of them constitute the whole of humanity, but only relative totalities with geographic frontiers and divergent histories.[35]

The sadness and violence that are associated with these frontiers and divergent histories are all too clear to us.

God's call to Abraham includes the prediction that God will make of Abraham a "great nation," in a particular land, for the blessing of all people (Gn 12:2-3). That is, this nation will help reconstitute the order that had been broken. Israel was called by God to become a distinct people. But this reality, though realized through certain historical events, was not grounded in biology, or even, strictly speaking, in descent. The word *Hebrew*, in fact, comes from *apiru*, which referred to a particular social stratum of the Ancient Near East—landless people, often political refugees or displaced persons who did not fit into normal society. Norman Gottwald tells us:

> The people with whom Yahweh was in bond did not have a biologically traceable descent, or even a unified pre-history, but were a composite people whose newfound unity was expressed, in spite of their heterogeneous origins, by means of the socio-political artifice of the "family tree."[36]

As Christopher Wright notes, what set Israel apart was not its ethnic heritage or its ancestors but the special relationship that it enjoyed with God. At every level of society, moreover, the social structure was meant to reflect this relationship. The tribes themselves were a loose, non-centralized structure held together by mutual obligation springing from shared religious convictions.[37] The clan was intended to preserve the economic viability of constituent families, whereas the judicial role was performed by elders in the extended family. In general, then, the economic system was geared to broadly based equality and self-sufficiency of families and to protection of the poor (13). The structure itself is theologically significant: "The kind of society he desires and commands is based explicitly on the kind of God he is" (16). All of this was to reflect the system of relationships that were outlined in the law:

> So now, O Israel, what does the LORD your God require of you? Only to fear the LORD your God, to walk in all his ways, to love him, to serve the LORD your God with all your heart and with all your soul, and to keep the commandments of the LORD your God, and his decrees which I am commanding you this day, for your own well-being. (Dt 10:12-13)

Human relational existence also includes the created context—the seas and mountains, the fertile and arid lands, the savannas and forests—all of which become the raw materials for the formation of ethnic identities. Israel's connection with the land became central to its obedience to God—the law was given for the time of the land (Dt 6:1). A primary protective measure was the inalienability of the land, based on the fact that God was the ultimate owner (Lv 25:23). While Americans often overlook the relationship between place and identity that is so important elsewhere in the world, they cannot avoid seeing, for example, the role of the frontier in their own cultural consciousness.[38] We are creatures made from and for the earth as well as for each other and God. We will see in the next chapter how our fallenness has distorted these earthly relationships.

Already we see elements of healthy and unhealthy understandings of ethnic identity. The Hebrews were people who joined themselves freely to God's project of forming a people that reflected God's purposes and character; their identity was partly received as a gift and partly chosen in their response of obedience. On the other hand, Babel and the incident of the golden calf reveal a people grasping their identity through idolatrous projects that defy God. Here, then, are two kinds of pluralism that need to be recognized. One has to do with our created diversity, which Richard Mouw and Sander Griffoen call associational pluralism, an "important positive feature of our created condition."[39] But this associational pluralism is invariably exercised in a particular direction that either promotes or undermines human flourishing. Mouw and Griffoen call these tendencies in a culture "directional pluralism."[40] Cultures and peoples need guidance, and if they do not find it in terms of God's purposes, they will create some alternative—and inevitably idolatrous—project to pursue in the name of the people.

This contrast between what is given (or withheld) and what is asserted appears everywhere in the literature of ethnicity today, and it lies at the heart of the contemporary struggle for recognition. Charles Taylor notes that this demand for recognition in American culture today constitutes the major issue in discussions of multi-culturalism.[41] Previously people located their personal moral worth in terms of *honor*, which involved a system of mutual recognition. Honor has now been replaced by notions of *dignity*, where the good is located entirely within ourselves (and is rooted in our feelings).[42] This sense of personal dignity, which Taylor traces back to Rousseau, has become the basis of modern ideas of nationalism and ethnic pride—which demand the recognition of a corporate dignity (31). Interestingly, this sense of dignity is developed dialogically through interaction with significant others and has led to what Taylor calls a "politics of difference," which calls for "distinctions on the basis of differential treatment" (39).

But what are the supposed grounds for this distinctive recognition? The motives are clear: despised or mistreated groups demand treatment that will allow them to replace a "demeaning sense of self with another" (65). But, asks Taylor, can we assume the equal worth of all cultures? Can we be forced to find something of value in every culture (69)? Are recognition and respect simply a matter of power politics and taking sides (70)? If so, we are not as far from Rwanda as we like to think we are. It might be true that all cultures must be taken seriously, but how do we learn this from the study of cultures? How is this grounded?[43]

Christianity claims that the communion of God within the Trinity and the reflection of this in the good (but interrelated) diversity of creation provide ample grounds for valuing human diversity. This gives us a perspective form which to approach one important and representative discussion about identity in America: the African-American search for an afrocentric cultural identity. Recent black American writers have proposed rewriting African-American history in terms of their own reading of their past. For too long, they say, they have read history and literature that were written by someone else and that, if they were lucky, included them in a footnote.[44] Now they are insisting that their story be rewritten from the perspective of those who lived it. The radical version of this insists with Molefi Asante of Temple University that all modern culture emanated from Africa. But others insist that their story, while not better or worse than white history, is different from it. Africans start from a different center and have a history that distinguishes them from other groups. Recentering people within their own story allows them to become subjects of their own future rather than simply objects of a story told by another.[45]

The legitimacy of such a claim rests, it seems to me, on the understanding that our existence as human beings is communal. We are formed in and by the relationships that nurture and sustain us. These relationships have been given to us as a gift of God, reflecting God's own internal richness. Therefore we can fruitfully learn and recount the history of our ethnic relationships with gratitude and sometimes with pain, much as our family ties are strengthened by our holiday storytelling. The act of telling these stories need not be seen as separatist or hostile. Indeed, when they strengthen identity and provide resources for mutual encouragement, these stories can be accepted as part of God's good gifts. In making this claim for a separate identity, African-Americans are simply saying, Everyone stands somewhere, this is where we happen to stand.

As Cornel West explains this, black identity is neither exclusive nor does it deny eurocentric dominance in the academy. "Instead we recognize Black humanity and attempt to promote the love, affirmation, and critique of Black humanity, and in that sense we attempt to escape the prevailing mode of intellectual bondage that has held captive so many Black intellectuals of the past."[46]

But there are those, even in the black community, who raise a caution at this point. We can tell our stories and remember our history, but we must oppose the "essentialism" that is a carry-over from European colonialism. It was this Enlightenment universalism, they argue, that marginalized blacks (and other minority groups) in the first place. Henry Louis Gates reminds us that ethnic identities are all social constructs, they are "tropes"—metaphors in the language we have been using. They remind us that we belong together, but these instruments of solidarity can all too easily become weapons we use against others. We can use these, Gates says, to will a sense of natural difference into our formulations that does not exist.[47] Such purist constructions exacerbate ethnic differences and separate people in artificial ways. While many black writers feel Gates undervalues the rage that blacks often feel about the injustice of American life, his reminder of the constructed character of ethnicity is important. "These terms are arbitrary constructs," he notes, "not reports of reality."[48]

Even more important is Gates's insistence that our language not create barriers that do not exist in fact. This reminds us that language about ethnicity is irrepressibly moral. It can bring people together, but it can also push them apart. Our construction of our identity, comprising the stories we inherit and recount, has validity when it does not become a means of denying relationships that we also sustain with others. Equally critical to our understanding of ourselves is how we construe the "other." There is nothing wrong with claims to ethnicity if they help people recover a sense of self that was taken from them—nothing, that is, if one remembers the metaphoric nature of ethnicity. It expresses the reality that we are members of one another, like God, the Father who is in the Son who sends the Spirit. But the reality of our interconnections, while reflected in our ethnicity, is larger than this. A helpful way of describing this reality is to recognize that our identity includes but also transcends our ethnicity. So, while we do exist somewhere in a particular social and ethnic setting—and this setting is to be taken seriously—we do not exist *solely* in that setting. To use Miroslav Volf's terms, we stand somewhere, but we do not stand in one place only.[49]

When this is forgotten, ethnicity can be used to exclude rather than understand the "other." Gates spoke of the rationalizing essentialism of the Enlightenment. Paul Gilroy similarly cautions blacks not to learn the tricks of "cultural protectionism" from their oppressors.[50] He prefers to think of black culture in terms of a ship that crosses and recrosses the Atlantic (16, 17). Black settlers form a compound culture—from disparate sources—that remakes wholesale the culture of Africa. What he calls the Black Atlantic—black culture in Europe, the Caribbean, and America—is made up of a variety of layers—African, colonial, European, technological. It is a nontraditional tradition, irreducibly modern (195). This is a helpful reminder of our common human condition. We all have layered identities, because we do not stand in only one place. We are mongrel, as Michael Lieber put it. Another way to say this is that although we have a primary group, in the end, whether we like it or not, "we are all members of multiple 'groups'—crosscutting, overlapping and, ever-evolving."[51]

Forgiveness and Hospitality

More important than what group we belong to is what we propose to do with our identity. In light of these relationships we are called upon to exercise our agency. When looking at ourselves in relation to the "other," the question is the same: What will I do with this "other"? Here we recall that communities of descent are in part socially constructed. They inevitably involve human agency and their formation is intrinsically moral. The place where this agency is most in evidence is in attitudes toward outsiders. Do I have any responsibility outside my family or tribe? Of course I can deny that the relationship even exists and turn inward to my own group. This is a temptation if my experience with the "other" has been painful, and I feel the need to retreat into the comfort of my group to lick my cultural wounds. The dynamics that lead from this to the awful expression *ethnic cleansing* are all too clear. Because the pain of my history is so great, I must deny the relationships that in fact exist between me and my neighbor and that reach to the level of our shared DNA. I can try to turn back the evolutionary clock in the vain search for ethnic purity, but then what have I done? Croatian Miroslav Volf, reflecting on his own return to Croatia after its "independence," notes that the "others" are not in some distant land. They are "our colleagues and neighbors, some of them even are our spouses. The others are among us; they are part of us. Yet they remain others, often pushed to the margins. How should we relate to them? Should we celebrate their difference and support it, or should we bemoan and suppress it? The issue is urgent."[52]

We can seek to efface the "other" in our promethean attempts to become pure. We can, however, respond to this urgency in another way. We can recognize that our relationship with the "other" is not only unavoidable but the very means of our salvation. Emmanuel Levinas has argued eloquently that our relationship with other people is fundamental to our very being. He notes that this connection is pre-theoretical and given. The "other" appears to us as a face we cannot evade; it stands there before us and makes its appeal. Contrary to the dominant Western notion, Levinas argues, spirituality does not reside in our knowing.

> In starting with sensibility interpreted not as a knowing but as proximity, in seeking in language contact and sensibility, behind the circulation of information it becomes, we have endeavored to describe subjectivity as irreducible to consciousness and thematization. Proximity appears as the relationship with the other, who cannot be resolved into "images" or be exposed in a theme.[53]

This proximity, as we have been arguing, is irreducibly moral. It places us in a situation of responsibility for the face that appears before us. "My responsibility for the other is the *for* of the relationship" (90). To ask with Cain, "Am I my brother's keeper?" only has meaning "if one has already supposed that the ego is concerned only with itself, is only a concern with itself" (107). But this ignores the "pre-history" of the self, which is already a "hostage," as Levinas puts it, to the "other." This is not a choice that we can make or not make, as Enlightenment thinking would have it; this is a given of our being. "What is at stake for the self, in its being, is not to be. Beyond egotism and altruism it is the religiosity of the self" (107).

What makes Levinas's plea important is the fact, which Martin Buber failed to see, that the self exists in a situation of unequal relations. Therefore to open ourselves up to relationships leads inevitably to injury and persecution. Levinas, though a Jewish philosopher, virtually repeats the words of Jesus in noting that to give our cheek for insult "is not to draw from suffering some kind of magical redemptive virtue. In the trauma of persecution it is to pass from the outrage undergone to the responsibility for the persecutor, and, in this sense, from suffering to expiation for the other" (101). This exchange lies at the basis of human interaction. Persecution is not something added to subjectivity but "the very movement of recurrence" (101). Communication, then, is the process of opening ourselves up to the "other." But, in words that recall Charles Taylor's politics of recognition, "the openness is not complete if it is on the watch for recognition. It is complete not in opening to the spectacle of or the recognition of the other, but in becoming a responsibility for him" (108).

Levinas's discussion is instructive in two ways. First, he underlines the inescapably moral relationship we share as humans. This is a given to our created reality, and—though Levinas does not stress this point—a clear reflection of the divine image in us. But we need to stress in a way Levinas does not that our present existence gives us very little empirical evidence for these claims. On every hand people seem to exist in a state of denial of this kind of responsible existence. So we conclude in scriptural terms that Levinas is describing the situation God has created us to enjoy, but which we have forgotten. This moral accountability is a state from which we have fallen irreparably away. So the deep and rich argument of Levinas is a call back to a treasure that we have long ago misplaced.

Second, this act of displacement of ourselves from the central place, what Levinas calls "substitution," is something that we cannot do for ourselves. Though he does not use New Testament language, Levinas's thought echoes Paul's in many places. Paul insists, "Let each of you look not to your own interests, but to the interests of others"(Phil 2:4) and "Bear one another's burdens" (Gal 6:2). But in each case Paul ties this practice to what Christ has done in and for us. In the first passage Paul launches into what is one of the most important New Testament Christological passages: "Let the same mind be in you that was in Christ Jesus, who . . . emptied himself . . . and became obedient to the point of death" (Phil 2:5, 7, 8). In the second Paul notes that bearing one another's burdens is fulfilling the "law of Christ"(Gal 6:2). In Romans Paul makes this connection clear: "Each of us must please our neighbor for the good purposes of building up the neighbor. For Christ did not please himself; but, as it is written, 'The insults of those who insult you have fallen on me'" (Rom 15:2-3). In other words, the practice that is central to the New Testament (and to Levinas), that we must become "responsible" for others, is tied in the Christian view to the death of Christ on our behalf. As Christ tells his disciples: "Whoever wishes to be first among you must be slave of all. For the Son of Man came not to be served but to serve, and to give his life a ransom for many" (Mk 10:44-45).

As God has created us in relationships from which we have fallen away, so Christ came to reestablish these fundamental ties. The Christian scriptures make clear that these ties between God and ourselves, and among ourselves, are intimately related. For the exclusion of the "other" from our presence reflects the fact that we have denied that we live in the presence of God. This is why John ties our active love for God and our neighbor together—"Those who do not love a brother or sister whom they have seen, cannot love God whom they have not seen" (1 Jn 4:20). But Christ came to break down the barrier that excludes us from God's presence and also the walls that we have built between ourselves. We who were strangers and aliens, "having no hope and without God in the world, . . . have been brought near by the blood of Christ," Paul says (Eph 2:12, 13). But what Christ did in bringing us "near," at the same time, also breaks down the dividing wall that exists between Jew and Greek. That wall is very real, having been constructed by hostility and fear. But Christ has overcome the enmity and the resultant hostility between us "that he might create in himself one new humanity in place of two, thus making peace, and might reconcile both groups to God in one body, through the cross, thus putting to death that hostility through it" (2:15-16). This having been done, Paul can say, in words that recall Levinas's decentering of the ego, "It is no longer I who live, but it is Christ who lives in me. And the life I now live in the flesh I live by faith in the Son of God, who loved me and gave himself for me" (Gal 2:20).

This relationship with Christ creates new possibilities with respect to my neighbor—in some cases unheard-of possibilities. The New Testament is realistic enough to recognize that our neighbor may also be our enemy. The first words out of the mouths of some groups who have suffered at the hands of another group are often: "You do not understand what awful things they have done. I cannot bear to look at them when I remember what they have done to my family." This is true, and no one who has not experienced this can understand it fully. But Christ, who did not revile but suffered abuse, has put humanity in a new situation. His forgiveness of us and our sin is irrational, just as our forgiveness of others may appear irrational. "The perpetrator," notes Miroslav Volf, "*deserves* unforgiveness." But whatever the other person deserves, the fact remains that we are still responsible agents. We may respond by contributing to the spiral of violence and unforgiveness—indeed, that often seems the "noble" way. But we can also, against all evidence or reason, "let go" of the offense. "Could it be," Volf asks, "that the word of forgiveness that must be uttered in the depths of our being if it is uttered at all, is an echo of Another's voice?"[54]

The work of bringing people together is more than just forgiveness, though it cannot happen without that. It is the creation of a space where they can feel welcome. This is work the New Testament calls "hospitality." As opposed to seeking to purify who we are by excluding the "other" (for whatever righteous reasons), in the work of hospitality we create a place in the world we know for the stranger. The forgiveness Christ has extended to us puts us in a situation in which we can take the initiative; we need not stay in the place of either the victim or the oppressor. On the basis of the fact that the barriers which we have created—the "hostility," Paul calls it in Ephesians—have been broken down, a new opportunity and a new place of responsibility have been created for us to entertain the "other." In order for this to happen we must act on the forgiveness that Christ has extended; indeed, the New Testament implies that our forgiveness is not real until we are prepared to do this.

Hospitality is an important idea in the New Testament generally, but it is especially central in the life and teaching of Jesus, right through to the last supper in which he plays host to his very betrayer. But in Luke 14, while at dinner in the home of a leader of the Pharisees, he describes the new opportunity being created for hospitality. "When you give a luncheon or dinner, do not invite your friends," he begins (Lk 14:12). In other words, do not follow the usual pattern of mutual gift giving—if you do this for me I will return the favor ("in case . . . you will be repaid," v. 12). Instead, invite the "poor, the crippled, the lame, and the blind. And you will be blessed, because they cannot repay you, for you will be repaid at the resurrection of the righteous" (vv. 13-14). In New Testament times these folks were not simply strangers, people on the margins of society, but they were those who would automatically be excluded from such invitations because of their ritual impurity. Christ was introducing his followers to a new situation in which spaces could be created, even for such as these. The ordinary cultural and religious laws were now to be read from the perspective of the One who came to seek and to save those who were lost. This is why Christian practices of hospitality—which ignore traditional boundaries between insiders and outsiders[55]—have been central throughout the church's history. This has become possible because forgiveness allows us literally to rewrite the story we have told about "others," and consequently, the story we tell about ourselves—often resulting in a radical rearrangement of who occupies the center and who is pushed to the margins.

References to the marginalized in a culture remind us of people whose identity is so deeply challenged that there seems to be no place for them in the world. Refugees, immigrants, children of mixed-race marriages—many people find themselves homeless in some fundamental way. They have been excluded from the normal relationships that people enjoy and cut adrift. They experience in particularly painful ways the alienation among peoples that exists in our fallen order. Two examples might be given. Among immigrant groups in America many have come to sense their homelessness within the dominant culture. Korean-Americans, for example, especially those of the second generation, feel deeply their "in-betweenness." They are no longer a part of their home country, Korea, but they feel they are not accepted by other Americans. Where do they belong?[56] In the Caribbean today people also have a sense that they have no future in the world. People of this region, writes Dieumeme Noelliste, represent a "disparate band dislodged from its original habitat, transplanted and scattered into a new hostile and incoherently constituted environment." What hope is there for a people who are without a story—or whose story is too painful to recall? This past "has no positive content and thus cannot constitute the basis for any new departure. Void is the only starting point; but what can result from emptiness except nothingness?"[57]

We have argued that the challenge for those who have a home lies in opening to the "other." To those who find themselves homeless in different ways the challenge is quite different: how to find the way home. Two insights from Korean theologian Sang Hyun Lee are helpful here. First, in the Christian view the metaphor of pilgrimage has come to stand for an important dimension of human life. While we are made for this created order, we are at the same time homeless, restless in it. This is because, as Augustine reminds us, we are also made for God. We are restless until we finally find our rest in the sabbath with God. Meanwhile, we journey along in faithfulness and trust in what God will do for us. As Sang Hyun Lee points out, this need not imply that we deny either this world or the next; rather, both can be seen in their appropriate positions. For people in marginal situations, the reality of life as "pilgrimage" may take on a meaning that the more settled members of the human community cannot understand.

Second, the gospel is good news. The good news for pilgrims is that they are, after all, in the right place because God is there with them, journeying along beside them.[58] God understands what it is like to be excluded from the centers of power, having experienced such exclusion on the cross, and can bring us through to a place we can call home. Wilderness, after all, is a necessary way-station en route to the Promised Land.

But can we actually find this comfort? Is there hope for the storyless neighbors in our midst? To answer this question we must move to our third theological category: embodiment.

Ethnicity and the People of God

While human community is a good that rests on the relationships that God built into creation, in the present situation—distorted as it is by human sin—the church as the people of God provides the norm for our understanding of human relationship. In a sense we will explore, all human relationships aspire to be the church; at the same time, the concrete reality of the church relativizes (even if it does not efface) our ethnic differences.

These claims seem difficult to make in the present situation because we do not often see the church fulfilling its role as a community of reconciliation. Indeed, the language we confess to describe the church is often denied in practice. But, as Gil Baillie points out, this is no surprise to those who understand the point of God's call to holiness and community, because repentance is the precondition of participating in the church. As Baillie notes: "Were there to be a generation of Christians that did not suddenly discover that it had been betraying the Gospels, it would ipso facto be betraying it in the worst way. Only in contrition does the Christian believer or the Christian community achieve lucidity."[59] Baptism, then, does not make a person perfect by removing the stain of original sin; rather, it is rather a confession of our sinfulness and an introduction into a new set "of personal relationships in a community ordered around the justifying death of Christ."[60]

Let us examine each of these two claims in turn. First, we have said that in this period of history all human relationships aspire to be the church. That is to say, the community that gathers in Christ's name is the direction human community is pointed, whether it recognizes this or not. This does not mean the church is the only valid form of community or that ethnicity and cultural solidarity have no value. They have value because of the created gifts of God and God's sustaining presence among the nations of the earth. But these gifts and this presence find their highest embodiment in the communities from every tribe and tongue and nation that gather to worship the risen Lord by the power of the Holy Spirit.

Here we recall that our human relationships are primarily tactual and concrete. Moreover, as we have seen, the moral imperative of relationships is not added later but present from the beginning. We are called by our very proximity to moral responsibility—we are our sister's and brother's keeper. That is the way things are. But now the Christian church as the community of Jesus' disciples exists because that moral order God established has, in Jesus, taken a particular historical shape. The existence of the church is based on the assumption that God's will can be known and done in the created and relational world we inhabit, and moreover that this will is seen (and done) in Jesus Christ.[61] As Colin Gunton puts it:

> [According to the New Testament], human community becomes concrete in the Church, whose calling it is to be the medium and realization of communion: with God in the first instance, and with other people in the second, as a result of the first.[62]

Our insistence on the centrality of the church rests on the fact that the community where God's word is preached and heard embodies the reality of the reconciling grace of God as this is revealed in Christ. Were the words of Paul in Ephesians 2:15 or in Galatians 3:28—that we two have become one in Jesus Christ—to remain an attractive ideal to be striven for, we would never actually understand what human community was meant to be. But when this is embodied—when, for example, white Afrikaaners and black South Africans can embrace with tears; when Korean Christians can embrace the very Japanese who imprisoned them during Japanese rule—then we can begin to understand the potential of human relationships. For in Jesus human relations have been recast on a new basis that breaks the cycle of punishment and vengeance.[63]

This claim also rests on the fact that the Christian community forms a locus of moral reasoning that allows for both individual dignity and the corporate identity of humanity. Here is the recognition that "a stick alone does not burn," that we need the corporate wisdom of all God's gifts to see our way ahead. As John Howard Yoder maintains, in the community we can recognize that God has gifted agents of direction, of memory, of linguistic self-consciousness, and of order and due process. All of these together in the hands of the Holy Spirit, who indwells Christ's people, work to bring the whole body to the maturity that begins to reflect the Lord. "The way of discipleship is the way for which we are made; there is no other 'nature' to which grace is a superadditum."[64]

The church provides a safe place to stand, which can give the believer moral leverage for transformation of life and work. We have noticed that moral discernment is more often called for than provided. This is because human order is inherently moral, and the human observer cannot keep from making moral judgments on everything from child prostitution to gender equality. But the question always comes back to this: Where is the moral ground on which one can stand to make (and live out) such moral judgments? The answer the New Testament gives is that the church is that moral space. From this perspective the whole of life opens out as a potential field for God's grace to operate, so that new ways of living, working and relating become actually—and not simply theoretically—present and historically embodied.

The Christian claims that "all social life has its basis in redemption whether it is prepared to acknowledge it or not."[65] Of course this claim appears scandalous to those who have not come to know the grace of God in Jesus Christ. As Yoder says: "Only from within the community of resurrection is the cruciformity of the cosmos a key rather than a scandal."[66] This all rests on belief in a God who created all things and orders them according to the divine will. Most educated Westerners, we have allowed, no longer assume this ground. And this has brought our culture to its present crisis. As Charles Taylor points out, the challenge to Christianity that the modern person raises is this: How can we believe in God any longer? But humanism, he notes, faces even more serious questions: So what? Why should these differences matter? [67]

This brings us to the second claim that was advanced at the beginning of this section: the concrete existence of the church as a historical community relativizes our ethnic differences. There are two places in the New Testament where ethnicity appears on center stage. The first is in the final commission of Jesus to his disciples to "make disciples of all nations [*panta ta ethne*], baptizing them . . . and teaching them to obey everything that I have commanded you" (Mt 28:19-20). That is, they are to form people into communities where the new possibilities of service and worship that Jesus has introduced are embodied. This work will be in direct continuity with

Jesus' own creation-altering life and death, a fact underlined by Jesus' promise, which concludes Matthew's commission: "And remember, I am with you always, to the end of the age" (Mt 28:20).

In a second major New Testament reference to ethnicity Paul claims that God "made all nations [*pan ethnos*] to inhabit the whole earth, and he allotted the times of their existence and the boundaries of the places where they would live, so that they would search for God and perhaps grope for him and find him" (Acts 17:26-27). Just as a central calling of Christians is to make disciples of the nations, so a major function of ethnicity is to locate the search for God, to be that locus in which God might be found and known. Here the validity of Donald McGavran's point may be acknowledged: ethnicity does provide a lens, an indispensable one as we have seen, in terms of which the grace of God may be seen and grasped. This calling, which all nations are given, reminds us that our differences, however real and valuable they may be, are going to be brought together in a higher and more wonderful setting. To put it another way, however important the projects pursued by various ethnic—and other voluntary affiliations[68]—there is a larger and more comprehensive project in which they find their meaning: the Kingdom of God.

The Bible in both the Hebrew and Christian scriptures underlines this universal character by referring to this new entity God is forming simply as God's "people" (Hebrew, *am*; Greek, *laos*). When Jesus raised the widow's son from the dead and fear seized the people, they glorified God saying, "God has looked favorably on his people" (Lk 7:16, quoting Ps 106:4). Whatever their background and despite the wounds this background might have caused, people now in Christ are given a place in the presence of God. As Peter says,

> Once you were not a people [*laos*],
> but now you are God's people;
> once you had not received mercy,
> but now you have received mercy.
> (1 Pt 2:10)

This shows the final truth about ethnicity: to be a people within a particular created context is to be related to God and to experience God's salvation.

CONCLUSION

We have argued that ethnicity represents the social groupings that result from a variety of historical and genetic factors. These groups clearly reflect the relational abundance and diversity of God's creation, but they also reveal what people have made of that creation. *Ethnicity* is not only something that is given in creation, but it is also socially constructed. It allows people to join together to work for historical (and civilizational) projects that contribute to human and creational flourishing. But it also allows people to attempt idolatrous towers that reach to heaven. Each people has its own unique gifts to bring to the larger human project, and each also has things to learn from others.

With the coming of Jesus Christ, ethnicity is placed in a new setting. Community now is given a particular direction; it is leading to the end that God has promised creation. Many worthy projects may still be appropriately pursued; all have validity because of the good order and purposes of God's creation. But at the center of these projects now is the most comprehensive of all our human work: bringing people together into the family of God. And each people has its own part to play here as well. The present shape of the body of Christ is imperfect, of course, but not only because of our fallenness. It is incomplete because "what we will be has not yet been revealed" (1 Jn 3:2). Though we are already the children of God, John says, in that day "when he is revealed, we will be like him for we will see him as he is" (1 Jn 3:2). And as John says in another place the "we" in that day will be made up of a heavenly chorus of people from every tribe and people.

> After this I looked, and there was a great multitude that no one could count, from every nation, from all tribes and peoples and languages, standing before the throne and before the Lamb, robed in white, with palm branches in their hands. They cried out in a loud voice, saying,
> "Salvation belongs to our God who is seated on the
> throne, and to the Lamb." (Rv 7:9-10)

This hope controls and guides the practices of the community of faith in this period of history, for it implies that the final truth about things will be revealed to all the tribes together, and not to any one of them alone—that, in the words of John Milbank, "peace no longer depends upon the reduction to the self-identical, but is the *sociality* of harmonic difference,"[69] so that at the end each people will bring its ethnic glory into the heavenly kingdom to lay at the feet of the Lord (Rv 21:24, 26). Meanwhile, we insist that no one group alone will see clearly how to proceed. As Miroslav Volf says in his discussion of justice: "For people from different social groups and traditions to agree on justice they need to practice enlarged thinking, which is to say that they need to make space in themselves for the perspective of the other, which in turn means they need to be willing to embrace the 'other.'"[70] To take a single example, inter-ethnic marriage in a Christian setting can be a symbol of the fact that our identity can and does extend beyond our immediate cultural group. Such marriages can embody this enlarged thinking in a very concrete way. Indeed, the space where this enlarged thinking is most clearly visible is meant to be the community of faith. For here are those who through Christ's sacrifice by the Spirit are lifted up to God "to create a living echo of the communion that God is in eternity."[71] This people shows that ethnicity is ultimately constituted by praise.

5

Ecology

Ecology—or the study of the relationships between living things and their environment—has recently come to be identified with the problems associated with our human management of God's creation. How the gift of God's good creation—the beauty of mountains and clouds, or the awe inspired by vast forests and sunsets over ocean beaches—has come to be considered a problem, even a battlefield of competing interests, may be difficult to understand. But global warming and oil spills, and the debates they engender, are realities that confront us almost daily in the media. The June 1992 UN Summit on the Environment and Development in Rio de Janeiro, Brazil, and the 1995 Summit on "Social Development" in Copenhagen gave environmental problems and their social impact new visibility.

For the Christian these discussions have become especially difficult because influential voices declare that environmental problems are a direct result of Christian teaching and practice. What is worse, even if that charge can be met, those taking the initiative in addressing environmental problems often do so out of a religious framework that is clearly at odds with Christianity. Indeed, in the popular imagination, ecology and what is called New Age thinking have become virtually synonymous—as the polemic of Cal Thomas quoted in chapter 1 illustrates (see page 2). Our purpose in this chapter is not to consider the state and extent of environmental problems—many sources are available for that[1]—but to think about the historical background of the discussion and then, as we have done for other questions, apply the theological categories we are developing to the issues that are raised.

The real roots of the present crisis are not in Christianity's view of creation but in the views about human autonomy that have developed in the West. Indeed, neither creation nor humanity can be properly understood outside of its relationship with God. Within this context humanity is called to responsible stewardship by God's continuing presence and activity in the earth, especially as this is seen in the redemptive life and death of Jesus Christ and in the gift of the Holy Spirit.

As in the case of ethnicity, the awareness of environmental problems has grown dramatically in the last generation. Probably the Club of Rome report in 1972[2] and the oil crisis that came soon afterward did more than anything else to bring these things to the popular imagination. But long before this, scientists had become alarmed over the impact of human activity on the natural order. In 1967 Lynn White, Jr., stated bluntly that "the Christian axiom that nature has no reason for existence save to serve humanity" is the cause for the growing ecological crisis.[3] This view has been modified in subsequent discussions but continues to dominate the thinking of secular environmentalists. The issues today, however, are framed in terms of a more recent and equally important discussion. In the 1980s a debate evolved between two groups. One, represented by J. L. Simon, argued that the ingenuity of humans will continue to "create" resources and that therefore the so-called ecological problems were being exaggerated. The second group, including people like P. R. Ehrlich of the Ecological school, believes the ecological limits are very real and see technological attempts to extend those limits as creating more problems than they solve. Those on the side of Simon, called Exemptionalists (because they see humans as exempted from ecological limitation) really continue the anthropocentric paradigm that White attacked, the paradigm which has become deeply entrenched since the rise of industrialization. The Exemptionalists have recently become politically active, forming lobby groups that target the environmental activists. Called the Wise Use Movement, they promote the use of resources for human development and often characterize environmentalists as "tree worshipers."[4] The ecologists, on the other hand, also called the neo-Malthusians because they associate ecological problems with unchecked human population growth, insist that the way of life that has resulted from seeing human interests as paramount is threatening both local and global ecosystems. This view has come to be identified with the so-called Green paradigm.[5] In a 1991 article that outlines this view, Greg Knill states that the "real cause of the environmental crisis is the inappropriate human-nature relationship" that has religious roots in Christian and other sources. Moreover, "only a fundamental alteration in this relationship will produce a permanent solution to the problems."[6]

This debate can serve as a useful starting point to our discussion. Even these brief comments reveal that these issues reach to the level of fundamental commitments and that their solution will not be technical or scientific alone. While not everyone would speak of a religious solution, observers are convinced that any solution will involve assumptions about the nature of reality and especially the human role in the earth's management.

While Christians were quick to respond to White's accusations,[7] those who have thought deeply about these things admit there is an ambiguity both to the biblical teaching and to the practice of Christians. In his inaugural address at Oxford, John MacQuarrie pointed out the complexity of Hebrew thinking about the earth. There is the monarchical view of human domination, which White pointed out, but there is also a more organic and interactive view, which has often been lost sight of in Christian history.[8] H. Paul Santmire similarly has pointed out that there are two theological motifs present in the history of the church.[9] The first, the spiritual motif, understands the human search as seeking to transcend earthly limitations and to find a home in God. This tradition, represented by Origen and the early Augustine, found expression in medieval theology—especially in Dante—where to ascend to God means to leave materiality behind. Though countered by the secularization brought about by the Renaissance and Reformation, which focused on this world as the focus of divine and human attention (121), this spiritual tradition has experienced a revival in the twentieth century in the works of Karl Barth and Teilhard de Chardin, for whom the material is merely the context for spiritual reality (145).[10]

But there is another equally important tradition, paralleling what MacQuarrie calls the organic view in the Hebrew scriptures, which Santmire calls the ecological motif. This stream is associated with Irenaeus, the later Augustine, and with Celtic and Benedictine spirituality. These Christians understand human life as a promising journey to the good land God has prepared for it. In the Middle Ages, St. Francis represented this tradition with his emphasis on the wonder and love for God's creation as a "brother or sister" of humanity.[11] The Reformers provided a theological grounding for this by denying that we could ascend to God, insisting rather that God in Christ descended to be with us on earth.[12] Santmire calls upon Christians to develop this second, ecological stream, but his survey indicates that the role of Christianity in the discussion is not as simple as either White or his Christian respondents would like to think.[13] Clearly both traditions have something to contribute to Christian ecological reflection and action.

It is possible that the anthropocentric bias blamed on Christianity has its roots more in the modern intellectual tradition, which both Christians and secular environmentalists share, than in the Christian tradition itself. In the area of ecology, even more clearly than in questions of culture and race, the turn that occurred in the scientific revolution has had far-reaching results. We have described that as a transformed world view that began to see the world in its own terms rather than in terms of God and God's purposes. Clearly the biblical and Christian traditions have little in common with the radical anthropocentrism of Descartes's starting point—sitting alone with his thinking in a darkened room. Rosino Gibellini, in fact, argues that Descartes inverted the biblical notion of dominion from one that is responsible to God to one that is autonomous in character.[14] It is not hard to see that this understanding of dominion may have more to do with the exploitation of the earth than any simple reference to human responsibility.

But there is an equally serious result that follows from Descartes's narrowing of human understanding to "what can be thought with certainty." As we will explore in more detail in the next chapter, this focus ignores not only the bodily but the earthly context of our human life. How then is there any place for human responsibility to care for the earth? Does this not, Odil Steck asks, "perceive too little—dangerously little—from the point of view of our survival? . . . Does [it] not lead to serious deformations with regard to the object of our knowledge—i.e., the natural world and environment—and with regard to the perceiving subject?"[15] The abstraction of self from the world not only divides up and ignores the relationships of creation, but, as a result, denies that fundamental link between the subject and the object.

This rational autonomy is probably seen most clearly in the rise of industrialization and the triumph of technology. Raymond Williams points out that beginning early in the nineteenth century the idea of culture as the expression of human values became divorced from society, with its focus on urban and industrial development. The former, under the influence of Romanticism, developed a more refined and superior sensitivity; the latter perceived human activity as dominating through the development of technology.[16] In many respects the twentieth century marks the triumph of technology as the supposed instrument of human (and rational) liberation. It is not hard to see this as a descendent of Descartes's search for what can be known with certainty and of the Baconian quest to employ nature in the service of human development. As Jacques Ellul writes in his classic study of technology:

> The twofold intervention of reason and consciousness in the technical world, which produces the technical phenomenon, can be described as the quest of the one best means in every field. And this "one best means" is, in fact, the technical means. It is the aggregate of these means that produces technical civilization.[17]

Technology from one point of view is only an instrument and cannot be blamed for all that is wrong with the human relationship to the environment. Indeed, as Loren Wilkinson and his colleagues argue, technology is able to widen our knowledge of God's creation and can become a means to our stewardship of it.[18] But we often have the sense that the machine has broken our natural links with the created order. Romano Guardini laments: "Materials and forces are harnessed, unleashed, burst open, altered and directed at will. There is no feeling for what is organically possible or tolerable in any living sense."[19] And when this machine-like order functions autonomously—that is, outside the responsible relationships in which the human creature lives—it often takes on a destructive life of its own. Responses to both the Rio Summit and the Copenhagen Summit include references to the irrationality of the world economic system, which appears to have taken on the character of the sorcerer's apprentice. Julio de Santa Ana describes modern economic culture as "a culture trying to dominate and control everything, without limits, in accordance with the 'Faustian' spirit driving it."[20] For people of all religious persuasions, or those with none, these particular developments in Western culture have contributed to the problems with which we struggle at the end of our century.

Whatever their roots, both the problems and this historical context are now inescapable. As we have noted above, there is a consensus developing that the solutions to ecological problems are spiritual as well as technical. Indeed, we are all more or less disabused from the idealistic notion that we can solve all our problems by the application of science and rationality. There is a growing realization that for the past two or three centuries something has been missing from our corporate lives, something we would call, in some sense, spiritual. Indeed, Charles Taylor argues, the earth is one of the last remaining spiritual sources available to the modern person. This widespread feeling for nature, which took an expressivist turn with Romanticism, has come to have a particular spiritual—even mystical—tone. As Taylor says of the source of ecological ethics, "To have a proper moral stance towards the natural order is to have access to one's inner voice."[21] Care for the earth has a dimension of ultimacy about it; our human flourishing depends on it. But can the Christian say more about these things?

THEOLOGICAL PERSPECTIVES ON THE EARTH

The Relational Character of Creation

The earth exists with God. We have stated that creation is, from one point of view, the limits that God has placed on himself. If we cannot agree completely with Jürgen Moltmann that creation is "the withdrawal of God into himself," it clearly prefigures what later takes place in Jesus Christ, his kenosis (emptying).[22] This limitation of God not only defines God's relation to creation but it also frees the creature to be itself, to have its own integrity. Thus, in the Christian view, the freedom of the creature is not the freedom of autonomy but the freedom that is realized in relationship with God.

That a constitutive relationship can be liberating is a reflection of the fact that God exists in a communion of loving and giving in which the richness of each person is fulfilled in the trinitarian relationship. That relationship is reflected, we have asserted, in God's relationships with the world. Jürgen Moltmann's thesis expresses this well: "It is this trinitarian concept of life as interpenetration or perichoresis which will therefore determine [an] ecological doctrine of creation." For the creation also exists in community, though its relationships are both similar to and different from those within the Godhead.[23] The asymmetrical character of the creature's relationship with God is essential to our understanding both of God and the world (see the Introduction, above). The world is dependent on God in a way that God is not dependent on the world. But the Trinity, especially in its works in history, gives us an indispensable clue to the relationships among creation. This is because God's presence in creation reflects what God is. God's presence is relational, active, and embodied in the creation itself.

As we have seen, the creature continues to have its existence, to draw its nourishment as it were, from God. God, in turn, continues to act in the world to bring about God's purposes. Samuel Terrien discusses this active, and for the creature constitutive, relationship as the Hebrew theology of presence. In the Hebrew scriptures spaces and times remain dependent on a free and sovereign God, "whose transcendence was never divorced from a 'pathetic' concern for the welfare of human and even animal life."[24] God continues to be present for the creature in a personal way, acting both from "below" and from "above," that is, both by sustenance and miracle. Moreover, this presence is caring and supportive, even as it is non-coercive and respectful of the dignity of the creature.

The implications of this for our "management" of the earth are large. For the goodness, what Genesis 1 calls the "blessing" of the earth (Gn 1:22, 28), while it includes the human couple, also preexists them. The Genesis account begins in fact, not with the human purposes but with God and God's purposes. God works for a full "week" before even considering the human creation. God has called the earth to its blessed responsibility, what is later called fertility, long before humanity appears. Indeed, the rule of the man and woman is to be placed firmly in the context of this productive and blessed order.

But the order exists not for the creatures' sake, not even for human sake, but for God. Psalm 104, which is closely linked to the creation account, underlines God's centrality not only in maintaining the earth's processes but, above all, in taking delight in it all:

> May the glory of the LORD endure for ever,
> May the LORD rejoice in his works. (Ps 104:31)

For the modern person, who understands the world in its own terms, the creature is encountered as an object either to be used or preserved. In either case—whether we carefully protect the earth or carelessly exploit it—it is we, human creatures, who magisterially decide what is to be done. If the world is a natural order that must simply be respected, what is the problem? Why worry about disorder? or the disappearance of species?[25] By contrast, in the biblical view that we are considering, the order has a goodness that derives from its creator and therefore deserves respect and protection. As Odil Steck says, "Life is first of all an event of the continual inclining of Yahweh the creator, a movement toward the world which comprehends it and mankind, and which . . . offers the provision of life's necessities to all living things."[26]

This ownership of the earth becomes a dominant theme in the Hebrew scriptures and determines, in principle, all of Israel's land-management policies. God says through Moses: "The land shall not be sold in perpetuity, for the land is mine; with me you are but aliens and tenants" (Lv 25:23). This principle, given in the context of Jubilee instructions, determines Israel's basic attitude toward the land as stewardship.[27] So the goodness of all the earth and its processes—not simply the human good—are constantly in view.

Intercropping (growing one crop between the rows of another) to increase yield is forbidden (Lv 19:19); fruit trees are not to be harvested until they are established (Lv 19:23-25); the sabbath regulations specify a fallow year for the land (Ex 23:10-11); animals are always to be treated with respect, as even they are included in the sabbath rest (Ex 23:4-5, 12).[28] All of this reflects the fact that God is the ultimate owner and wants the good order at every point to reflect the divine interests. This goodness exists quite independently of human concerns, as God pointedly reminds Job (Jb 38–39), and it is meant to reflect God's own glory. John Calvin describes this "theater for his glory": "There is no spot in the universe wherein you cannot discern at least some sparks of his glory. You cannot in one glance survey this most beautiful system of the universe in its wide expanse without being completely overwhelmed by the boundless force of its brightness."[29]

We will consider presently the responsibility the human creature inevitably carries with respect to creation. Here we note that biblical teaching puts this in the larger context of God's own care and interest in creation. This means that the first movement in human relationships toward the earth is not active but passive. This is underlined in the reality of creation as given by God, "fore-given," as Odil Steck says, "unreservedly favorable for the promotion of life, and . . . as such precedes all specific activity on the part of the living."[30] Again, this places Christians in the clearest possible contrast to secular environmentalists. In the Western tradition the earth is encountered as an object that must be managed, without any larger context in which it can simply be received. Emmanuel Levinas develops this discussion by reminding us that "it is not by chance that Plato teaches us that matter is eternal, and that for Aristotle matter is a *cause*, such is the truth of the order of *things.* Western philosophy," he goes on, "which perhaps is reification itself, remains faithful to the order of things and does not know the absolute passivity, beneath the level of activity and passivity, which is contributed by the idea of creation."[31] Creation, as the work of God, is first of all received as a gift that speaks to us of purposes and interests that transcend our own, and thus should be received with humility. If we are observant in the way encouraged by Calvin, this will first evoke our wonder, and then, if we read the clues in the right way, it will move us to worship—that ultimate act of active reception—the One whose glory is evident there (cf. Rom 1:17ff.). Christians then will be insistent that our work in the world, in ecology as in all our work of stewardship, will begin and be carried out in the context of worship.

Creation lives in community. One of the fundamental axioms of the emerging science of ecology is the interconnection of all living things. In Christian thinking this has come to be identified with the integrity of creation. Larry Rasmussen elaborates this relational ontology as follows:

> We live into one another's lives and die into one another's deaths in a way that displays all connections on a curved and closed planet as

> "integral" one with another. Life thus carries a fateful "integrity" from the inside out. Effects may and do vary widely. Some are life-giving while others are deadly. But nothing is without effect.[32]

This has several implications for understanding and interacting with the earth. One is that creatures must always be respected and treated in the context of their environment. This word, *environment*, which has come to be used in the singular, ought to be understood as radically plural. That is, each living thing belongs to a very particular ecosystem to which it contributes and from which it derives its life. Within this context living organisms thrive and, more important, have their moral worth. This is a very important discovery, because the Western intellectual tradition has proceeded to knowledge by way of abstraction and analysis (which means separation). Now ecologists are reminding us that value consists in the order of the whole, in seeing and putting things together. This implies that, in ecology, wisdom comes through seeing things in their natural relationships.

Such thinking has led to a new field of ethics, founded by naturalist Aldo Leopold, which he calls a "land ethic." He defines the basic principle of this ethic as follows: "A thing is right when it tends to preserve the integrity, stability, and beauty of the biotic community. It is wrong when it tends otherwise."[33] This moral admonition is based on the assumption of the communal character of nature, but it also implies that there is an integrity to this community. Scientists speak of this as the basic self-organizing capacity of the natural world, from the atom's self-organization to that of the star or galaxy.[34] It is represented, for example, by the natural order, which the doctor ultimately trusts—aided by whatever interventions are appropriate—to heal the body. The awareness of this participatory ordering of reality, the Christian believes, is consistent with both the goodness of creation and God's presence within it. As Larry Rasmussen puts this theological claim: "This moral ordering is God's own creating, that indeed the inner secret of creation is the indwelling of God's presence and power within it."[35]

This claim has two important corollaries that contemporary environmental ethics is recognizing. On the one hand natural objects have value in themselves; they must be respected. This land ethic has been developed by Christopher Stone.[36] In 1972 he argued that there is a moral (and thus) legal right that lakes, rivers, and forests have which derives from their value to the overall order (and the presumed goodness) of things. This view has actually led to suits against companies for damages to these natural entities, on the basis of what Stone called their "moral considerability." That is, even when there is no damage to a human plaintiff, these entities retain their "moral considerability." Thus they can be considered legal entities, and cases can be brought on their behalf.

Notice, on the other hand, that though this value is attributed to an entity—a tree, or a lake—the goodness is not recognized apart from its contribution to the good of the larger order. Value and goodness relate to the context and position a given entity occupies; they are not absolute or intrinsic. This principle of ecology, which has long been recognized in economics, has great implications for human life and stewardship of the earth. The view that the value of goods and services is positional has been foundational for economics. There the value of a good or a service is defined in terms of the market, which, as Adam Smith defined it two hundred years ago, is a network comprised of individual decisions made by consumers all pursuing their own self-interest. Here what counts as a good is a matter of shared—and negotiated—interests.

The market recognizes, to an extent, the contextual nature of value. The problem, as we are becoming aware, is that it operates on too narrow a view of *value*—in the terms of our discussion it is not contextual enough. It does not recognize and honor *all* the relationships in which an entity exists. As Loren Wilkinson points out, modern views of the market leave out our crucial role as keepers of the goods of the earth (and thus of the broader interests of our neighbors).[37] The market considers only producers and consumers taken out of their context as members of a community and keepers of the goods of the earth. Ultimately the value of goods or services not only should but does reflect this larger context. In this relational view the comprehensive relations in fact determine operative values whether we recognize this or not. Present economic exchanges, for example, may choose to ignore their impact on the ozone layer, but someday we or our children will have to "pay" for the damage that is being done to our atmosphere. Another example, people who can only afford to live on the edges of cities on land polluted by industrial waste are "paying" costs that were not covered in the industrial processes that produced the waste. This is because these relationships are actually determinative of value. That is the way God made the world to work.

This realization has led to a broader conception of the relationships among creatures than that even envisioned by Aldo Leopold. This "social ecology" recognizes the central role that human communities play in the ecosystems. This newer way of thinking informs the important papers collected by Leonardo Boff and Virgil Elizondo in *Ecology and Poverty* (1995). Western campaigns to "save the whale," for example, ignore the larger system of relationships in which, in some parts of the world, as much as one-third of the human population is threatened with extinction on a daily basis. The "option for the poor," José Ramos Regidor notes, must now be exercised "within the more general option for life, for the integrity of creation, especially where life is most threatened."[38] This place that is being deprived of life is where the poor of the earth are living; it is also often the place where the environment has been most damaged. This has led to a consideration of ecological issues in a larger framework, called social ecology. The tenets of social ecology include the following:

a. Human beings interact intensely and continually with the environment. Neither can be studied in isolation from the other, because each determines aspects of the structure and functioning of the other.
b. The interaction between human and environmental systems is dynamic and develops in time and space.[39]

This recognition of the special role of humanity in the developing science of ecology raises again the question of the ambiguity of Christianity toward the earth. Whatever may be the human role in the processes of environmental degradation, this "cry of the poor" reminds us that here is an aspect of the created ecosystem as threatened as any other. What moral consideration must we give to this fact? It seems to me that answers to these difficult questions can be found only in the context of the biblical perspective of creation. On the one hand, God is interested in the good order of things quite apart from human interests narrowly conceived (Ps 104; Jb 38–39). On the other hand, human efforts do threaten the goodness of the order—and both human and nonhuman creatures suffer from this disorder. This is why the psalmist at the end of that most ecologically sensitive Psalm 104 calls out to God:

> Let sinners be consumed from the earth,
> and let the wicked be no more. (Ps 104:35)

Only this will return good order to the chaos that God keeps at bay (cf. vv. 3-5). This leads us then to the next principle that grows out of our theological assumptions.

Creation, in its present condition, cannot sustain itself. So far there is little debate among people who work with the earth and are concerned about its future: the fabric of life is an interrelated whole that must be respected. But along with this affirmation a further claim is often advanced. Not only is the earth a single, self-regulating community, but the ideal is to achieve what is called *homeostasis*. Holmes Ralston, III, who proposes this term, insists we have a duty "to stabilize the ecosystem through mutually imposed self-limited growth."[40] Similarly, James Lovelock, in his immensely influential Gaia hypothesis, proposes that the earth is best thought of as a single, large, internally related, living organism. His description of *homeostasis* is the "maintenance of constant conditions by active control."[41] Lovelock, a respected NASA scientist, was obviously puzzled by the outpouring of support for his modest proposal and wrote *The Ages of Gaia* to respond to some of the questions his earlier book raised. He reiterates that "the Gaia hypothesis said that the temperature, oxidation state, acidity, and certain aspects of rocks and waters are at any time kept constant, and this homeostasis is maintained by active feedback processes operated automatically and unconsciously by the biota [the animal and plant life of a region or period]."[42] But this does not imply that Gaia is indifferent to human efforts. "She is stern and tough, keeping the world warm and comfortable for those who obey the rules but ruthless in her destruction of those who transgress."[43]

The classic dilemma of the naturalistic interpretation of the earth is here demonstrated with Lovelock: How does one derive an *ought* from an *is*? Does the fact that the earth appears to be self-regulating, imply that human efforts *ought* to be directed to that end? Clearly there is an implication that communal processes ought to be respected because when they are, the fertility of the earth is increased. Contrariwise, human greed and unbridled use of technology has had a negative effect on the earth's processes. John Cobb is probably the most prominent theologian to mount a theological argument for adapting our social and economic lives to the limits imposed by the earth's resources. "The finitude of our planet requires us to work toward a human society that accepts limits and seeks a decent life for all within them."[44] Cobb believes, with Lynn White and others, that the basic threat to proper care of the earth is the dualism implicit in a transcendent God and the resultant exploitative and unjust economic system. He argues that we must manage the earth on a more human scale in terms of *bioregions*, areas where self-sufficient economic systems can develop that are more harmonious with the natural order.

This call to the centrality of human responsibility is linked with Cobb's openness to "the future and unlimited power of transformation that is the grace of God" (11), and that is immanent in the created order. *Sustainability* is an important attempt to persuade people that this vision is the only way to move toward a hopeful future and to avoid the disasters that seem to threaten. But Cobb seems to imply that the immanent activity of God (and God's human image) must be bought at the cost of any transcendent control. As Max Stackhouse notes in his review, Cobb's "theological program tends to make economy into local culture, press culture toward nature and identify nature's becoming with the divine."[45] It would seem that an emphasis on sustainability tends both to overemphasize human intervention—Stackhouse worries about the "massive violation of human rights" Cobb's program implies—and to underemphasize God's sovereign interventions both within and at the end of history.

Sustainability, for many contemporary observers, is an important ideal toward which human efforts may usefully be directed. But the most thoughtful exponents of careful stewardship of the earth's resources are aware that, ultimately, sustainability is in impossible ideal. On the most basic level the law of entropy implies that energy is being constantly changed from usable to unusable forms.[46] All energy used is eventually converted into heat energy, which is radiated out into space, and there seems to be no way of stopping this. In addition to this natural running down of the universe, there is the gradual and very unnatural depletion of fossil fuels and mineral stocks. There are, of course, short-term ways of increasing our energy supply using solar power or even volcanoes or tidal power. But, as Loren Wilkinson notes, "all of them are deficient in one way or another."[47] James Lovelock twenty years ago might have doubted the negative long-term impact of human life and development on the earth, but to do so is becoming increasingly difficult. All the recent data indicate, for example, that global warming is a result of human activity. A September 1995 report in the *New York Times* said: "The warming of the last century, and especially of the last few years, 'is unlikely to be entirely due to natural causes and that a pattern of climatic response to human activities is identifiable in the climatological record.'"[48]

So the earth appears threatened in its natural order, and it is groaning under the weight of population growth and urban and industrial pollution. From one point of view this is simply an instance of the threat that the Bible sees to the created order, which, the Hebrew scriptures seem to imply, has to be kept from the chaos that threatens it on every hand. In the Old Testament wild animals threatened people (see Jacob's worry that an animal had attacked Joseph in Genesis 37:33). If no one would live in the land it would soon "become desolate and the wild animals would multiply" (Ex 23:29; see also 1 Kgs 13:24, 2 Kgs 2:24, 2 Kgs 17:25). In other passages, of course, God is seeking to preserve the life of animals: "You save humans and animals alike" (Ps 36:6) and the wonderful ending of Jonah notes God's concern for the cattle (4:11).

The basic threat of nature has been recognized throughout human history. Santmire quotes the ninth-century writer Sedilius Scotus: "Old ocean mutters, and the hard rocks groan. The unrule north wind hollow the vast air, its horse voice whines here, now bellows there." Seventeenth-century American colonist and printer William Bradford described what settlers in Plymouth found: "It was winter, and they that know ye winters of ye cuntrie know them to be sharp & violent, & subject to cruell & fierce stormes,,, Besids, what could they see but a hidious & desolate wildernes, full of wild beasts & wild men?"[49]

But beyond this natural disharmony that threatens human comfort, in the biblical view, the earth suffers and rebels because of human sin.[50] In the Hebrew scriptures the land became threatening because of Israel's unfaithfulness. The Lord gives rain in the autumn and spring, but, says Jeremiah:

> Your iniquities have turned these away,
> and your sins have deprived you of good.
> (Jer 5:25)

And Hosea notes that because they have not kept the covenant

> Therefore the land mourns,
> and all who live in it languish;

together with the wild animals
  and the birds of the air,
  even the fish of the sea are perishing.
(Hos 4:3)

In Job's speech in his own defense, he lets us know that he understands very well what we now call social ecology:

"If my land has cried out against me,
  and its furrows have wept together;
if I have eaten its yield without payment,
  and caused the death of its owners;
let thorns grow instead of wheat
  and foul weeds instead of barley."
(Jb 31:38-40)

Obedience carried the promise of fruitful lands and crops, and wise management of the earth could increase its yield, but all of this implies that life on the earth is more a call to responsible stewardship than a self-regulating process.

Wilkinson and his colleagues do note one way in which the problems of energy depletion and pollution may be addressed, that is, by a massive change in lifestyle on the part of the 20 percent of the earth who use the vast majority of its resources. As they put it, we may voluntarily lower our consumption or we (or our children) will do it of necessity.[51] But this too implies that the earth needs, indeed calls out for, the intervention not only of human effort but ultimately of God to set right the relationships that have gone wrong. So the creation is not a closed system, but, as scientists recognize, an open system. Above all, it is open to the future that God has purposed for it. As in the case of ethnic groups, the community character of creation needs direction. It can be injured by improper use of the relationships that sustain it, or it can be nurtured and moved in the direction that the Spirit of God calls it. But in either case something must happen to move it toward or away from its true purposes. It is the nature of God's creation to be open to this agency.

The Responsible Character of Creation

Though creation was pronounced good, its goodness needed to be tended and nurtured. This responsibility was given to the first couple as a special calling (Gn 2:15), but it was also to be the continuing work of God, who continues to work in, with, and under the processes in a way that respects their good creaturely character. We have considered the situation that soon emerged, described in Genesis 6, by which God was so grieved that he decided to "blot out from the earth the human beings I have created—people together with animals and creeping things and birds of the air, for I am sorry that I have made them" (Gn 6:7). This implies that judgment was one response that God considered—an appropriate one, after all, in view of God's good purposes and absolute ownership of the earth. Indeed, since the moral order was built into creation—what the Bible calls "righteousness"—the correction that judgment represented was in one sense necessary to the survival of the earth (we have noticed this in God's response to the Tower of Babel). But, in the event, this was not what happened: "Noah found favor [*hesed*] in the sight of the LORD" (v. 8). On the basis of this favor God promises after the flood:

> "I will never again curse the ground because of humankind, for the inclination of the human is evil from youth; nor will I ever again destroy every living creature as I have done.
>
> As long as the earth endures,
> seedtime and harvest, cold and heat,
> summer and winter, day and night,
> shall not cease." (Gn 8:21-22)

So God promises to preserve the good order, no longer strictly speaking in the role of creator of the earth but rather now as its savior, as one who loves it and will show it favor. Something of this surprising mercy that lies at the center of God's being is seen again in Hosea, when God recounts the wickedness of Israel:

> My people are bent on turning away from me. . . .
>
> How can I give you up, Ephraim?
> How can I hand you over, O Israel? . . .
> My heart recoils within me;
> my compassion grows warm and tender.
> I will not execute my fierce anger. (Hos 11:7, 8-9)

However the promises of the prophets about the Messiah are interpreted, God promises to come to the people in the role of savior of the earth. But in this role it is not as though God once was creator and now is savior. Rather, God's work as creator has been extended to include this new role, that of savior:

> For I will pour water on the thirsty land,
> and streams on the dry ground;
> I will pour my spirit upon your descendants,
> and my blessing on your offspring.
> They shall spring up like a green tamarisk,
> like willows by flowing streams. (Is 44:3-4)

The earth had reached such a state that it called out for a new intervention—a new Exodus, a new creation. These dominant images are intertwined in the prophets. The intervention that is represented by Jesus picks up both of these themes and develops them further. Jesus is the *savior* who will deliver his people from Egypt and give them a new law (Mt 2:15, 5-7); but he is also the *creator* who calls the earth back to its creative purposes (Col 1:15-20; Eph 1:10).[52] So with the darkness over the cross and the bodily resurrection of Jesus the massive correction in the relational character of the earth has begun. Jürgen Moltmann says it well: "The movement of God in the raising up of Christ and his ascension to heaven sets the whole universe on the move toward the coming kingdom of glory."[53]

Joseph Sittler, more than anyone else, has helped us see the importance of the cosmic dimension of Christ's role for our understanding of the earth, beginning in his famous New Delhi speech of 1961, "Called to Unity." There and in subsequent writings Sittler insists that Christianity has reduced the work of God's grace in Christ to personal salvation, so as "to shrink to no effect the biblical Christology of nature."[54] Since then, as we have seen, many biblical scholars have concluded that creation theology is the broad horizon for salvation and that reconciliation of the earth was included in Christ's redemptive and mediatorial role.[55] Christ continues as savior to mediate between the creation and God, holding us and the whole creation together in love (i.e., non-coercively) before God.

Evidence for this is also to be found in the pouring out of the Holy Spirit to renew God's people and the earth. When Peter quoted Joel 2 and concluded that the passage was being fulfilled in his day, he certainly had in mind the passage's full context:

> Do not fear, O soil;
> be glad and rejoice,
> for the LORD has done great things!
> Do not fear, you animals of the field,
> for the pastures of the wilderness are green;
> the tree bears its fruit,
> the fig tree and vine give their full yield.
> O children of Zion, be glad
> and rejoice in the LORD your God;
> for he has given the early rain for your vindication.
> (Jl 2:21-23)

Joel goes on to speak of the threshing floors that are full and the defeat of the "swarming locust" which God calls "my great army," so that the people will know, God says, "that I am in the midst of Israel" (v. 27). At that time "I will pour out my spirit" (v. 28). In other words, the Spirit is being sent for the earth—for the soil, the animals, and the trees, as well as for God's people.

In the light of the coming of Christ and the pouring out of his Spirit the earth has been put into a whole new situation of responsibility. Whatever else Romans 8:18-25 means, the central thrust is that the nonhuman creation is now included, as Odil Steck put it, "in the saving event opened up in Christ. Here man and the world of creation belong together."[56] Steck goes on to note the implications of this for the earth. First, the natural order has again become the sphere of the creative activity of God. Notice how the "nearness" of salvation takes on a deeper and richer meaning in this context (cf. Rom 13:11). But the natural world, at the same time, shares potentially the sphere of human self-centeredness; it may refuse to acknowledge the new creative work of God. As the earth may suffer over the human rebellion, so too the earth is now the sphere in which faith can be active and alive (cf. the Book of James). With the coming of Jesus and the presence of the Spirit, "God's salvation is already manifested in the existing world in the form of signs" (268, 274, 278). As we will see below, a central aspect of these signs involves our care of the earth, as well as our care of our neighbor.

It is in this new context that *human agency* is to be understood. As we saw, the biblical understanding of the image of God includes the relationships with God, people, and the earth, and the way those relationships are enacted in our communal life. The call to till and keep the earth (Gn 2:15), with the coming of Jesus, is now to be understood in the light of our role as "salt and light" (Mt 5:13-14). That is to say, since the order of the earth has been disturbed, we cannot simply tend and take care of the earth—indeed, the earth itself calls for a more radical restructuring. This God has provided in events associated with Easter and Pentecost. Because of this our work with the earth takes on a new dimension: we are called to reflect the redemptive intervention of Jesus.

As at the beginning, human presence on the earth today exists at a critical juncture, between, one might say, fertility and decay. The fertility has been built into things. God saw (and sees) to that. But decay is also possible. We can nurture the earth, but we can also injure it. Now, with the victory of Christ and his continuing rule through the Holy Spirit, the blessing of fertility has been given a new impetus and a larger context. For better or worse, we still have a responsibility to the earth, but now the stakes have been raised. Disobedience is now possible to the new order as well, with consequences which, if anything, are even more dire than they were before. Notice that Paul in Romans 1, just after his announcement of the revelation of God's righteousness in Jesus Christ (v. 16), goes on to speak of disobedience to the Creator (and the creation) in terms of idolatry. Those who do not honor God "exchanged the glory of the immortal God for images" (v. 23). Idolatry was possible since the beginning of creation, but now it is seen in terms of the "revelation of God's righteousness" in Christ (see Rom 1:17 and 3:21-22). As Romans 8 makes clear, because of this revelation, creation itself, in a new way, shares in the suffering that this idolatry causes; it too longs for the full revelation of that firstfruit of the Spirit, which is now at work in us (8:22-23). The pain of this idolatry is all too clear in the contemporary treatment of sex, business, art, and, yes, of the earth. These all have their own particular goodness, but they also offer their unique moral challenges. Today the call of the earth comes to us with new urgency.

We have commented frequently on the fact that morality is not added to creation but is built in. But now we are in a position to answer the question, In what way is morality built in? Morality is inherent in creation for two reasons. First, morality is inherent in creation because the goodness of creation is a call to responsible stewardship. What we have in our hand may be shared, and nurtured or it may be wasted and destroyed. Second, the order is moral because God is there. All we do with creation is done in the presence of God. This is to say, the human response to the earth is both necessary and moral. As God's image we are standing responsible before God and creation (and now the new creation), and we are called to respond. Creation in its patterned relations calls out to us; we must handle it. Even to do nothing is a moral act, for the weeds will overtake us and the fruit will rot on the trees. In an important sense the whole creation is waiting for our answer. And because of the interrelated character of creation, the future also depends on our response. As any actor knows, at a certain moment the whole world of the play rests on whether the actor remembers his or her part. Just so the world waits for the human actor.

I would like to speak of this responsible agency in two parts: Christian stewardship and wisdom, and stewardship and the gospel. We noted that our role as the children of God has the character of salt and light—metaphors which speak of the interventionist nature of our life in the world in this new situation. Our discussion in the last section led us to the conclusion that the earth cannot sustain itself. It waits, it calls, it is open to human and divine activity, which can help it reach its true end (or, of course, can stand in the way of that goal). Recent studies indicate that this "call" resides in the earth as a part of its intrinsic nature.[57] Its freedom and ours relates to this mutual responsibility. As Emmanuel Levinas says: "This freedom enveloped in a responsibility which it does not succeed in shouldering is the way of being a creature."[58] The earth not only has moral "standing," as we saw in the work of Christopher Stone, but its rights and expectations make claims on us. As any farmer knows, if we care for the earth, it will care for us. What Carol Gilligan says of our relationships with other people relates also to our care for the earth:

> As a framework for moral decision, care is grounded in the assumption that self and other are interdependent, an assumption reflected in a view of action as responsive and, therefore, as arising in relationship rather than the view of action as emanating from within the self and, therefore, "self-governed."[59]

It seems to me that the ambiguity in scripture and in the tradition over the place of humanity in creation is grounded in the unique moral situation into which humanity is introduced as God's image. Created from the dust as part of the organic life of creation, humans are also called to responsibility for creation before the Creator. Franciscan tradition has stressed the former, the spiritual tradition the latter. But the truth of both traditions must be kept in view. For humans carry out this tending and keeping from within the order, not from outside of it. Their leadership will in its human way reflect God's own non-coercive servant-like presence, working to bring creation to its highest end, as a vehicle for God's glory.[60] Just as God both dwells within creation and is also sovereign over it, so the human creature has a special role both within and over creation, even if he or she does not constitute the final purpose for creation. That role is to be responsive to the call of the Creator, to work to bring out of creation the goodness the creator has hidden there.[61]

Being responsive involves listening carefully to what the creation is saying, a practice that is central to the whole Wisdom movement. The psalmist notes that the "voice" of "the heaven . . . and the firmament . . . goes out through all the earth, and their words to the end of the world" (Ps 19:4). Listening to this voice, we have argued, is related to listening to God. As James Crenshaw writes in describing Old Testament wisdom: "God has constituted the universe so as to reward virtue and punish vice."[62] Moreover, it is this moral order that grounds any meaningful construal of history. Christian Link maintains that "in the context of Wisdom especially, historical thinking reaches its most radical expansion, and pervades the natural *roots* of human existence."[63] We so often hear of the damaging effects of human activity on the earth that we sometimes forget that the relationship between humanity and the earth, when it is properly ordered, is mutually enriching. The valid aspect of homeostasis and sustainability, which Christians must not lose sight of, is this: when human agents remember their role, listen to the earth, and respond appropriately, the earth can be enriched.

Recent investigation has uncovered many instances of this wisdom at work in contemporary ecology. In an important study from West Africa, James Fairhead and Melissa Leach have concluded that, contrary to what is commonly thought, the activity of villagers in Guinea has "deliberately accelerated processes of forest island formation."[64] This positive process, which includes increasing the diversity of species in forest and savanna, is halted when villages are abandoned (25). Their finding is consistent with the contemporary movement away from the idea that there is one perfect climax forest state. In this older view "the actual landscape appeared as a set of anthropogenic sub-climaxes containing within them the seeds and foretastes of apocalypse to come" (31). Rather, based on the well-known observation that no ecological condition is permanent, Fairhead and Leach suggest we think in terms of multiple stable states related to mutually advantageous human and natural interaction. They conclude:

> Human activity may alter the balance of interacting factors and initiate a shift between stable states. . . . For example, through simultaneously improved soils, seed sources and fire control, people may facilitate the establishment of forest vegetation which (for lack of necessary rare conjuncture) might otherwise never have occurred. . . . People thus "work with nature," serving to secure by ratchet effect, those transitions that are to their advantage. (32)

Examples of this kind could be multiplied. Sri Lankan C. R. Hensman describes "the close interconnections between the newly empowered, life-appropriating social practice of *the people*, all over the world, and the renewal of the living Earth."[65] In his own Sri Lanka, for example, ordinary people, knowledgeable as they are about particular terrains, weather patterns, and techniques, have been able to develop as many as twenty-eight hundred rice-production cultivars (strains and varieties of plants developed by humans).[66] Recent studies of Amazonian agriculture have shown that the itinerant practices of indigenous Amazonians "is the only system adapted to the characteristics of the ecosystems of the wet tropics."[67] That these practices are currently being disrupted by government relocation projects underlines the fact that the struggle for wisdom is a part of a larger spiritual battle, one that Christ came to engage, and that we by his Spirit continue to wage.

Stewardship and the gospel—a new economic order. We have said that our responsibility toward the earth, which reflects our creation in the image of God, has been placed in a new context with the coming of Christ. With the resurrection of Jesus a horizon of hope has been opened for the creature. For our part, we are placed in a new situation of responsibility. This responsibility is represented by our call to "make disciples of all nations . . . teaching them to obey everything that I [Jesus] have commanded you" (Mt 28:19-20). When placed in its full biblical context, this work of announcing the new covenant is seen to have great ecological implications. As Hosea describes this new covenant, it is clear that all the earth is included. God says:

> I will make for you a new covenant on that day with the wild animals, the birds of the air, and the creeping things of the ground; and I will abolish the bow and sword, and war from the land; and I will make you lie down in safety. (Hos 2:18)

Reconciliation of the earth with people will be the essence of this new covenant. In Hosea's context, God wants Israel to turn from the Canaanite Baal fertility cults—not unlike the New Age monism of our own day—to the true fertility God.[68] This covenant will revitalize the relationships that characterize the creative order:

> On that day I will answer, says the LORD,
> I will answer the heavens
> and they shall answer the earth;
> and the earth shall answer the grain, the wine, and
> the oil. (Hos 2:21-22)

Paul's words in Romans 8 are a New Testament echo of this very idea: "For the creation waits with eager longing for the revealing of the children of God. . . . We know that the whole creation has been groaning in labor pains until now; . . . while we wait for adoption, the redemption of our bodies" (Rom 8:19, 22, 23).

One of the ironies of Christian history is that evangelism—the act of proclaiming the good news that God has reconciled the world to himself in Jesus Christ—has sometimes been seen as a retreat from the problems posed by the environment. These scriptures and our entire argument have shown that nothing could be further from the truth. Our environmental responsibilities not only include evangelism, but they must start there. The Christian assertion is that it is only now, because of the cosmic Reign of Jesus Christ and the presence of the life-giving Spirit offering the creation up to the glory of God, that these earthly problems can be meaningfully addressed. The announcement of the gospel is itself, as Odil Steck says, "a proclamation of the saving intention of God toward everything he has created."[69] Living in the light of the gospel provides a new way of imagining the world and thus makes possible a new set of practices.

We referred in chapter 2 to the evidence for this new perspective provided by Frances Young and David F. Ford, who have argued that Paul in 2 Corinthians is working with a central economic metaphor. Metaphor, they remind us, works at the boundary of the actual, "opening it up to new possibilities."[70] The actual for the Corinthians was an economic order that Bruce Malina has described as the "limited good economy."[71] In this order one sought to find an "equilibrium" in which life became sustainable. Now, however, Christians find themselves in a new "economy"—in terms of our argument, an economy that recognizes a larger order of relationships. Now God has reconciled the world to himself, and we find ourselves in an altogether different "economic order." Now there is more than enough for everyone: grace overflows (2 Cor 9:14), extending to more and more people (4:15), leading to mutuality in ministry (5:20), and, really the heart of Paul's argument, to *koinonia,* the free exchange between believers in Macedonia and needy believers in Jerusalem (see 2 Cor 8 and 9). Paul concludes: "You glorify God by your obedience to the confession of the gospel of Christ and by the generosity of your sharing with them and with all others" (9:13).

Local matters, Young and Ford conclude, have been taken up into the heart of the gospel.

This practice demonstrates nicely what believers are called to do with the goods of this created order. Because of the new imaginative vision provided by the good news of Christ's work of reconciliation, we can imagine another way of relating to the earth. We can work for a sustainable order; that is, one in which the processes of earth are respected and nurtured. But we do this in the light of a world in which Christ has been raised from the dead and where Christ will return to reveal the new creation he has begun. In Christ the righteousness that makes the world good actually has been made manifest in bodily form, a form that is meant to be expressed in the lives of his people. And so we work ultimately not simply to sustain but to renew the earth, knowing that however often we may fail, this renewal has actually begun and will one day be revealed, when Jesus Christ returns. So our practices have a different direction and are based on a different hope.

THE EARTH WILL BE FULL OF THE KNOWLEDGE OF THE LORD

A central element of our argument is that this direction and this hope relate in a fundamental way to the earth. In the Christian view, the embodied and material character of the earth is no obstacle to God's self-revelation in and through it. Indeed, this revelation is central to the event of Christ's life, death, and resurrection. Here, however, I would like to look at things from the other direction. Because of our Platonic heritage, Western thinking has privileged the mind and its processes. This tendency, we have argued, probably has more to do with the misuse of our environment than tendencies inherent in the Christian tradition. It certainly is one of the causes for our neglect of art and aesthetics, as we will discuss in the next chapter. But even if we allow our material context to play a role in our faith—for example, as the sphere for us to show something of God's goodness—we do so grudgingly. The earth is, after all—from John Bunyan to Karl Barth—still only a kind of backdrop for the real drama, which is the journey of the human soul to God.

It should be clear by now that this is a seriously distorted reading of things, not only leading to the neglect of our physical environment, but, more seriously, producing a biblical myopia. For a close reading of scripture makes it clear that God's program grows from within the material world, it is not simply inserted into it. Odil Steck has been helpful in pointing out this inward perspective of God's program. "In the formative framework of a view of the world seen from within, a view which is close to experience and deeply affected by life itself, man sees himself included in the event of the gift of life, an event which neither he nor other living things has any control over, but which Yahweh freely brings about."[72] God is present in the smallest event and works from below as well as from above. While still separate from the world and transcendent in the divine purposes—for this reason we avoid expressions like the "world as God's body"—God works from inside. This view, to which feminist theologians have contributed so much, is critical to the "task of recovering the biblical and theological depth associated with the earth (and with it of the body and the senses)."[73] Because of God's presence, Christ's sustaining, and the Spirit's renewing work, the theology of the earth will have its own contribution to make to the theological enterprise. As theologians join with the wise people in every culture who learn from the earth, so they will also have to learn from anthropologists and artists.

Anthropologists, for example, in turning their attention to the Hebrew scriptures have helped us see how the ritual practices of Israel became expressive and efficacious of God's redemptive activity. Since they could imagine, indeed had experienced God's delivering presence, Israel's rituals could celebrate and "re-present" this. As Mary Douglas said in her pioneering study, "Livestock, like the inhabited land, received the blessing of God. Both land and livestock were fertile by the blessing, both were drawn into the divine order. The farmer's duty was to preserve the blessing."[74] And in a recent article Douglas argues that the purity laws of Leviticus, as reflected in the structure of the book, have a positive theological function.[75] These rules have a comprehensive function of including everyone (and everything) in the benefits of purification (240). Through parallelism and analogy, the author sought to extend the protection of the holiness of God into all relationships. Douglas concludes: "In this structure impurity enters as the reasoning by the via negativa and is clearly subordinated to the positive view of the theistic universe against which it is balanced. The central place in the teaching is given to righteousness; impurity is the foil for displaying the meaning of righteousness. More than a literary foil, it is a statement about the nature of existence in a sacramental universe, a religious ontology" (255).

As the farmer needed to follow the best wisdom he knew—to learn to know God, so to speak, from within the created order—so we too must listen as carefully as we can to the earth and respond patiently to what we hear. But now our practice goes with the grain of a new order, which Paul calls the new creation, which we have experienced in our own lives and families.

This theological depth is what gives poets and artists their material. The great artist Paul Cézanne understood that the meaning of things lay in their depth: "Nature is not on the surface but in the depths; the colours are the representation of the depths on the surface; they spring from the roots of the cosmos."[76] Jesus proposed the central ritual practice for Christians when he took the bread and wine, saying, "This is my body." In this act the grain and vine, and by extension the whole created order, are placed in a new relational context. As historian William Irving Thompson says, when Jesus takes the bread and wine, he "is a poet with an ecological vision of life."[77]

In this central practice Christians "re-present" their own fellowship—with the Savior, who is present by his Spirit; with the body of believers both present and absent, and in their participation in (and celebration of) God's created gifts. This practice and the relationships it sustains, grounds Christians in a new form of life. This form of life is expressed in a new way of being human, seen in the generous exchange Paul facilitated in the collection for Christians in Jerusalem. And it can be seen in practices that Christians today develop to express their care for the earth, as salt and light. We do not join in recycling and reuse programs because they have become politically correct, nor do we reject these practices because their exponents have bad theology. We participate because care for the earth is a Christian practice. And these simple acts—such as weekly recycling—can be seen as rituals that enact a new order that God is bringing to pass. In the Christian view, creatures can become expressive not only of their created goodness but of the new creation. And our treatment of them can become small parables of redemption.

Sometimes views of the future are presented as a kind of sloughing off of the inessential, a paring down of reality until we reach a kind of pure spiritual reality. Nothing could be further from the biblical view of eschatology. The Bible presents God's future in terms of plenitude, a gathering up of all good things into a final concert of praise. In this final vision—both Isaiah and John's Revelation concur—the earth (and the body) will not so much be unmade as remade. Isaiah's vision of the new creation in Isaiah 65 pictures a new Jerusalem in which people live out their years, build houses, plant vineyards, and eat fruit; where their offspring are blessed; and where the wolf and the lamb shall feed together. The picture concludes:

> They shall not hurt or destroy
> on all my holy mountain,
> says the LORD.
> (Is 65:25)

We have argued that the ecological concept of relationships, in which each living thing has its own place prepared for it, is closer to the biblical vision than to Newton's view of space as receptacle. When Jesus promises to prepare a place for each of us in John 14:2-3, he is speaking of the perfection of these ecological relations. When he tells us to pray daily that God's will be done on earth as it is in heaven, he is telling us to pray for the coming of the Kingdom in which those relations are perfected. As Jürgen Moltmann points out, heaven is currently God's living space, but the goal toward which creation moves is the renewal of heaven *and* earth, which will together become God's dwelling. This is why John in Revelation 21 and 22 mixes imagery of heaven, the temple, and creation, for in the final celebration all these are brought together in the new heaven and new earth. Jürgen Moltmann sums up this vision:

> The kingdom of glory is the indwelling of the triune God in his whole creation. Heaven *and earth* will become God's dwelling, the surroundings that encompass him, and his milieu. For created beings, this means that—all together, each created being in its own way—they will participate in eternal life and in the eternal bliss of God who is present among them.[78]

CONCLUSION

Let us summarize our argument. We began by pointing out the growing consensus that environmental problems must be seen as part of a larger spiritual or religious crisis—a crisis that Christianity itself has come to share. The roots of this, however, lie not so much in the supposed anthropocentrism of Christianity as in the view of human autonomy coming from René Descartes and Francis Bacon.

The solution is to recover the full context of earthly relationships: with God and the whole creation. In the biblical view all of creation has value, but only in the context in which it has been created—creatures in their interrelationship with each other, with humanity, and with the Creator.

The problems of caring for the earth result, then, from either seeking value in objects outside of their full network of relations or failing to relate them properly to God's purposes.

But creation must not be seen only as a set of relationships; it is also an unfinished project. Creation's goodness and order are given to us and precede our efforts. This grounds our work in a humble receiving and a careful listening to the call of creation. We have called attention to the claims that this order makes and the moral responsiveness it displays. This makes possible a wise stewardship that contributes to renewal as well as to a sustainable environment. But these efforts point out the larger need for an intervention that renews the earth at its center, a renewal the New Testament claims is in view with the coming of Christ. Because of Christ and the presence of the Holy Spirit as firstfruits of the new order, human activity can reflect this redemptive reality. Human efforts can result in substantial healing,[79] and this is especially true as these center on and grow out of a proclamation of the gospel that expresses God's intention to bless the whole earth.

God's intention is seen finally in God's intent that the divine glory cover the earth as the waters cover the sea, that the earth embody God's splendor. That purpose is manifested in the coming of Jesus Christ and his redemptive work, but it is also reflected in the call to make disciples of all nations. All creation is now called to account before the Creator's intervention in Christ. His presence through the Holy Spirit anticipates the day when God will "make all things new" (Rv 21:5). This same presence Christians embody by the form of life the New Testament calls "being in Christ." Donald Worster has argued recently that the ecological imagination has Christian roots even when this is not recognized.[80] He notes four values that grew from the American Protestant tradition and underlie the environmental movement. He sees a moral activism, which comes from Calvin and Knox and issues in a shared moralizing energy; an ascetic discipline that reflects Jonathan Edwards's reaction to the sensuous gratification of European culture; an egalitarian individualism that does not lose sight of the smallest and least; and finally an aesthetic spirituality that believes, as Jonathan Edwards taught, that one can find the glory of the Creator (and be delivered from evil) by contemplating the beauty of creation.

Sadly, environmentalists have retained the virtues but lost sight of their rationale. In exulting in the wonder and beauty of creation, however, they are responding as God did in saying of creation: "It is very good." What better opportunity to introduce them to the Creator, who loves them along with all creation. But this can happen only if Christians reclaim their own heritage, which, throughout Christian history, has taken its nourishment from the biblical vision of the shalom God intends for creation. Susan Bratton, in her wise comments on Donald Worster's study, proposes that these virtues be put back within the New Testament context of diaconal ministries, where the creativity and gifts of the whole body may be applied in every area of responsibility toward the earth, from the least to the greatest.[81] As in the other areas of culture, grounding our Christian responsibility in this special "form of life" that the Christian scriptures describe, and which has reference to all areas of human life, is the only thing that can give us vision and hope for a renewed world.

6

Art

Art embodies the human longing to express, to "re-present," in sensuous form the deep splendor and agony of creation. The activities of making art may include what we must do to live and make a living, but they always go beyond these things—in the same way that God's purposes in creation went beyond what was merely useful for humanity. In the history of Christianity art has figured prominently both in bringing joy to human life and in reflecting God's larger purposes—even going so far as to mediate God's presence. Augustine, for example, came to believe that delight was the mainspring of human action. But it is precisely this ability to cause delight, he believed, that lies beyond our control and speaks of our need for God.

> The fact that those things that make for successful progress towards God should cause us delight is not acquired by our good intentions, earnestness and the value of our own good will—but is dependent on the inspiration granted us by God. . . . Surely our prayers are, sometimes, so lukewarm, stone-cold, indeed, and hardly prayers at all: they are so distant in our thoughts that we do not even notice this fact with pain—for if we were even to feel the pain, we would be praying again.[1]

Augustine's connection of delight with prayer is a good illustration of the fact that art, before the modern period, was consistently connected to worship, both as vehicle and motivation. This connection also reminds us of the purposes God had in making the earth. As Calvin put it: "Let us not be ashamed to take pious delight in the works of God open and manifest in this most beautiful theater," and, "There is no spot in the universe wherein you cannot discern at least some sparks of his glory. You cannot in one glance survey this most beautiful system of the universe without being completely overwhelmed by the boundless force of its brightness."[2]

Human life, like creation itself, exists for the sake of delight, both the delight that life brings when fully lived and the delight that God and the creature take in each other. For this reason the sabbath in the Hebrew scriptures stands as a central symbol of God's purposes in creation (and in redemption). *Sabbath* comes from the Hebrew "to stop," and so speaks of our human ability to reflect God in stepping out of the temporal. As is clear from the creation account God takes a continuing delight in creation—"It is good"; "It is very good"—and culminates his work by resting from "all the work that he had done in creation" (Gn 2:3). As described in the later sabbath legislation, the seventh day is for the sake of rest, but even more for enjoyment and celebration—and especially for worship. The sabbath is creation's party, its "gallery opening," when the artist and the work are celebrated together. This sabbath rest of God, Karl Barth argues, not the creation of humanity, is the goal of creation. This goal points toward the greater value of the whole, with its harmony and God-relatedness.[3] But it also speaks of the primacy of event and culmination over the drift of the biblical story. Better, it grounds that story in the being and rest of God. This, we will argue, is central to a Christian aesthetic.

It is important to understand how this discussion fits into the larger structure of the book. We asserted that Christian reflection on culture is best seen in terms of certain relationships and practices that reflect (or distort) the presence and activity of God. But human practices, at their best, have a certain inclination toward the symbolic—toward the expression of what must be celebrated. The melody of everyday life and the work place calls us out of those practices into something bigger and greater. This call is a call to know and celebrate God. Art, then, may be the best place to understand the meaning of our life in the world, or at least it is a good place to start.

This place of rest and celebration is what our harried culture seeks more than anything else—a place where we may be perfectly at home and see ourselves and the world with a new clarity. Great art has always had this effect because it reflects the greater experience of standing in God's presence. It is a rest that calls us to Rest. This is because God made the world as a home and vehicle of the divine brightness. In the new creation God has remade creation in Jesus Christ and poured out the gifts of the Holy Spirit to further embody God's purposes. In the body of Christ, God gives us space to celebrate these gifts and their Giver where we can stretch our weary legs and dance before the Lord. Because God has already made this place through the re-creative work of Christ, we do not need to work for it; we need only receive it as a gift and enjoy it. We need now to develop the theological categories that support this view of art, but first we turn to a brief discussion of the shape of current dialogue.

INTRODUCTION

Art has always been dependent on the givenness of creation. All the classical theories of art have recognized the underlying connectedness of reality that art reflects. Plato understood that the best artists know the proper "measure" of ultimate reality and seek to make this visible in their work. "Had [a good poet or artist] learned by rules of art, he would have known how to speak not of one theme only, but of all."[4] But, since ultimate reality—this measure of all things—lay behind the world of appearances, Plato could not understand how these rules could come to expression in material reality. Indeed, he became convinced that this was possible only in a lower or defective way. As he expressed this in the *Timaeus*: "Now the nature of the ideal being was everlasting, but to bestow its attribute in its fullness upon a creature was impossible" (par. 37). Since the visible world was made by the Demiurge in the image of this invisible world of the forms, the artist only makes a copy of a copy—a view that has had enormous influence on the subsequent history of art, especially Christian art. Plato's notion of "copy" or "mimesis," however, should not be dismissed too easily, for it suggests that art can actually imitate—or, as he put it, "enact"—the cosmic order of reality.[5]

Aristotle took Plato's notion of "copying" further in two ways. First, since for him the "measure" of reality can come to expression in material shape, art could make a kind of universal statement about the way things are. As he put it in his *Poetics*: "By a universal statement I mean one as to what such or such a kind of man will probably or necessarily say or do."[6] This means that truth—or the way things are—can actually come to expression in the various sensuous forms of art.[7] It implies not only that the imitation (mimesis) of art can adequately present reality, but that art can be a means to real knowledge. Second, Aristotle believed that art could be mimetic in this way because there was a kind of natural affinity between the way things are (or should be) and the artist and/or spectator. As he says in the *Poetics*: "Imitation then being natural to us—as also the sense of harmony and rhythm . . . it was through their original aptitude, and by a series of improvements for the most part gradual on their first efforts, that they created poetry out of their improvisations."[8] The artist is able to bring the natural connections in reality to expression in sensuous form.

While these classical ideas may sound strange to modern ears, they have a certain congruence with biblical ways of thinking. For in the Bible the beautiful and the good—the line between these is frequently impossible to draw—usually express normal and healthy relations and processes of creation.[9] Because God was understood to be the source of beauty (cf. Wis 13:3), words for beauty and splendor in the Hebrew scriptures are particularly associated with worship in the Temple and tabernacle. It is not accidental that God's spirit is said to endow Bezalel with his ability to create artistic designs for the tabernacle, the first reference to the spirit coming upon someone for a particular task (Ex 31:2-11, cf. 28:3). Whatever the "beauty of the LORD" might be (see Ps 27:4), it clearly implies an experience of wonder and joy associated with the Temple cult.[10] This verse also implies that the presence of God is associated with what we now call an aesthetic response, not only with its wonder but its terror as well. As G. von Rad puts this: "The descriptions of theophanies are undoubtedly the most central subject of an OT aesthetic, for they reveal more clearly than all else how the special experience of God undergone by Israel became normative for the special features in the experience of beauty."[11] Thus words for beauty and awe are not only used of Temple worship and the experience of Moses on Mt. Sinai, but even of God's acts of deliverance more generally; these can be called "triumphs of the LORD" (Jgs 5:11b; Hebrew: "righteous acts"), or they can be referred to as "beautiful" (Ez 16:13-14) or "glorious" (Is 63:12). Because they had encountered God, in the Exodus and on Mt. Sinai, God's people were able to recover a sense of the fullness and integrity of the whole created order, even to see there God's own loveliness.

Evidence for this is to be found in the frequent identification of what is "beautiful" or "glorious" with what we would simply call fitting. Praise "befits" the upright (Ps 33:1b), holiness "befits" God's house (Ps 93:5), the messengers' feet are "beautiful" (Is 52:7), an old man's gray hair is his "crown of glory" (Prv 16:31), the righteous finish their years in "pleasantness" (Jb 36:11). By contrast fine speech is "not becoming to a fool" (Prv 17:7), nor is honor "fitting" for a fool (Prv 26:1). This aesthetic dimension of God's ordered reality is occasionally lost in our English translations, as when the RSV translates Psalm 141:6: "When the wicked are given to those who shall condemn them, then they shall learn that the word of God is *true* [Hebrew: *pleasant* or *lovely*; cf. NRSV]."

Clearly notions of beauty and the role of art cannot be separated from the larger purposes of God in creation and redemption. Beauty relates to goodness, which encourages us to take up a course of action that reflects the allegiance of our heart. Beauty can lead us to God and worship, but it can also become deceitful (Prv 31:30). It relates to truth, because it reflects the ordered whole of creation—God has made everything "suitable for its time" (Eccl 3:11). Notice above all that in the Hebrew scriptures truth and goodness naturally find expression in the material world God has made; materiality is nowhere pictured as a barrier either to goodness or to God's presence. Indeed, the prophets look forward to a day when

> the earth will be filled
> with the knowledge of the glory of the LORD,
> as the waters cover the sea. (Hb 2:14)

This point must become the starting point of any understanding of the role of beauty in the New Testament. There is a continuity between the testaments on many levels in their treatment of what we call aesthetics. For example, there is a direct line extending from Abraham's experience in Genesis 18, through Moses' encounter on Sinai and the visual glory of God in the Temple, to the visions of Isaiah and Ezekiel, and finally to the appearance of God in Jesus Christ both in history and at its culmination. This is the line that the transfiguration clearly intends to emphasize. But, beauty in the New Testament, as in the Old, like its counterpart goodness, does not call attention to itself. This has led some interpreters to believe these things have no importance in Christ's work. In the Christian scriptures what is good and beautiful does not occupy a separate territory. Rather, it is seen in the ordinary splendor of a life lived according to God's purposes. Interestingly, the Greek word most frequently used for "beautiful" (*kalos*) can also mean "good"; indeed, in most cases it means both together. *Kalos* describes every tree that brings forth good fruit (Mt 3:10), the ground that yields a good harvest (Mk 4:8), the woman's "good service" in anointing of Jesus' feet (Mk 14:6), the Old Testament law (1 Tm 1:8), every creature of God (1 Tm 4:4), and above all the works that are to characterize God's people (Ti 2:7; Jas 3:13). This humble aesthetic fits well with the One who came not to be served but to serve. In fact, at the very point where we might expect some spectacular reference to awe and delight in the New Testament, it is missing. When something of Christ's divine glory is glimpsed, it is more likely to strike terror than delight. In Matthew's account of the transfiguration the disciples "fell to the ground and were overcome by fear" (Mt 17:6); they were terrified when Jesus walked on the water (Mt 14:26); and when John had a vision of the splendor of the risen Christ, he "fell at his feet as though dead" (Rv 1:17).

While some (at least in the Protestant tradition) have argued that aesthetics plays a minor role in the enfolding program of God, in the history of the church its place can hardly be overemphasized. Early Christian art, for example, often assumed to be largely an adaptation of Greek and Roman motifs, has recently been seen as a powerful expression of a whole new way of seeing the world. Throwing off inhibitions, painters, sculptors, and mosaic workers sought to encompass the whole of Christ's rule. Thomas Mathews claims that "their success spelled the death of the sacred imagery of classical antiquity and the birth of a new, Christian art."[12] By all accounts the humble creation-centered theology of St. Francis inspired Giotto to turn to natural settings in a way that opened up the world and prepared for the Renaissance. The Reformation and its emphasis on Christ's redemption of all of life inspired painters, especially the Dutch painters, to find glory in the common vistas of rivers and fields, or the ordinary interior of a peasant home, or even in a well-laid table or floral bouquet. This repertoire of motifs came to determine the dominant themes of the modern period.

So Christianity has not been without influence on the development of art or disinterested in aesthetics in its own life and worship. But since the Enlightenment, at least, the relationship between art and religion—in a way not dissimilar to that of religion and science—has become problematic, even antagonistic. What has gone wrong? The story is far too complicated to recount here, but we might recognize two important influences on this development: one within the history of Christianity itself, the other in the particular development of modern ideas about art. In the first place, Christianity in particular and Western culture in general have sometimes distrusted the sensuous as a distraction from literal truth and, in the case of mystical Christianity, as a snare keeping the believer from communion with God. Augustine's background led him to fear that human enjoyment might distract the soul from the supreme delight found only in God. "The eyes love fair and varied forms, and bright and soft colors. Let not these occupy my soul; let God rather occupy it, who made these things, very good indeed, yet is He my good, not they."[13] In the twelfth century the Cistercians took a similar stance in their reaction against overly luxuriant church decoration. St. Bernard argued: "We who have turned aside from society, relinquishing for Christ's sake all the precious and beautiful things in the world, its wondrous light and color, its sweet sounds and odors, the pleasures of taste and touch, for us all bodily delights are nothing but dung."[14] The centrality of the word, both preached and read, in the Reformation fueled a similar reaction against the excess of medieval imagery and issued in a distrust of all kinds of visible ornamentation. This led Ulrich Zwingli to argue that "[images] can portray only the accidents, not the substance of Christianity, as they are given in the relativities of time and history." And so, he concluded, "the prime symbol of true belief is the Word, invisible and heard; the prime symbol of false belief is the image, visible and seen."[15] While this suspicion of the image has moral roots, as we have implied, in its subsequent development it came to be expressed simply as a preference for the literal expression of truth over any metaphorical diversion. This tendency found expression in the logic of Peter Ramus, in the plain style of Puritan preaching, even in such apparently diverse developments as the empirical epistemologies of Locke and Hume and Georg W. F. Hegel's view that only concepts purified from any unclarity associated with pictures can bring us to truth.

Even this brief survey shows us that though this iconoclastic temperament has Christian roots, at least in part, it has come to characterize Western civilization more generally.[16] As David Richards comments: "Western art is constructed upon [the] problem of representing that which it cannot, while effectively dismissing the actual body as an inconsequential means to the end of an impossible representation."[17] This reference leads us to the second major cause of problems in relating Christianity and art: the particular development of modern ideas about art. What is the "impossible representation" of modern art? Perhaps we might summarize this search by saying that modern artists have developed their own pictorial ways of pursuing the Enlightenment search for ultimate reality, even—dare we use the word?—for salvation.

As with the natural world, indeed in a way related to it, beauty is one of the few things that draws a religious response from the modern secular person. Simone Weil believes there are three ways that people are drawn to God: through affliction, religious practices, and by experiencing beauty. The first two have been effectively eliminated from modern life, leaving, she believes, the third. Among white races, she argues, "the beauty of the world is almost the only way by which we can allow God to penetrate us."[18] But while they respond to beauty, modern people frequently leave God out of account, and so the development of modern art involves a quest for ultimacy without God. In a way analogous to Descartes's systematic doubt, artists have progressively sought to find the "truth" by sloughing off dimensions of reality. In the eighteenth century the certainties of religious narratives, royal power, and even classical mythology began to fall to the "critical mind"; thus they were gradually eliminated from the artist's repertoire. In the nineteenth century the "critical eye" represented by Gustave Courbet began to paint what was in front of his eyes, while Claude Monet took delight in the light and color of his luxurious garden. In the movements of cubism and surrealism in our own century artists have surrendered their connection with the natural world altogether, seeking in abstract forms or dream motifs to discover some cosmic order. Not all modern artists, of course, believe that there is such an absolute or final reality worth searching for—Dadaism developed this denial into an entire art movement, and the contemporary post-modernists have apparently given up the search altogether. But the difference between the pre-modern and modern use of art could well be summarized by this testimony of Julian Schnabel, one of the most celebrated artists of the 1980s:

> Duccio and Giotto were painting in a society in which there was actually belief in God. . . . People had religious experiences in front of paintings. The painters were connecting people to something bigger than their individual experiences. I think people still have religious experiences in front of paintings. The only difference today is that the religion isn't organized or prescribed—it's consciousness. To get religion now is to become conscious, to feel those human feelings.[19]

"To feel human feelings" comes as close as anything to David Richards's "impossible representation." But this experience is to be found not in connection with God, other people, or even natural motifs; Schnabel's most famous pieces feature a concatenation of broken plates pasted on the canvas. No, modern minimalism has effectively dismissed any actual way of embodying this salvation. These feelings are to be found, if at all, in the purity of individual consciousness that art elicits. What is involved, as H. R. Rookmaaker put it a generation ago, "is a whole way of thinking that leaves out of account, and so largely negates, vital aspects of our humanity and our understanding of reality."[20] But this negation has gone hand in hand, at least up until post-modernism, with the dead serious quest for connection with some absolute or final reality. Frank Burch Brown in his comments on modern art notes the similarity between discussion of modern art objects and the eucharist; both are felt to mediate a transcendent experience. But, he notes, references to the eucharist are at least more honest, since they acknowledge mystery from the beginning! "The doctrine of Eucharistic transubstantiation . . . sounds scarcely more mysterious than does modernist talk about the ineffable presence and ontological depth of a poem or painting that has already been declared to be self-contained and devoid of reference or meaning."[21]

That the elements of the eucharist can embody, in the Christian view, the grace or even the very presence of God speaks of the critical role that symbolic objects and aesthetic experience have played in Christian history. But, as Schnabel's confession implies, even though this faith is lost, one might argue that it is the memory of these connections that allows modern art to retain its allure. I have often noticed in exhibitions of modern art that even the most minimal expressions of artistic sensitivity—the bright cut-outs of Matisse or the brooding colors of Franz Kline—can move me deeply. Why is this? I believe it is because even these bits and pieces that the artist has preserved—the flotsam and jetsam of more holistic views of life—carry with them the remnants of their connections with other things. They still hold resonances of other days when we felt the connections with things larger than ourselves and when hope was still alive. In the words of the psalmist, "the firmament proclaims his [God's] handiwork" (Ps 19:1), whether we believe it or not. Try as we might, while the earth remains we cannot shut out this Voice.

Thus Christianity and modern art have important things to say to each other. Our work in the theological discussion that follows is to articulate what some of these things might be, and more important, to try to reopen a conversation that has been allowed to lag.

THEOLOGICAL CATEGORIES FOR AESTHETICS

Artists Are Embedded in Creation

At the center of the biblical notion of creation is God's delight in the splendor of what God has made, and the way the creature, even after the Fall, continues to exhibit this glory (Ps 19:1). The glory exists not in any particular aspect of creation but in the effulgence of its rich interrelationships and in its continuing dependence on the Creator. So in talking about the work of the human creator, we do not begin with either the artist or the world but in the way both are related, and in the way the human creator can embody and respond to these relationships with delight. Moreover, we do not find a value in these relationships and then, afterward, remember that God somehow made things this way. Rather, these relationships are constituted by the continuing presence and work of God, a reflection of God's trinitarian reality. This is seen especially in Christ, who having restored integrity to creation continues holds it together, and in the Holy Spirit, who works in the creature to tune its heart and make it a fit vehicle of God's praise.

Now in putting matters this way we are flying in the face of all discussions of aesthetics since Immanuel Kant, though not those of the classical theorists. Kant insists in his *Critique of Judgment* (1790) that judgments of taste are completely disinterested; that is, they are isolated not only from the judgments of others but from other faculties. "Since the delight is not based on any inclination of the subject (or any other deliberate interest), but the Subject feels himself completely *free* in respect to the liking which he accords to the object, he can find as reason for his delight no personal conditions to which his own subjective self might alone be party."[22] The biblical materials insist on the moral, integrated character of our involvement with creation. Kant, by contrast, says we are not to take up any position with reference to possession, or with any view of its moral praiseworthiness; the experience of taste is merely that experience which gives us immediate and disinterested delight. Notice Kant's emphasis on freedom from attachment and even from any reason which might be offered—the free play of the imagination is, Kant believes, requisite for cognition in general. So the artist and the spectator in this view of things are free, but their freedom is one of radical dissociation. This independence is further developed in the Romantic image of the artist and is enshrined in the counter-cultural notion of the "free-spirited" avant-garde artist.

These modern understandings of art are even reflected in the institutions that promote what we call art—museums, galleries, research fellowships, and even fine-art auctions. Progressively these institutions have moved art, and its contemplation, into an increasingly rarefied atmosphere. Anyone who has studied this world in any detail realizes how jealously this elite guards its prerogatives in owning and controlling aesthetic objects. Art, then, is separated *spatially* from life, restricted to the special places designed for its viewing, and it is separated *psychologically* by focusing, since Kant, only on the particular emotion associated with aesthetic experience. It is even separated *socially* and *economically*, far removed from the experience (and the pocketbook) of most people.[23]

As with other dimensions of human culture, what we have relentlessly abstracted we must now struggle to reintegrate. For if one of the dominant characteristics of modern art has been its alienation from the world around it, another has been its anguished search for some new Archimedean point. Because twentieth-century artists could no longer affirm reality, Suzi Gablik says, in their thinking, "a work of art was an independent world of pure creation which had its own, essentially spiritual, essence."[24] But it is not likely that, having progressively eliminated the spiritual connections that previously existed in the created world, we will be able to satisfactorily endow our own creations with the spirituality for which we now long.

It is our claim that the spiritual encounter we yearn for is to be found in the ordered connections of reality and, especially, in our awareness of God, who sustains that order. Frank Burch Brown maintains that our aesthetic perceptions themselves reflect these multiple connections and thus are multilayered, interdependent, and simultaneous. We know that the presentation of a meal, the position of the table ("Would you prefer to sit by the window?"), even how people are seated, are as important to the experience of eating as the taste of the food. We enjoy the experience on many levels. The reaction to a piece of music, for example, takes place at the level of sense and intellect, at an aesthetic level in the pleasing harmony, but it can also, for the believer, be an awareness of something more in the music, which Brown calls "tacit awareness of theology," perhaps the composer's love of God.[25]

We have already argued that our relationships in the world are intrinsically moral. Another way of saying this, relevant to a discussion of art, is that all our relations are conditioned by our human interests, our purposes, and especially our feelings. These multifaceted relationships are the way that we come to know the world, a point developed further below. What we stress here is the interrelated character of these relationships. Our human ability to *name* these realities allows us to fix them in some articulated form, which we might call knowledge or in some cases art. Following Knud Løgstrup, over against Kant, we argue that art consists of attuned impressions of these relationships that usually contain an articulation of knowledge. "We know what we call things that happen in the world," Løgstrup says. "In the attuned impression, on the other hand, we are open to a meaning in what we sense and meet with."[26] Aesthetic activity, then, has to do with the attuned impression, which we make or respond to, that issues in delight. What is good in the aesthetic dimension has to do with the pleasing (or arresting) perception of the sensuous (embodied) dimension of God's good creation. So our discussion focuses not on either the production of an art object or the experience and use of such objects, but on both. We are after the theological meaning of these realities—which can be applied equally to what we call low or high art—not merely a strategy for making and using art.[27]

Since our response to an object or an experience takes place on many levels, reflecting the variety of connections that informs our experience, our aesthetic experience will reflect this diversity. This leads Frank Burch Brown to speak of an *aesthetic milieu*, in which "everything in focal or subsidiary awareness . . . , within a particular context, is either immediately or mediately aesthetic in effect."[28] In some contexts, a worship service for example, the aesthetic level of experience may not always be the focal level, but in a museum the same object—say, a bejeweled crucifix—may be viewed in a different light. Our personal commitment to God, which is expressed in our worship, is inevitably bodily and interpersonal (i.e., social) and so will invariably include an aesthetic dimension even as it is always moral. But it is not possible to reduce the practice of our faith to this aesthetic response—the deepest aesthetic experience does not in itself constitute an encounter with God—any more than it can be reduced to our moral behavior. In the same way, our experience with God may include our ritual encounter with the eucharist and the social interaction with God's people ("sharing the peace"), but it cannot be reduced to these. The actual encounter with God may be mediated in various ways, but it is always a separable and distinct reality of our religious life.[29]

But the insistence on the goodness of the aesthetic dimension of creation (and of our creations) argues that material objects can have intrinsic value, we might say they have an "integrity" that is not reducible to their "relationships." Rembrandt's *Supper in Emmaus* (1648) refers, in a historical sense, to Christ's dinner on the evening of his resurrection; on another level it honors the gift of hospitality and the joy of discovery on the faces of the disciples; above all, it makes a theologically profound statement about God's incarnation in the man Jesus. But it does all of this in the particular pictorial space in which the artist has put these four people; that space includes the great arch that rises above the figure of Jesus, who is breaking the bread, and the way the light focuses on the central figure. All these connections become visible in a unique way in this particular arrangement of form and color. But while these outside references enrich the content and the delight we can take in the picture, Rembrandt's work cannot be reduced to these references.

What exactly does the artist do with these relationships in which he or she exists? Again in stark contrast to the modern notion of abstraction, our being in relationship to creation and ultimately to God, is, at the same time, a being responsible to what is there. The only way for us to know what is there is to become involved with it, to interact with it. Consistent with the modern notion of abstraction and knowledge as conceptual, modern people have mistakenly come to believe that they know something by passively watching or listening and then ordering what they see and hear. But in the biblical view we come to know by involving ourselves with the object of our knowledge. Jeremiah says to the sons of Josiah concerning their father:

> He judged the cause of the poor and needy;
> then it was well.
> Is not this to know me?
> says the Lord." (Jer 22:16)

So artists in a certain sense enable the created relationships to come to expression in various sensuous media. In these forms artists cast out lines across the world, especially across its empty spaces, connecting entities that may throw light on each other. In this way artists participate both in our dominion (our "naming") of the earth and in our comprehension of it. While they are not primarily making moral judgments on what is there, their work cannot help having a relationship to our moral life, simply because we exist in all these relationships at once—one or the other cannot be suspended while we enjoy the beautiful form, even if, as Polanyi puts it, one becomes focal while the other is tacit. Artists, then, have a certain responsibility to what is there and to the relationships in which they exist. Calvin Seerveld reminds us that "truth is the way God does things." So "to experience or declare what is true gets one actively caught up in the fabric of protecting, [and] strengthening sense opening communion with the Almighty Holy One."[30]

The artist, then, has a critical role to play in articulating the way in which we actually "indwell" our relationships. Michael Polanyi, especially in his book *Personal Knowledge*, has helped us understand that all knowledge is ultimately personal; it is conditioned by our human interests and our bodily sensibilities. Moreover, we know more than we can tell, because our feelings and intuitions are telling us things that we have not yet learned to describe. Artists bring these sleeping images to the light.[31] With their attuned imaginations they help us "see" or "hear" things our senses passed over. But their discovery goes to the heart of what is actually there. We "see" more each time we look carefully at a painting by Rembrandt, just as we are always learning more about what it means to live in this world. Indeed, following Polanyi, it is probably better to speak of "knowing" in terms of "learning." And we might describe a critical role of our growing discipleship as discovering connections both with God and with creatures, imagining—even proposing—what these connections might look like.[32]

One of the most telling illustrations of this point is recent work on educational reform. Students of the field have suspected for a long time that there is a link between the way students learn and the development of their imagination. Consistent with the quest of education in the West for "true knowledge," so-called arts programs, when tight budgets have not eliminated them altogether, are ordinarily considered to be a kind of recreation and are relegated to periods late in the day. But recent research has made it clear that children exist in a number of patterned relationships and need to be taught to function in as many of these as possible. Moreover, what we call intelligence varies greatly among individuals when applied in these various domains.[33] It is becoming clear that the arts play a critical and usually overlooked role in developing these mental aptitudes and in making connections between these domains. In a recent study done in Providence, Rhode Island, Martin Gardiner of the Music School enrolled a group of underachieving five to seven year olds in a special program that emphasized the systematic development of musical and artistic skills in addition to the standard curriculum. After seven months these students had caught up to their peers in reading and were outperforming them in math. The conclusion the researchers drew was that

> when students discover that participation in arts activities is pleasurable, they become motivated to acquire skills in the arts . . . with two types of results. First . . . students' general attitude toward learning and school can improve. Second learning arts skills forces mental "stretching" useful to other areas of learning.[34]

In other words, poetry, dance, and drawing may help students learn to indwell the various dimensions of their experience and—if God wills—see the delight that is meant to touch the whole.

If the norm to which the arts is accountable is ultimately truth as "the way God does things," as Seerveld suggests, then the criteria that the biblical discussion suggested appears compelling: art best achieves its purpose when its sensuous form is "fitting" to the relationships that it reflects. Part of the reason people believe the Bible is profoundly uninterested in aesthetics is that they have come to believe that art is simply about beauty and its contemplation. Beauty, of course, is a part of the fitting coherence in which creation exists, but, at least since the Fall, it is often missing, or better, hidden. Beauty as we understand it today derives from Plato's notion of proportion, and, since Romanticism, has become "set in stone," even idolized. Understood in this way, beauty has often served to drive people apart rather than bring them together. This is true whether it is found in the Hollywood cult of the body or the "feel good" glitz of pulp fiction. But, as Seerveld points out, there is no intrinsic reason why art must be subservient to this notion of beauty; "God's glory is not principally an aesthetic question for it lies equally under and behind and involved in all aspects of creation."[35] Or at least, it is not *simply* an aesthetic question, for the aesthetic is best understood as an aspect of the embodied relations in which God has created the world and to which our human sensitivities are best ordered. In this way beauty may be understood in a more contextual, a more biblical way. In the words of Simone Weil: "The beauty of the world is not an attribute of matter in itself. It is a relationship of the world to our sensibility which depends on the structure of our body and soul."[36]

This fittingness may account for the fact that our irreligious century has preferred an irreligious art, just as earlier ages felt comfortable with religious art. As Nicholas Wolterstorff says, there is clearly a fittingness between Frank Lloyd Wright's humanism and his architecture, between the spare white interiors of colonial churches and their rational theology, between Gothic architecture and Scholastic theology. This characteristic may account for our century's preference for incoherence and discord. On this point Wolterstorff is insightful:

> The twentieth century . . . has witnessed the invention of radically new strategies for securing the rest and stability of completeness. But also . . . it has witnessed the diminished interest in securing unity by means of completeness, and a willingness to make do with coherence. Could it be that this is connected with the quality of human experience in our age—restless and unsettled as it is? Could it be that here we find one more example of fittingness between aesthetic quality of works of art and the dominant quality of human experience in a certain age?[37]

Artists Are Caretakers of the Relationships of Creation

In making things that delight, artists are exercising their God-given responsibility of having dominion ("naming" the earth), loving their neighbor, and praising God with their mind, soul, and strength. This is their responsible (re)action to the relations in which they are created. But we have argued before that implicit in the responsive character of human life is the dimension of—no less active—reception.

We stand before the world, or before a work of art. The first responsibility, indeed the beginning of all moral and aesthetic sensitivity, is to be genuinely open to these experiences. This is not as simple as it sounds. As C. S. Lewis points out in *Experiment in Criticism*, most people "use" works of art, just as they use the created world, for their own practical purposes. That is, people are open primarily to their own receiving; they are not open to the ideas of the work.[38] This is safer, of course, because then they do not have to change. But to be genuinely open to the world is to make oneself vulnerable. In this sense, as George Steiner says, attention is the natural piety of the soul. And as Kathleen Norris reminds us, it is the prerequisite of conversion.

Attention is central to biblical piety as well. The commandment upon which all other commands "hang," according to Jesus, is "love the Lord your God with all your heart, and with all your soul, and with all your mind . . . and you shall love your neighbor as yourself" (Mt 22:37, 39). This kind of love demands a fair amount of attention, to what we and our neighbors feel and think, and to the shape our love ought to take. I have always been struck by the way people who love something spend their time looking at it, paying close attention to it. While on vacation French artist Georges Rouault would sometimes spend more than an hour on one city block, peering intently into store windows, picking something up from the ground, taking in every detail. Architects spend a great deal of time looking at old houses; forestry researchers look at trees day in and day out; composers fill their empty hours listening to other people's music. They are open to these things because, unlike others ("What does she see in those old houses?"), they are always seeing something new, something they had not noticed before.

Of course, this is not the end of the matter. Artists in particular are always restless before what they see. What they touch, taste, hear, or see becomes grist for the imagination, which, starting with these hints, throws imaginative lines out across the empty spaces of life, building pontoons across the abyss. At this point the real struggle begins, because the words are not flexible enough, the colors are not quite right, the tones seem flat.

> Words strain,
> Crack and sometimes break, under the burden,
> Under the tension, slip, slide, perish,
> Decay with imprecision, will not stay in place,
> Will not stay still.[39]

But for poets, these words, however fragile and thin, are the only materials there are. They must be led along in a conversation with these stubborn adverbs and adjectives, coaxing out their meaning. As an artist I make do, grabbing the hand that this color or that form holds out to pull myself up to a place where I see the world differently.

The conversational, dialogical character of this work—both with the materials and the natural motifs—is seen clearly in Vincent Van Gogh's description of one of his drawings:

> I believe that the way to acquire strength and power is to observe faithfully. As you will see, there are already several planes on this drawing, and one can look around it and through it, in every corner and hole. What is still lacking is vigor . . . but that will come. . . . The real thing is not to make an absolute copy of nature, but to know nature so well that what one makes is fresh and true; that is what is lacking in many.[40]

What is made can be fresh and true because it finds leverage in the order of what is there—an order vivified in the human construction and reconstruction of these relationships. The artist stands on the shoulders of this order, as it were, to throw out the line farther than it has been thrown before. He or she exists in the dynamic interplay that reflects God's own involvement and non-coercive immanence in the creation through the Holy Spirit. Just as God's presence is an active one, so our presence in the relations of creation is necessarily active. Listen to Knud Løgstrup's expression of this again:

> The mind does not exist without being in tune, without being a sounding board for everything that exists and occurs in the world and nature in which human beings with their senses, eyes, and ears are embedded. And unless there is attunement, nourished by things in nature, there would be no zest and energy for a single life manifestation.[41]

So the attunement is actually nourished by the interaction with the world that fulfills our creation mandate. This coherence is possible because God made the world through one who was to become incarnate, and so it is a fit place for human beings to live. This is why Christian artists see their discipleship, whatever else it might involve, as fundamentally the comprehension of the world through their sight, touch, hearing, taste, and smell.[42]

The human imagination does not leave things as they are. There is always arrangement, discovery, even at times deconstruction. Part of the reason for this is that though coherence is possible and relationships are meant to allow human persons to flourish, human experience is as often painful as it is delightful. So artists are not only responsive to their environment, but they seek to make something of it, to do something with it. This is consistent with our normative categories that, first, humans exist in a dynamic set of relationships that define their reality, and that, second, they find themselves necessarily committed to doing something about these connections. In the case of art, what they do always has a symbolic dimension to it. That is, the objects they make—the poem, the dance, the painting—constitute sensuous forms that embody their interests. They express a longing for a loved one:

> My love will come
> will fling open her arms and fold me in them . . .
> she'll run dripping upstairs, she won't knock,
> will take my head in her hands,
> and when she drops her overcoat on a chair
> it will slide to the floor in a blue heap.
> (Yevgeny Yevtushenko, "Waiting")

or even a prayer:

> Come, Holy Spirit,
> bending or not bending the grasses . . .
> I am only a man: I need visible signs.
> I tire easily, building the stairway of abstraction.
> (Czeslaw Milosz, "Veni Creator")

In all cases they express the wish or hope that things were otherwise—or the fear that the pain will return in the morning. In this way aesthetic objects are taken up into the purposeful life of people, becoming in their own way tools of these purposes. Artists have sometimes ignored this. Picasso allegedly said: "I put whatever I like into my pictures, and the objects, so much the worse for them, they simply have to put up with it." But still Picasso registered what may be one of this century's most powerful protests against the inhumanity of war in his painting in response to the Spanish Civil War, *Guernica* (1937). According to T. S. Eliot, Charles Baudelaire, the nineteenth-century critic, understood that the issue in art, as in all of life, was good and evil, even salvation and damnation. "So far as we are human what we do must be either evil or good."[43]

So art must be, at least, a protest against evil and not just a hymn to beauty. But some artists and critics, especially those influenced by Marxism, believed that art could do more than simply protest; it could become an instrument of human liberation. Herbert Marcuse, for example, argued:

> The radical qualities of art, that is to say, its indictment of the established reality and its invocation of the beautiful image of liberation are grounded precisely in the dimensions where art *transcends* its social determination and emancipates itself from the given universe of discourse and behavior while preserving its overwhelming presence.

> Thereby art creates the realm in which the subversion of experience proper to art becomes possible: the world formed by art is recognized as a reality which is suppressed and distorted in the given reality.[44]

Notice that art not only achieves a freedom from the givenness of ordinary reality (this derives, as we have seen, from Kant), but it also provides a kind of moral energy that can work toward liberation.

What happens when the Marxist vision of where society is heading breaks down, when utopias of all kinds are to be had at a discount? The responses to this void left by the eclipse of all utopian projects, whether Christian or Marxist, are typically of two kinds. On the one hand are those who understand deeply what has been lost and recognize the void that has been left. While their prescriptions are sometimes vague, their descriptions of the problem are often riveting. We have already referred to Suzi Gablik, but another critic writing from this perspective was the late Peter Fuller. He could not bring himself to accept a religious perspective, though he recognized the moral and spiritual bankruptcy of his own historical materialism. He concludes an important essay, "The Christs of Faith," with these words:

> Christianity remains a scandal and a stumbling block to the "historical materialist" interpretation of history. It is not just that [these] methodologies have so conspicuously failed to explain why it is was Christianity, specifically, which rose to dominance; or how it managed to survive and develop in almost every known kind of social formation. . . . The problem runs deeper still: the whole question of the historical Jesus, and the beliefs which accrued around him, should cause us historical materialists to consider just how far we are from understanding the *positive* role which such great and consoling illusions play in determining man's ethical, cultural and indeed his spiritual life.[45]

A second response to the breakdown of the utopian imagination, more characteristic of mainline critics, is to hold out for some critical though not prescriptive role for art. Examples of this perspective may be found in the recently published anthology *The Traffic in Culture: Refiguring Art and Anthropology*, which seeks to assess the function of art and anthropology in a post-modern situation.[46] George Marcus and Fred Myers point out in their introduction that the holism of anthropology provides a corrective to the autonomy of modern art since Kant (6). Consistent with the post-modern perspective, there is no utopian vision that can be harnessed by either art or anthropology. What then remains of the role of art? Its role apparently is still critical; art is able to confront the nature of modernity itself, providing both moral commentary and alternative perspective (6). What is the source of this alternative perspective or this moral commentary? The privileged source, apparently, which both art and anthropology feature, is the "otherness" of other cultural perspectives (14). So both disciplines have a common "historical project" that involves "cultural critique" of the world we take for granted (27). Neither art nor anthropology, of course, has any privileged perspective; no one any longer would claim such a thing. But by allowing art and anthropology to work off the perspectives of each other, the hope is that we will be able to ratchet ourselves up to a place where the air is purer—to a place where "critique" is still possible.

But criticism in the name of what? Our century carries on this project in the name of modern secular saints, Marx, Nietzsche, and Freud, who applied Descartes's project of doubt to the whole of our Western tradition. But where did they get the moral energy to turn their withering critiques on social practices, even on religion? Why bother? Merold Westphall has convincingly argued that their energy is a leftover from a larger perspective on good and evil:

> In calling Freud, Marx and Nietzsche the great secular theologians of original sin I have suggested that the hermeneutics of suspicion belong to our [Christian] understanding of human sinfulness. The self-deceptions they seek to expose, like those exposed by Jesus and the prophets, are sins and signs of our fallenness. If we are to deepen our understanding of our sinfulness with their help, we need to remember at the same time the larger theological context in which the doctrine of the fall is properly placed, between the doctrines of creation and redemption.[47]

So, in holding out for a "critical" perspective, we argue, art preserves the memory of a grander cultural project, one initiated by Jesus and the prophets, who were able to speak a critical word to their own culture and its practices. But this was not a critique for its own sake. It was a critique in the name of a higher vision of human reality. Amos, the shepherd of Tekoa, spoke in terms of this critique,

> Take away from me the noise of your songs;
> I will not listen to the melody of your harps.
> But let justice roll down like waters,
> and righteousness like an ever-flowing stream.
> (Am 5:23-24)

as did Jesus,

> "The Spirit of the Lord is upon me,
> because he has anointed me
> to bring good news to the poor.
> He has sent me to proclaim release to the captives
> and recovery of sight to the blind,

> to let the oppressed go free,
> to proclaim the year of the Lord's favor."
> (Lk 4:18-19)

But in speaking of this larger vision we have already gone beyond the "critical" function of art, important as this may be. To understand fully the importance of this larger perspective to the work of art, we need to develop a final claim.

The Artist Is Able to Project a World that Embodies Hope

Artists, we have said, shape their materials into symbolic forms that project a world. Artists, Nicholas Wolterstorff argues, project a world for our consideration that is normally incompatible with the actual world.[48] Indeed, the artist's imagination, while it feeds on the actual world, is finally restless, even ruthless, with what is there. Artists take the sounds and colors they find around them and melt them down, so to speak, so that what remains is their own imaginative world. Because these worlds become so compelling—who is not dazzled by Mozart's *Requiem*, or Monet's gardens, or even the world of *West Side Story*?—they often have been distrusted by those who are deeply religious, even as they have been revered by the irreligious. The one fears the allure of sensuous forms will obscure the vision of God; the other finds there a vision of ultimacy that modern secular people have lost (cf. Julian Schnabel).

How do we respond to this "allure" of art in a Christian way? We might decide to avoid this temptation and keep ourselves from art, as from an idol. Indeed, in the minds of many Christians—from the medieval mystics to the Reformers and modern Puritans—idolatry has been the chief danger of art. The honor and attention that a person gives to lovely or striking form, these believers argue, is something that is reserved for God alone. This view has been vigorously argued by some of the finest minds—and with some of the finest prose (cf. Augustine, St. Bernard)—Christianity has produced and should not be dismissed out of hand. It is based on the important biblical premise that the human person, to use Augustine's phrase, is made for God and is restless with anything less than God. It has some apparent support in the parables of Jesus, where finding God is called the "pearl of great price." In order to purchase this surpassing treasure we must "sell everything," even or especially those things of great value, which would keep us from possession of the one thing that matters, God.

Immanuel Levinas presents a striking form of this argument in his essay "Reality and Its Shadow."[49] Art is not reality, it is a shadow, he argues. Art deflects people from face to face encounter and responsibility. This weakness is inherent in the nature of art, which in Sean Hand's words "freezes time within images" (129), but it is also the result of the unique history of modern art, which Levinas recounts. Art has progressively been taken out of its context of reference to the earth, out of its ritual context in the community, and what is worse, out of its context of the worship of God, which has nurtured art from time immemorial. God has created us in real relationships, Levinas insists, which involve an inherent moral obligation to the presence of the "other." Perceiving the image requires passivity and thus neutralizes these concrete relationships, which must be grasped through action. "Art does not belong to the order of revelation. Nor does it belong to the order of creation, which moves it in just the opposite direction"(132). To paraphrase Kierkegaard, the aesthetic retreats from reality, the moral makes for it. Levinas concludes: "Art, essentially disengaged, constitutes in a world of initiative and responsibility, a dimension of evasion" (141). We have spoken above about the disinterestedness of contemplation. Levinas goes further, he calls it the "disinterestedness of irresponsibility" (142). The literary genre of criticism, on the other hand, exists on the "hither side of the world which is fixed in art, it reintroduces that world into the intelligible world in which it stands, and which is the true homeland of the mind"(142). In its pointing it directs us back to our relation with the "other," "without which being could not be told in its reality, that is, in its time" (143).

We might respond to the "allure" of art, then, by contrasting it with the actual encounter with the "other," and finally with God. This is a view with a significant pedigree in the history of faith, but it is not the whole story. There is another way of construing the power of art: an encounter with an art object, rather than deflecting attention, can direct the viewer to God. One who has best described this other way is George Steiner.[50] Steiner argues that in one sense the position we have just described is a capitulation to the modern imagination. Creativity in this view is premised on the absence of God, that is, on freedom. The natural response of the believer, then, is to see such a process as idolatrous. Steiner, however, proceeds from the reverse assumption: "Any coherent account of the capacity of human speech to communicate meaning and feeling is . . . underwritten by the assumption of God's presence" (3). In other words, aesthetic meaning is, in fact, based on the "real presence" of the "other" in the work of art. In this encounter we must "wager on transcendence" (4). So, contrary to Levinas, who sees art as an evasion of responsibility, Steiner believes art demands responsibility. Hermeneutics properly understood is answerability (8). We listen to a work, and if we hear what is there, we can "translate" it by acting out "the material . . . so as to give it intelligible life" (5). This is why Steiner believes the best reading of a work of art is not criticism—our captivity to this is a symptom of our life in the shadowlands—but another work of art, whether a performance or a new work altogether. "We are answerable to the text, to the work of art, to the musical offering in a very specific sense, at once moral, spiritual and psychological" (8).

The reason all of this sounds so strange, Steiner notes, is that in European culture between 1870 and 1940 a fundamental rupture occurred between the word and the world. What he calls the "logos order" was broken. "It is this break between word and world which constitutes one of the very few genuine revolutions of spirit in Western history and which defines modernity itself" (93). Modern artists, of course, regularly defy the emptiness that has resulted, going so far as to insist, Prometheus-like, that the truth of things *depends* on the absence of a world above and behind this one (what is called disparagingly *heteronomy*). But even this claim, Steiner reminds us, has theological implications. On what grounds does this skeptic ascribe meaning? "What conditions, if any, would enable the uttermost skeptic to believe that he can communicate to us his suspensions or refusals of belief?" (102).

Rather, art as language exists because there is the "other," first another, who speaks to us in the work. Finally, beyond this, the Other who stands behind and above all. "The archetypical paradigm of all affirmations of sense and of significant plenitude—the fullness of meaning of the word—is the Logos model" (119). This is why art is intrinsically moral; it "queries the last privacies of our existence" and tells us to change our life (142). The otherness that enters us really wants to remake us, making us (an)other (188). In order for this to happen we must wager on this real presence, both of the person in the work, and, beyond this, of the Logos. So, the gravity and pathos of art are ultimately religious, even if our positivism and technology have done their best to filter out these frequencies. Ours is the art of a long black Saturday, says Steiner, after the death of love on Friday, and before any hoped for liberation (232).

The attraction of art, then, is an echo of a deeper call that goes out through all the world. This way of understanding the "allure" that we spoke about seems to me to be ultimately more satisfying. This is because it bases the indubitable power of art on something real. Of course, there are those who, in the name of religion, either deny the power of aesthetic experience (is it the case that our faith sometimes *closes* our eyes to such things?) or attribute it to an evil power.[51] But thoughtful people know better. They know that these queries of our existence are real, and that their power for good and evil are intrinsic to our humanity. And they are right in their assessment, because aesthetics has a dimension of epiphany to it. Reality "shines through" it.[52] But, we claim, this Presence that is felt so deeply is personal. On one level it represents the other imagination that reaches out to us in the enlivened order of things that the artist presents. Here we believe the personalism of Steiner needs supplementing. We have argued that the imagination of the artist feeds on the splendor of the ordered whole that God created and sustains, and causes it to speak with a particular human accent.

Beyond the personal presence of the artist there is a further dimension to the reality that shines through: the continuing presence of God. Here we connect with the larger argument of this book. To speak of the Logos, as Steiner does, is to make an important claim, but one that needs further elaboration.[53] The artist working with the sublime and the depths of human life, even when he or she inspects the glory that is hidden in the ordinary, is working with live wires. This is not only because the human person is made in God's image and all of creation bears the vestiges of its creator, but because Christ the mediator of this creation has actually become embodied in it to confront its evil on the cross and triumph over it in the resurrection. Whenever artists dream of another world or of transforming what is before them, they engage in a struggle in which Christ himself is implicated. In this sense the chief basis of all craft is Christological. As Paul puts it, "All things have been created through him and for him, . . . and in him all things hold together" (Col 1:16-17). Beyond this the Father (in the name of the Son) has poured out the Holy Spirit upon "all flesh" (Acts 2). Indeed, Romans 8 implies that the Spirit's presence is echoed in the groaning of all creation. The reason for this is that the special role of the Spirit is to work in creation, through the gospel (notice how the firstfruit of the Spirit in the believer in Romans 8 is given a special role), to transform creation into a fit vehicle of God's glory. "It is that very Spirit bearing witness with our spirit that we are children of God, and if children, then heirs, heirs of God and joint heirs with Christ" (Rom 8:16-17).

Colin Gunton has followed T. F. Torrance in suggesting the imagery of priesthood for the human role in working with creation. "To image the being of God towards the world, to be the priest of creation, is to behave towards the world in all its aspects, of work and of play, in such a way that it may come to be what it was created to be, that which praises its maker by becoming perfect in its own way."[54] This statement encompasses a broader range of human activities, which helps us understand the role of art in the context of our whole life before God. The fact that the world, in Gerard Manley Hopkins's words, is "charged with the grandeur of God" is what makes art possible at all. But this possibility, however wonderful and moving in itself, exists to serve a higher purpose: to glorify God. In this it is taken up into the larger drama of good and evil, of sin and redemption, of everyday encounters as well as dramatic episodes.

Note carefully that what is embodied in a successful work of art is not simply beauty or goodness but beyond this the struggle of human life in the world in all of its interrelations. "When I curse Fate, it's not me, but the earth in me."[55] So art is not simply about contemplation, but it is a dimension of the larger project of being human. So the Christian artist can have both a more comprehensive vision of art and, at the same time, see a more modest role for it. H. R. Rookmaaker wrote a generation ago: "Christian art is nothing special. It is sound, healthy, good art. It is art that is in line with the God-given structures of art, one which has a loving a free view on reality, one which is good and true."[56] But to be good and true is a difficult and high calling. It means that the world—in all its pain and its delights—must be taken seriously. When these are felt deeply, the artist then seeks, in Steiner's terms, to enact them—in dance or paint or words. The artist as believer stands between the world and this creation, seeking to "translate" what is there. This gives the role of art as cultural critique, which post-modern art critics seek to retain, a new and higher calling. Hans-Georg Gadamer has described this transaction well:

> As the work of art as such is a world for itself, what is experienced aesthetically is a world for itself, removed from all connections with actuality. The work of art would seem almost by definition to become an aesthetic experience: that means, however, that it suddenly takes the person experiencing it out of the context of his life, by the power of the work of art, and yet relates him back to the whole of his existence.[57]

The work of art, while separate from life and in some ways opposed to it, when it is successful can connect us back with that world. In fact, Gadamer implies, the fullness of meaning of the work stands in the place and on behalf of the meaningful whole of life. But this can only happen if the world of the art and the world of our lives mutually interpret each other. This happens, we suggest, not because the artist has some Christian content which he or she wants to get across, but because the human and earthly reality that grasps the artist is ultimately related, through God's creating and sustaining work, to the everyday world that we all inhabit. In this the Holy Spirit plays a role, not by giving some supernatural content, but, John Taylor says, "by opening our eyes. The Holy Spirit is that power which opens eyes that are closed, hearts that are unaware, and minds that shrink from too much reality."[58]

CONCLUSION

We have been arguing that what humans do with God's creation, like that creation itself, has ends which cannot be comprehended in what is useful or even moral—though it will ordinarily relate to these things.

We noted in the first place that the glory of creation exists in the splendor of its harmony; what is lovely, like what is good, is what suits the order God has made. Beauty in the Bible, like goodness, does not call attention to itself but "rejoices in the truth" (1 Cor 13:6). The artist's calling, then, in the second place, is to explore the nooks and crannies of these relationships—as an explorer of fittingness. He or she allows the splendor of what is there (or what should be there) to come to sensuous expression. The practice of art becomes a critical component of our learning about the world (as recent literature on school reform argues). But third, artists do not leave things as they find them. They construct, reconstruct, and arrange what they find, scaling the sheer face of a rocky world to reach a place where they can see more clearly. And if God wills, they can create a critical vision that does not distract from God but may open the way back to God's presence.

Utility, morality, even human development are all things that are important to God, and so they are important vessels to bring to the abundance of creation. But even these sometimes overflow and our work breaks into a song or a dance that speaks of the sheer delight that God's presence calls forth at the center of things. This melody, or two step which we practice and struggle to learn, is a kind of foretaste, an intermediate expression of a final chorus we will perform standing before the Lamb, singing and dancing our perfected praise. Or perhaps it is a cry of despair over the distance we still feel from that moment of peace. In other words art can be a rest (or even a restlessness) that speaks of Rest. It is a "wondering" that is meant to lead us to the final wonder over the depth and breadth and height of God's goodness. In its depth it may even reflect some of the urgency of the Book of Hebrews, which warns: "Therefore, while the promise of entering his rest is still open, let us take care that none of you should seem to have failed to reach it" (Heb 4:1).

This is important, because the sense for this "rest," the allure that we have spoken about, remains alive and well in late-twentieth-century people. As Simone Weil expresses it: "A sense of beauty, although mutilated, distorted and soiled, remains rooted in the heart of man as a powerful incentive. It is present in all the preoccupations of secular life. If it were made true and pure it would sweep all secular life in a body to the feet of God."[59] "If it were made true and pure"—that is the challenge. For the modern person can no longer imagine such a view of things. The violence and cruelty of our century has killed our dreams, threatening at times to take art and culture down with them. But there are moments when we stand before a painting by Monet, or hear a fragment of a minuet by Mozart, and we glimpse the outline of another world—and turn away transformed. Our jaded neighbors must somehow hear that there is Someone who has come to open the way to that world and thus to liberate not only our souls but our imaginations.

Conclusion

Human Life as Embodied Worship

When Paul, in anticipation of his visit, appeals to the Roman Christians to present their bodies as a "living sacrifice, holy and acceptable to God" (Rom 12:1), he adds enigmatically, "which is your spiritual worship [or service: Greek *latreia*]." As the rest of the chapter makes clear he does not have in mind primarily the Sunday liturgy but rather a full-orbed life in the world. "Spiritual worship," according to Paul, means wholehearted love, enthusiasm, and rejoicing; it embodies compassion and hospitality (even of your enemies!); it is leavened with weeping and laughter. This worship springs from an inward renewal of our minds that allows us to discern and practice the good in the whole of life (Rom 12:2).

Catherine LaCugna says: "The language of praise is the primary language of Christian faith and for that reason the liturgy is sometimes called 'primary theology.' . . . The worship and praise of God is the living context, the precondition even, for the theological enterprise."[1] Academic theology, which works largely with concepts, is called secondary theology; it elaborates and explains this life of faith. Theologians have not always avoided the temptation to reverse this order of things and see their abstractions as the "real thing" that ordinary Christians need to study and apply. The Orthodox and Catholic traditions with their rich emphasis on the worship of the congregation sometimes make a different mistake and restrict this praise and worship to formal liturgical practices. Of course our worship focuses here, but it inevitably spills over into all of life. As LaCugna argues, only in "doxology does the inner life of God make any sense whatsoever."[2]

That we have trouble as modern people seeing all the activities of our life and culture as worship is the result, so we have argued, of our having intellectualized and dichotomized our lives. Rather than placing this everyday world into a larger portrait—as Dante, for example, was able to do[3]—we have shrunk reality to the cramped confines of our human world. We have pointed out that our century's recovery of narrative and the dramatic movement of God's loving search for us have given us important tools that help us put the pieces back together. Narrative has allowed us, in Erich Auerbach's words, to discern a larger "figural interpretation [of] our everyday contemporary reality."[4] This is crucial because life is seen by many educated people today as a quest, a journey toward some heartland of faith. These pilgrimages—whether to Harvard for wisdom or to the "old country" for roots—have become an extroverted and secular mysticism. But as Victor and Edith Turner note, for the modern person these quests have lost any deep or transcendent dimension. "Life has become one long pilgrimage, without map or goal."[5]

A map and a goal. Interestingly, these are images that reflect both ways of doing theology that we have examined. Theology has either been understood as the loci that together make up the intellectual map by which life is construed, or, more recently, it describes the journey and goal of the human pilgrimage. Important as these images are, they must be placed in a more comprehensive framework. Spatial and tactual dimensions must be added to our intellectual map and our spiritual journey. We have described these depth and breadth dimensions in three ways. First, we have pointed out that, underneath and round about, our lives are constituted by relationships with God, each other, and the physical creation. Second, these relationships inevitably call us to responsible action that is modeled after and responds to God's own world-shaping actions. And third, these relationships and actions are invariably expressed in our embodied life in the world; our (renewed) lives are meant to bring about something altogether fresh: a fellowship reflecting the trinitarian life of God producing works that will not be lost but brought into the heavenly Kingdom. All human life in the world is meant to find its orientation in the project that God has inaugurated in creation and embodied in Christ. In Colin Gunton's summary, the "end of all human action is praise of the creator," rendering God due response for divine goodness and giving us a "common light to illuminate all the dimensions of human culture."[6]

These realities, it turns out, are reflected in all the major summaries of God's project in scripture. The Ten Commandments, for example, though rooted in the Exodus narrative, represent a cross section, as it were, of that story. They describe the fundamental relations we enjoy—with God, our work, our family, our neighbors—and the responses that are appropriate to those relationships—worship (without idols), remembering, honor of parents, and respect for life and property.[7] In the Christian scriptures Christ provides a summary of these instructions in terms of a full-bodied, clear-headed love of God and neighbor. Paul too describes the Christian life—in view of God's mercies—as presenting our body as a living sacrifice—reasonable, everyday, embodied worship. Sacrifice in this vision of things turns out to provide the key to a flourishing cultural life. In the Hebrew scriptures, of course, sacrifice necessarily included giving up something, even a death, as payment for the estrangement sin had caused. This necessity found its final embodiment in Christ's own life and death on the cross. But now, after Christ's resurrection and the pouring out of the Holy Spirit, sacrifice becomes a celebration of mutual gift-giving in the body of Christ (symbolized by the presentation of the gifts in the liturgy). Here we give ourselves and our talents to each other as God has given himself to us in Jesus Christ. So this new way of living is also, at the same time, a new way of knowing and loving God—all of which is symbolized in baptism and the eucharist. These sacrifices of praise find their echo in our life and work in the world. This "takes the form of that culture which enables both personal and nonpersonal worlds to realize their true being."[8]

We do not forget, of course, that these summaries of the form of life appropriate to God's people are placed in the context of what God has done and is doing, in the Exodus and in Christ. They are theologically joined to these events. But our argument is that a narrative of those acts, however complete, is ultimately inadequate. Its inadequacy lies in the fact that these acts are grounded in the eternal relations of love among the persons of the Trinity. Indeed, in Christ and his church Christians confess that the reality of creation is taken up into—joined to—that eternal reality. Theology as intellectual map and as story helps us see how things fit together and even shows us where things are headed. But it does not, in itself, help us see our work as gardeners or truck drivers as Paul's *latreia*—embodied worship. Work is service first to God, then to God's creation and image. The form of life, the cultural patterns, in which Christians live both reflects something of the divine character and will one day be made into a perfect vehicle of that glory.

The theological grounding of the Christian form of life is a crucial corrective to our century's attempts to restore or liberate creation. Theologians of the social gospel reflect an optimism about human ability to bring in the Kingdom; liberation theologians tend to link human liberation with particular political programs. We have learned much from both groups about the necessary social and political dimension of the gospel. But while both were linked with important biblical themes—the Kingdom on the one hand, and the Exodus on the other—they were not properly grounded in the being and purposes of God. One could make a similar criticism of the lively spirituality represented by the contemporary Pentecostal Movement. Our practices are grounded in and respond to the relations in which we are created and which themselves reflect in the inner-trinitarian relations of God. As God entered the world and drew it to the divine self, so our work is directed toward the world, seeking in love the good of the other, until the glory of the Lord shall be revealed.

There are two very important implications to what we are saying. First, the truly Christian mode of knowing, as of living, is not an abstraction from the world and a hankering after a mystical peak experience, but a concrete involvement and self-giving in the world's God-given physicality. Life involves a careful seeing in the midst of life, a collecting from it of the gifts God has put there and given meaning by the divine presence. Work and prayer, just as worship and witness, do not point in opposite directions but are together working toward what the Christian scriptures call the "revealing" of Jesus Christ.

Second, then, human life points toward the future God is planning for it, in which God and creation are perfectly integrated and God's trinitarian life perfectly displayed. Jon Levenson says that Jewish interpretation of the Torah aims, theologically, to understand and recover its "simultaneity"; that is, whatever its varying historical sources, as it stands, "Torah law is to be inferred only from its totality and . . . discrepancies are to be harmonized rather than exploited for theological purposes."[9] For, in the thinking of the Rabbis, the law not only looks back to Israel's dwelling in the land but ahead to the messianic future. That is to say, the narratives and laws are not only historically situated, but they also point forward to a time of fulfillment. In the Christian scriptures this "collection" of narrativity is a main characteristic of John's vision on Patmos. The best stories, we have pointed out, have a certain minimalist tendency—a focus on some particular actions and character. But in the Revelation of John the threads of biblical narrative are woven together into a final vision of God dwelling in a new creation with God's people. This is not a denial of the stories but their climax; it does not analyze the stories so much as collect them. It is not accidental that more hymns are found in Revelation than in any other book except the Psalms, for Revelation is a vision of a time when creation itself and its human underlord seem constantly to break into song. Symbols—bowls and trumpets, scrolls and seals—crowd in on one another. As might be expected, our analytic and cognitive mode of reflecting has mostly smothered this vitality, replacing its pulsating life with charts and principles. But this cumulative vision cannot so easily be suppressed. It concentrates and focuses the biblical stories, suggesting a "simultaneity" of their meaning in a final, and altogether new, creation. The "meaning" of these images is better reflected in a kind of Wittgensteinian family resemblance than in some single linear story—just as at the beginning of scripture the stories are piled on top of one another, pointing us to the awesome and wonderful presence of God.[10] We have referred to Dante, and it is fitting to end with this description of what he saw at the end of his journey:

> Like a geometer wholly dedicated
> to squaring the circle, but who cannot find,
> think as he may, the principle indicated—
>
> so did I study the supernal face.
> I yearned to know just how our image merges
> into that circle, and how it there finds place;
>
> but mine were not the wings for such a flight.
> Yet, as I wished, the truth I wished for came
> cleaving my mind in a great flash of light.

Here my powers rest from their high fantasy,
but already I could feel my being turned—
instinct and intellect balanced equally

as in a wheel whose motion nothing jars—
by the Love that moves the Sun and the other
Stars.[11]

Notes

PREFACE

1. D. Tracy and N. Lash, eds., *Cosmology and Theology* (New York: Seabury, 1983).

2. Jürgen Moltmann, *God in Creation: A New Theology of Creation and the Spirit of God,* ed. and trans. Margaret Kohl (San Francisco: Harper & Row, 1985).

1 GOD'S STORY AND GOD'S PRESENCE

1. Francis Fukuyama, *The End of History and the Last Man* (New York: Free Press, 1992).

2. This striking image was used in particular of the Balkans after the fall of Marshall Tito by Miroslav Volf in "When the Unclean Spirit Leaves: Tasks of the Eastern European Churches after the 1989 Revolution," *Cross Currents* 41 (1991).

3. *Los Angeles Times,* February 16, 1996, v. 15, p. B9, col. 3.

4. See Mark A. Noll, *The Scandal of the Evangelical Mind* (Grand Rapids: Eerdmans, 1994). Noll defines intuitionism as "the rapid movement from first impressions to final conclusions" (p. 245).

5. Stanley Hauerwas and William H. Willimon, *Resident Aliens: Life in the Christian Colony* (Nashville: Abingdon, 1989), pp. 69-71.

6. Belgic Confession (1561), article 2, as quoted in Noll, *The Scandal of the Evangelical Mind,* pp. 53, 54.

7. René Descartes, *Discourse on Method and Meditations,* ed. L. J. Lafleur (New York: Liberal Arts Press, 1950), p. 5.

8. This commitment to certainty and the alienation it has caused in the modern world is well described in Colin Gunton, *Enlightenment and Alienation* (Blasingstoke: Marshall, Morgan and Scott, 1985), esp. Part 2. Perhaps our evangelical tendency to make biblical authority mean an "inerrant Bible" is a part of our modern intolerance for ambiguity.

9. Augustine's neo-Platonic method is a predecessor of this modern view, but it was confirmed by Calvin, who began his *Institutes* with a discussion of the knowledge of self and the knowledge of God. Its relationship with Descartes's starting point is also evident. On this whole development see the classical statement by Krister Stendahl, "Paul and the Introspective Conscience of the West," in *Paul among Jews and Gentiles* (Philadelphia: Fortress Press, 1976).

10. George Ernest Wright, *The God Who Acts* (London: SCM, 1952). Subsequent page references to this book are in the text.

11. Exemplified for example, by Oscar Cullmann, *Salvation in History* (New York: Harper & Row, 1967).

12. The book which develops this point most clearly is Stanley Hauerwas, *A Community of Character: Toward a Constructive Christian Social Ethic* (Notre Dame, Ind.: Univ. of Notre Dame Press, 1981). A helpful overview of narrative theology is to be found in Stanley Hauerwas and L. Gregory Jones, eds. *Why Narrative? Readings in Narrative Theology* (Grand Rapids: Eerdmans, 1989).

13. See Gustavo Gutiérrez, *A Theology of Liberation* (Maryknoll, N.Y.: Orbis Books, 1973; rev. ed. 1988); the application to hermeneutics is illustrated by Hans Frei, *The Eclipse of Biblical Narrative: A Study in 18th and 19th Century Hermeneutics* (New Haven: Yale Univ. Press, 1974); also see Jürgen Moltmann, *The Crucified God,* ed. and trans. R. A. Wilson and John Bowden (London: SCM, 1974).

14. Erich Auerbach, *Mimesis: The Representation of Reality in Western Literature* (Princeton: Princeton Univ. Press, 1953; New York: Anchor Books, 1957). This book had a major influence, for example, on Hans Frei.

15. Frei, *The Eclipse of Biblical Narrative,* p. 280. See also, among others, Robert Alter, *The Art of Biblical Narrative* (New York: Basic Books, 1981), and John Dominic Crossan, *The Dark Interval: Towards a Theology of Story* (Sonoma, Calif.: Polebridge Press, 1988), which have done much to help us read the Bible (and think) in ways appropriate to the nature of narrative.

16. The statements of Vatican II are to be found in *The Documents of Vatican II: In a New and Definitive Translation, with Commentaries and Notes by Catholic, Protestant, and Orthodox Authorities,* Walter M. Abbott, general editor (New York: Crossroad, 1966). Paul D. Hanson, *A People Called: The Growth of Community in the Bible* (San Francisco: Harper & Row, 1986), developed this notion in an important study of the Old Testament understanding of community. Also see N. T. Wright, *The New Testament and the People of God* (Minneapolis: Fortress Press, 1992).

17. This has received its most important development in the work of Hans-Georg Gadamer and A. MacIntyre.

18. See Jürgen Moltmann, *A Theology of Hope: On the Grounds and Implications of a Christian Eschatology,* trans. James W. Leitch (London: SCM, 1967), and Hal Lindsey, *The Late Great Planet Earth* (Grand Rapids: Zondervan, 1970).

19. The way in which use of historical categories spans the theological spectrum is again illustrated by such diverse works on justice as liberation theologian Jose Miranda's impressive work *Marx and the Bible: A Critique of the Philosophy of Oppression* (Maryknoll, N.Y.: Orbis Books, 1974) and the fine evangelical treatment by Stephen Charles Mott, *Biblical Ethics and Social Change* (New York: Oxford Univ. Press, 1982).

20. Though interpreted differently, as we have noted, this historical approach has been adopted by both evangelical and mainline theologians. In 1957 George Eldon Ladd commented favorably on John Baillie's book *The Idea of Revelation,* which stressed that "God has done something . . . which place[s] men in a new situation." Ladd notes: "The historical character of biblical religion is one of the elements which determines both its distinctiveness and its glory." Though he goes on to insist that "revelation has not occurred in history alone; it has occurred also in the written Scriptures which preserve the divinely initiated meaning of act-revelation" ("Revelation, History and the Bible," *Christianity Today* (Sept. 30, 1957), pp. 6, 8). Langdon Gilkey a little later summarized the widespread view that "biblical religion was the response of faith to and the recital of the 'mighty acts of God,'" though he complains that theologians who speak like this often disbelieve in

the literal action of God in history, reducing this to the Hebrew confession about God's action. He argues for the recovery of a confessional-theological meaning for this language (cf. "Cosmology, Ontology and Biblical Language," *Journal of Religion* 41 [1961], pp. 195ff.). However interpreted, historical categories have by this time become the coin of the realm.

21. I have tried to introduce some of these theologies to a Western audience in *Learning about Theology from the Third World* (Grand Rapids: Zondervan, 1990).

22. This view is proposed by Jean François Lyotard, *The Post Modern Condition* (Minneapolis: Univ. of Minnesota Press, 1984; originally published in French, 1979), and his many followers.

23. A thoughtful example of someone taking this approach is David F. Wells, *No Place for Truth, or, Whatever Happened to Evangelical Theology?* (Grand Rapids: Eerdmans, 1993).

24. See Thomas Tracy, *God, Action, and Embodiment* (Grand Rapids: Eerdmans, 1984; Yale University dissertation, 1980), p. 77. Subsequent page references to this book are in the text.

25. See William Placher, *Unapologetic Theology: A Christian Voice in a Pluralistic Conversation* (Louisville: Westminster/John Knox, 1989), pp. 131 and 161ff.

26. David K. Clark, "Relativism, Fideism and the Promise of Postliberalism," in *The Nature of Confession,* ed. Timothy R. Phillips and Dennis L. Okholm (Downers Grove: InterVarsity Press, 1996), p. 120. Cf. essays of Fackre and Hunsinger in the same volume. This way of thinking lies behind our emphasis on embodiment below.

27. This truth has been recently underlined by the growing understanding that a proper understanding of history requires a theology of nature. This is the thrust of much of the discussion in D. Tracy and N. Lash, eds., *Cosmology and Theology* (New York: Seabury, 1983). Cf. their editorial reflections: "History cannot be understood without a relationship to creation; history cannot be understood without nature; the central categories of God and the Self (and, therefore, society and history) cannot be fully grasped without reference to the category of 'cosmos' or 'world,'" (p. 87).

28. James Barr, *Biblical Faith and Natural Theology* (Oxford: Clarendon, 1993), p. 77. This was given as the Gifford Lectures in 1991. This does not imply, as Barr appears to argue, that the idea of revelation has no normative role to play.

29. John MacMurray, *The Self as Agent* (London: Faber, 1957), pp. 105-12.

30. Jon Levenson, *Sinai and Zion: An Entry into the Jewish Bible* (New York: HarperCollins, 1985), p. 149; see pp. 148-51.

31. Ibid., p. 151. Similar things could be said about the fact that John sees the revelation of the end times and conveys the experience in ways that are richly visual.

32. Catherine LaCugna, *God for Us: The Trinity and the Christian Life* (New York: Harper, 1991), p. 322.

33. Since the time of Aquinas it has been common to distinguish God's self-relations, which are termed *real relations* from those God sustains with creation, which are called *logical.* LaCugna in her book has caused some consternation in questioning this distinction (see LaCugna, *God for Us,* pp. 152-57). Earl Muller has recognized that Thomas's distinction seems not to allow for a real incarnation, in which Christ clearly has a "real relation" with, for example, his mother. He thus proposes a third category, which he calls "subsistent relationality," in which Christ's

"filiability" could ground real relations with the creatures (see "Real Relations and the Divine: Issues in Thomas' Understanding of God's Relation to the World," *Theological Studies* 56 [1995], pp. 673-95, esp. pp. 688-90). This discussion underlines the growing recognition of God's intimate relation with creation and, important for our purposes, the impossibility of knowing God strictly in innertrinitarian terms.

34. Jürgen Moltmann has argued that the trinitarian concept of mutual penetration applies to the world. We prefer to say these relations are reflected in the world in their creaturely way (see chapter 5 below). The relations between God and the world are not symmetrical (see *God in Creation: A New Theology of Creation and the Spirit of God,* ed. and trans. Margaret Kohl [San Francisco: Harper & Row, 1985], p. 17).

35. LaCugna, *God for Us,* p. 324.

36. Colin Gunton, *Christ and Creation* (Grand Rapids: Eerdmans, 1992), p. 19.

37. LaCugna, *God for Us,* p. 324.

38. Gunton, *Christ and Creation,* p. 50. Cf. Jürgen Moltmann: "It is always the Spirit who first brings the activity of the Father and the Son to its goal" (*God in Creation,* p. 9).

39. LaCugna, *God for Us,* p. 324. One of the few weaknesses of LaCugna's splendid book is her failure to draw out the implications of this for our embodied life in creation.

40. Early members of this movement were Lucien Febvre and Marc Bloch, who influenced Fernand Braudel's famous work *The Mediterranean and the Mediterranean World in the Age of Philip II* (New York: Harper & Row, 1972). This work begins with a long section on the physical environment. This way of thinking had roots especially in the French Romantic historian Jules Michelet and owed something as well to Swiss historian Jacob Burkhardt.

41. Braudel, *The Mediterranean,* p. 16.

42. Hans-Georg Gadamer, *Truth and Method*, ed. and trans. by Garret Barden and John Cumming (New York: Seabury, 1975; rev. ed., New York: Crossroad, 1989).

43. See Alasdair MacIntyre, especially his *After Virtue,* 2d ed. (Notre Dame, Ind.: Univ. of Notre Dame Press, 1984), and his 1988 Gifford Lectures *Three Rival Versions of Moral Inquiry* (Notre Dame, Ind.: Univ. of Notre Dame Press, 1990). In *Whose Justice? Which Rationality?* (Notre Dame, Ind.: Univ. of Notre Dame Press, 1988) he notes: "Philosophical theories give organized expression to concepts and theories already embodied in forms of practice and types of communities" (p. 390).

44. Charles Taylor, *The Sources of the Self: The Making of the Modern Identity* (Cambridge: Harvard Univ. Press, 1989), p. ix.

45. This expression comes from Richard Lischer's helpful article "The Limits of Story," *Interpretation* 3:1 (1984), pp. 26-38. He suggests we need *parataxis* (placing things, without comment, side by side) in addition to *syntaxis*. In any synchronic view the possibility of discontinuity must be set alongside the historical emphasis on continuity. Gadamer with his emphasis on the continuity of tradition has been criticized at precisely this point. Emil Fackenheim begins a discussion of Gadamer (and Ricoeur and Heidegger) by saying these "never face up to the Holocaust, as an event by which historical continuity might be ruptured" (*The Jewish Bible after the Holocaust,* quoted in John Goldingay, *Models for Interpretation of Scripture* [Grand Rapids: Eerdmans, 1995], p. 229). In the case of genocide the historical categories

are clearly inadequate to come to terms with the irruption of the demonic. What theological categories make sense of this?

46. Following the classic trinitarian axiom that "the works of God outside himself are undivided," we insist that these categories together reflect God's trinitarian character; they are not meant individually to reflect one of the three persons.

47. Cf. "Analysis shows that a relation (always social) determines its terms and not the reverse" and an "individual is a locus of relationships" (Michel de Certeau, *The Practice of Everyday Life,* ed. and trans. Steven Rendall [Berkeley: Univ. of California Press, 1984], p. xi).

48. *The Levinas Reader,* ed. Sean Hand (Oxford: Blackwell, 1989), p. 82.

49. See Polanyi, *Personal Knowledge: Toward a Post-Critical Philosophy* (London: Routledge & Kegan Paul, 1962), pp. 99, 139ff. See also the excellent discussion of Polanyi in Gunton, *Enlightenment and Alienation,* Part 1, to which this section is indebted.

50. Knud E. Løgstrup, *Metaphysics,* ed. and trans. Russell L. Dees (Milwaukee: Marquette Univ. Press, 1995), vol. 2, pp. 293, 296.

51. Iris Murdoch, quoted in Gunton, *Enlightenment and Alienation,* pp. 74, 75. Gunton comments: "It is only as the woman gives her attention to what is actually there that possibilities for action become apparent." See Simone Weil, *Waiting on God,* ed. and trans. Emma Crawford (London: Routledge & Kegan Paul, 1951), pp. 97-100.

52. Gunton, *Enlightenment and Alienation,* pp. 49-53.

53. LaCugna, *God for Us,* p. 352. She notes that since God's personhood (To-Be-in-communion) is primary to God's substance (To-Be), God "would not be God without a pros, a toward-another, a relationship of communion with another."

54. Løgstrup, *Metaphysics,* vol. 1, p. 89.

55. Interestingly, Levinas criticizes Martin Buber at just this point. While agreeing that the I-Thou relation is primary to the I-It relation, Buber's intersubjectivity is understood in terms of reciprocity, as though it were always a friendly exchange. But this does not account for the asymmetry of the relationship in which I am always obligated ethically to act in relation to the other person, who may oppress me (Hand, *The Levinas Reader,* chap. 4; see Sean Hand's comment, p. 59).

56. G. Lessing argues: Supposing I do accept the fact of Jesus' resurrection. "To jump with that historical truth to a quite different class of truths, and to demand of me that I should form all my metaphysical and moral ideas accordingly, if that is not a transfer to another genus [Aristotle's famous category mistake], then I do not know what Aristotle meant by this" (*Theological Writings,* ed. H. Chadwick [Stanford: Stanford Univ. Press, 1957], pp. 54, 55).

57. See MacMurray, *The Self as Agent,* p. 12. Interestingly, John Aves has critiqued MacMurray in ways analogous to Levinas's critique of Buber; that is, he does not allow for relationships which may be asymmetrical (what Harvey Cox calls our urban I-You relations), or for relations that make moral demands upon us. But MacMurray's point still stands that action achieves a unity of knowledge and movement (see "Persons in Relation: John MacMurray," in *Persons, Divine and Human: King's College Essays in Theological Anthropology,* ed. Christoph Schwobel and Colin Gunton [Edinburgh: T & T Clark, 1991], pp. 132-133).

58. T. Tracy, *God, Action, and Embodiment,* pp. 65, 22-25.

59. Taylor, *The Sources of the Self,* pp. 56-58.

60. LaCugna, *God for Us,* p. 353.

61. Kallistos Ware, "The Unity of the Human Person according to the Greek Fathers," quoted in Aves, "Persons in Relation," p. 145.

62. See Brian Walsh and Richard Middleton, *Truth Is Stranger than It Used to Be* (Downers Grove: InterVarsity Press, 1995), p. 191.

63. Jon Levenson points out that this fact is emphasized even in the parallel descriptions of creation and the construction of the tabernacle (and Temple): "Since the creation of the world and the construction of the temple are parallel, if not identical, then the experience of the completed universe and that of the completed sanctuary should also be parallel" (Levenson, *Sinai and Zion,* p. 144). See the discussion below in chapter 2.

64. In this way it seems best to follow the lead of most Reformed theologians that even apart from the Fall it would have been God's purpose to enter fully into relationship with creation through the incarnation (cf., for example, Gunton, *Christ and Creation,* p. 96).

65. I owe my awareness of this expression to my beloved teacher Hans Rookmaaker, who often said it as we were standing in front of a painting by Rembrandt.

66. Hubert L Dreyfus, *What Computers Still Can't Do: A Critique of Artificial Intelligence* (Cambridge: MIT Press, 1992). Dreyfus's fundamental critique of artificial intelligence is that it makes knowledge wholly propositional; the role of the body and the situation is ignored. By contrast, he argues that "our sense of relevance was holistic and required involvement and ongoing activity." In artificial intelligence "representations were atomistic and totally detached from such activity" (p. xi). This, then, is at least one answer to Philip Sampson's question: "Is channel hopping any different from browsing through a bookshop? Is the paradigmatic experience of hyperspace in postmodern architecture and shopping mall really new?" ("The Rise of Postmodernity," in Philip Sampson, Vinay Samuel, and Chris Sugden, *Faith and Modernity* [Oxford: Regnum, 1994], p. 32). Yes, these experiences are new, for the fundamental reason that they are not embodied.

67. Margaret R. Miles, "The Revelatory Body: Signorelli's *Resurrection of the Flesh* at Orvieto," *Theological Education* 21:1 (Autumn 1994), pp. 75-90.

68. Ruth Hubbard, quoted in Miles, "The Revelatory Body," p. 86. Cf. T. Tracy: "Our charter of action is biologically stated" (*God, Action, and Embodiment,* p. 93).

69. Helmut Kuhn, "Personal Knowledge and the Crisis of the Philosophical Tradition," quoted in Gunton, *Enlightenment and Alienation,* p. 146.

70. Based on a kind of moral reasoning that Professor Patricia Benner calls "care ethics." See Patricia Benner, "A Dialogue between Virtue Ethics and Care Ethics," *Theoretical Medicine,* forthcoming.

71. See J. Metz: "The modern man's understanding of the world is fundamentally oriented toward the future. His mentality therefore is not primarily contemplative but operative" (*A Theology of the World* [New York: Seabury, 1969], p. 83).

72. Pierre Hadot, *Philosophy as a Way of Life,* ed. and trans. Michael Chase, ed. Arnold I. Davidson (Oxford: Blackwell, 1995), pp. 58-61, quotation at p. 59.

73. Cf. T. Tracy, *God, Action, and Embodiment,* pp. 22-25. This will be a primary theme of our next chapter. The term *project,* which we employ following Tracy, is ordinarily called *the Kingdom of God* by theologians, but *project* avoids some of the contemporary misunderstanding of that term.

74. Michael Buckley, *At the Origins of Modern Atheism* (New Haven: Yale Univ. Press, 1987), p. 361, cf. p. 67. James Turner makes a very similar argument about the defense of the faith in the nineteenth century. Because of the insistence on explaining the faith in scientific terms, the reality of mystery was lost (James Turner, *Without God, Without Creed: The Origins of Unbelief in America* [Baltimore: Johns Hopkins Univ. Press, 1985]).

2 CREATION

1. In his excellent study of these things, George Hendry argues that the place of nature in God's overall plan "has been virtually ignored for the past 200 years: nature has been dropped from the agenda of theology" (*Theology of Nature* [Philadelphia: Westminster, 1980], p. 11). Similarly, Gustaf Wingren notes that theology in Sweden has focused entirely on the second article of the Apostles' Creed in the twentieth century, ignoring the first article (in spite of the fact that many were studying Luther and Irenaeus!) (see Gustaf Wingren, *Creation and Gospel: The New Situation in European Theology* [New York: Edwin Mellen Press, 1979], p. 6). This situation has recently begun to change. Among the most important reflections on this area we find the work of feminist theologians Rosemary Radford Ruether, *Gaia and God: An Ecofeminist Theology of Earth Healing* (San Francisco: HarperCollins, 1992) and Sally McFague, *Models of God: Theology for an Ecological, Nuclear Age* (Philadelphia: Fortress Press, 1987); Joseph Sittler, *Essays on Nature and Grace* (Philadelphia: Fortress Press, 1972), Jürgen Moltmann, *God in Creation: A New Theology of Creation and the Spirit of God,* ed. and trans. Margaret Kohl (San Francisco: Harper & Row, 1985), Colin Gunton, *Christ and Creation* (Grand Rapids: Eerdmans, 1992), Paul K. Jewett, *God, Creation and Revelation* (Grand Rapids: Eerdmans, 1991); and the important study by Steven Bouma-Prediger, *The Greening of Theology: The Ecological Models of Rosemary Radford Ruether, Joseph Sittler, and Jürgen Moltmann* (Atlanta: Scholars Press, 1995). Recent biblical interest in creation is represented by J. G. Gibbs, *Creation and Redemption: A Study in Pauline Theology* (Leiden: E. J. Brill, 1971), Bernhard Anderson, ed. *Creation in the Old Testament* (Philadelphia: Fortress Press, 1979), and Jon Levenson, *Creation and the Persistence of Evil* (Princeton: Princeton Univ. Press, 1988; 1st ed., 1987).

2. 1 Clement 20:10-12, in *Early Christian Fathers,* ed. Cyril C. Richardson (Philadelphia: Westminster, 1953), pp. 53-54.

3. See Paulos Gregorios, *The Human Presence: An Orthodox View of Nature* (Geneva: World Council of Churches, 1978). The Orthodox human identity is grounded in the confession to God, "You made me," whereas Western Christians say, "By faith I am a child of God."

4. Hendry claims that what Thomas wanted to do was "to help [medieval Christians] relate their belief in God to the nature and condition of the world" (*Theology of Nature,* p. 14).

5. Martin Luther, quoted in Paul Althaus, *The Theology of Martin Luther* (Philadelphia: Fortress Press, 1966), p. 106. It is easy to see how this emphasis on God's "presence" led to Luther's famous view that creatures constitute "masks of God."

6. Calvin, *Institutes,* 1.5.5 (quoted and discussed in Bouma-Prediger, *The Greening of Theology,* p. 86). Calvin goes on to qualify the statement, showing that it is the sovereignty of God that he wishes to underline.

7. Gerhard von Rad, *Genesis,* ed. and trans. John Mark (Philadelphia: Westminster, 1961), pp. 43, 44. Cf. *Old Testament Theology,* ed. and trans. D. M. G Stalker (New York: Harper & Row, 1962).

8. Some of the more responsible discussions of the question, to their credit, do push the question of the naturalistic assumptions of the scientific world view and the question of absolute origins, which lies beyond scientific competence (see Phillip E. Johnson, *Darwin on Trial,* 2d ed. [Downers Grove: InterVarsity Press, 1993]). But the larger theological issues of God's continuing relationship and the theological meaning and end of the created order are still left unillumined by this narrow range of issues. This particular creation versus evolution debate will not occupy us further here because not only are Christians to be found on both sides of the issue, but it represents a case of Christians allowing themselves to be drawn into conversation on issues in which someone else, in this case the scientific establishment, has set the terms of the debate. For those interested, the debate has been featured in a special issue of *Christian Scholars Review,* vol. 24:4 (May 1995). This is not to say that the how and why questions are unrelated, but while science can tell us something about the former, the latter raises the more important theological questions. Science can only indirectly help us answer these.

9. R. J. Clifford, "The Hebrew Scriptures and the Theology of Creation," *Theological Studies* 46 (September 1985), pp. 507–23. Hans Urs Von Balthasar puts this point in a peculiarly modern way at the conclusion of his discussion of the modern history of what God has created: "Love loves Being in an a priori way, for it knows that no science will ever track down the ground of why something exists rather than nothing at all. It receives it as a free gift and replies with free gratitude" (*The Glory of the Lord,* vol. 5, *Metaphysics and the Modern Age* [Edinburgh: T & T Clark, 1991], p. 647).

10. Gunton, *Christ and Creation,* p. 16. Clifford's reference to the cosmogony of Genesis 2–11 is found in "The Hebrew Scriptures and the Theology of Creation," p. 520.

11. See Colin Gunton, *The Actuality of the Atonement* (Edinburgh: T. & T. Clark, 1988), pp. 17–28.

12. See Robert Neville, *God the Creator: On the Transcendence and Presence of God* (Chicago: Univ. of Chicago Press, 1968).

13. Aristotle, *Poetics* 1457b, 7-8, quoted in Gunton, *The Actuality of the Atonement,* p. 28. The most famous modern discussion of metaphor and the source of much subsequent discussion is Max Black, *Models and Metaphors* (Ithaca: Cornell Univ. Press, 1962). See also Paul Ricoeur: Metaphor "teaches something, and so it contributes to the opening up and discovery of a field of reality other than that which ordinary language lays bare" (*The Rule of Metaphor,* ed. Robert Czerny [Toronto: Univ. of Toronto, 1975], p. 148).

14. Descartes, quoted in Gunton, *The Actuality of the Atonement,* p. 30. Cf. Catherine LaCugna: "The systematic theologian needs to keep in mind that every concept, whether it be 'substance' or 'relation,' is fundamentally metaphorical, not a literal description of what is" (*God for Us.* p. 359).

15. S. J. Brown, quoted in Gunton, *The Actuality of the Atonement,* p. 37. See also S. J. Brown, *Images and Truth: Studies in the Imagery of the Bible* (Catholic Book Agency, 1955). In his discussion of these things Robert Banks points out that, because of this correspondence, "metaphor is more basic than concept" (*God the Worker: Journeys into the Mind, Heart and Imagination of God* [Sutherland NSW: Albatross Books, 1992], p. 20).

16. Thomas Tracy's observation is relevant here: "An agent's aim in his action will always be, most concretely and immediately, to carry through some pattern of performance, or 'project'" (*God, Action, and Embodiment,* p. 22). This suggests we can think of God as "performing" creation as well as merely constructing it (see Banks, *God the Worker,* pp. 50ff.).

17. See Bernhard W. Anderson, *Understanding the Old Testament,* 3d ed. (Englewood Cliffs: Prentice-Hall, 1975), p. 426. He notes: "The rhythms and refrains reflect years of usage in the Temple." The fact that the passage is meant to stimulate our imagination as well as our cognitive faculties underlines the futility of asking primarily scientific questions of the text.

18. Cf. Claus Westermann, *Creation* (Philadelphia: Fortress Press, 1974), pp. 18, 19. Westermann calls the human creation God's counterpart.

19. Levenson, *Creation and the Persistence of Evil,* p. 12; he is dependent on Clifford here.

20. Levenson does not answer the question of where these forces ultimately come from, but neither does scripture. Where does the evil influence on Adam and Eve in chapter 3 come from? From within creation. See the discussion of this below.

21. Levenson, *Creation and the Persistence of Evil,* pp. xvii, 14. Subsequent page references to this book are in the text.

22. George Mendenhall's work was formative. See the helpful review in John L. McCarthy, *Old Testament Covenant: A Survey of Current Opinions* (Richmond: John Knox, 1972). G. E. Mendenhall, *Law and Covenant in the Ancient Near East* (Pittsburgh: Biblical Colloquium, 1955), reprints the critical articles from *Biblical Archaeologist.*

23. I am dependent here on conversation and personal correspondence with my colleague Francis I. Andersen. He notes that "there is no place in the OT where all the components of a suzerainty treaty are found in a single text" (correspondence of July 8, 1995).

24. See John H. Stek, "'Covenant' Overload in Reformed Theology," *Calvin Theological Journal* 29 (1994), pp. 37–39.

25. Andersen, correspondence of July 8, 1995.

26. Notice that the order in this Hosea passage is the reverse, a kind of recapitulation, of the order of creation.

27. Brian Walsh and Richard Middleton, "Facing the Postmodern Scalpel: Can the Christian Faith withstand Deconstruction?" in *Christian Apologetics in a Postmodern World,* ed. Timothy R. Phillips and Dennis L. Okholm (Downers Grove: InterVarsity Press, 1995), p. 148. Even this formulation, however, bears the marks of von Rad's unfortunate legacy.

28. Francis I. Andersen, "Yahweh, the Kind and Sensitive God," in *God Who is Rich in Mercy: Essays Presented to D. B. Knox,* ed. David G. Peterson and Peter T. O'Brien (Homebush West, Australia: Lancer Books, 1986), pp. 41–88.

29. Joseph Sittler, in *The Gospel and Human Destiny,* ed. Vilmos Vatja (Minneapolis: Augsburg, 1971), quoted in Bouma-Prediger, *The Greening of Theology,* p. 68. See pages 204 and 205, where Bouma-Prediger notes the fuzziness in Sittler's concept of grace.

30. Gunton, *The Actuality of the Atonement,* p. 167. But this personal character of grace does not imply that grace must then be tied to election, as Barth insisted. "There can be no place in the doctrine of the divine being for a doctrine of providence above or even alongside that of the election of grace" (Karl Barth, *Church Dogmatics,* III/3 (Edinburgh: T. & T. Clark, 1960), p. 6. This assertion helps ex-

plain why in all of his six volumes Barth has little to say about our responsibility to and God's interest in the earth in itself. God is active, we will argue, in merciful ways in creation in a broader way than God's electing activity among God's people.

31. Michael de Roche, "Yahweh's Rib against Israel: A Reassessment of the So-called 'Prophetic Lawsuit' in the Pre-exilic Prophets," *Journal of Bibilical Literature* 102 (1983): 563–74. See F. I. Anderson and D. N. Freedman, *Micah* (Anchor Books, forthcoming).

32. John Calvin, *Institutes,* ed. John McNeil (Philadelphia: Westminster, 1960), 1.17.13, p. 227. Though Calvin uses the decrees to explain God's governance, he does it relatively rarely by comparison with later theologians. Cf. François Turretin, who organizes the whole of God's works around his decrees, which are "essential internal acts of God" that express the "certain determination concerning the futurition [*sic*] of things" (François Turretin, *Institutes of Elencthic Theology* [1669] [Phillipsburg, N.J.: R & P Publishing, 1992], part 4, question 1, p. 311).

33. Nancey Murphy, "Divine Action in the Natural Order: Buridan's Ass and Schrodinger's Cat," in *Chaos and Complexity: Scientific Perspectives on Divine Action,* ed. Robert John Russell, Nancey Murphy, and Authur R. Peacocke (Vatican City and Berkeley: Vatican Observatory and the Center for Theology and the Natural Sciences, 1995), pp. 326–57. Subsequent page references to this article are in the text.

34. See the Letter to Diognetus 7:4: "God sent [Christ] out of kindness and gentleness, like a king sending his son who is himself a king. He sent him as God; he sent him as man to men. He willed to save men by persuasion, not by compulsion, for compulsion is not God's way of working" (Richardson, *Early Christian Fathers,* p. 219).

35. Simone Weil, *Waiting on God,* ed. and trans. Emma Crawford (London: Routledge & Kegan Paul, 1951), p. 44.

36. Calvin, *Institutes,* 1.16.4, p. 203.

37. Martin Luther, quoted in Althaus, *The Theology of Martin Luther,* p. 107. Though Luther took this idea to the point of insisting that God's creative act was constantly creating the world out of nothing and that creatures were actually what he called the disguises of God (ibid., pp. 107–8). Cf. Gerhard Ebeling: "Creation [for Luther] is a mask which is nothing of itself or on its own account. It is only a veil for the creator who speaks the truth" (*Luther: An Introduction to His Thought* [Philadelphia, Fortress Press, 1970], p. 198).

38. See Kwame Bediako, *Christianity in Africa: A Renewal of a Non-Western Religion* (Edinburgh: Edinburgh Univ. Press; Maryknoll, N.Y.: Orbis Books, 1995), p. 101. Bediako goes on to note that this insight lies at the heart of Africa's potential contribution to our Christian understanding of the transcendent, and at the same time, our responsibility to the earth.

39. Julian of Norwich, *Revelations of Divine Love,* ed. and trans. M. L. Del Maestro (Garden City: Image Books, 1977), p. 88.

40. Brian Walsh and Richard Middleton have helpfully proposed that creation implies a "covenantal" epistemology of "call and response," though they do not develop the idea (*Truth Is Stranger than It Used to Be* [Downers Grove: InterVarsity Press, 1995], p. 168).

41. This plurality has been described variously as referring to the members of the Godhead (see Barth, *Church Dogmatics,* III/1 [Edinburgh: T. & T. Clark, 1958], p. 192) and as simply a concert of mind and action (Richard Mouw, *Politics and the Biblical Drama* [Grand Rapids: Eerdmans, 1976], pp. 24–27).

42. John Calvin: "Although God's glory shines forth in the outer man, yet there is no doubt the proper seat of his image is in the soul" (*Institutes* 1.15.3, p. 186).

43. Barth's discussion is in *Church Dogmatics,* III/1 (Edinburgh: T. & T. Clark, 1958), pp. 191ff.; von Rad's views are found in *Genesis,* ed. and trans. J. Mark (London: SCM, 1961), p. 60. For the Reformed view, see Mouw, *Politics and the Biblical Drama,* p. 27; cf. Walsh and Middleton, who see the image as an "invitation to covenantal responsibility" (*Truth Is Stranger than it Used to Be*), p. 152.

44. James Barr, *Biblical Faith and Natural Theology* (Oxford: Clarendon, 1993), p. 169. Barr's point is that these are just the issues out of which the pervasive tradition of natural theology in the Bible emerged. Cf. W. Dyrness, "The Imago Dei and Christian Aesthetics," *Journal of the Evangelical Theological Society* 15:3 (Summer 1972), pp. 161-72.

45. Mouw, *Politics and the Biblical Drama,* p. 27.

46. See Emil Brunner, *Man in Revolt,* trans. Olive Wyon (Philadelphia: Westminster, 1947), pp. 102-5.

47. Quoted in Mouw, *Politics and the Biblical Drama,* p. 27.

48. Cf. Robert Banks, "To be human is to become a gardener, following in the footsteps of the divine Gardener who established this setting in the first place" (*God the Worker,* p. 175).

49. See Herbert B. Huffman, "The Treaty Background of the Hebrew YADA," *Bulletin of the American Schools of Oriental Research* 181 (1966), pp. 31-38.

50. See John W. Cooper, *Body, Soul and Life Everlasting: Biblical Anthropology and the Monism-Dualism Debate* (Grand Rapids: Eerdmans, 1989). The physical dimensions of the image are discussed in G. C. Berkouwer, *Man, the Image of God,* trans. Dirk W. Jellena (Grand Rapids: Eerdmans, 1962), pp. 74–84. See reference to Psalm 139 above. Clearly the original meaning of *selim* (Gn 1:27) is a physical likeness, even a statue (see F. Brown, S. R. Driver, and L. A. Briggs, *Hebrew and English Lexicon* [Oxford: Clarendon Press, 1966]; cf. Am 5:26). So even in the physical image there is an assertion of what God is like, both as delegate and as deputy.

51. Barth, *Church Dogmatics,* IV/1 (Edinburgh: T. & T. Clark, 1956), p. 113.

52. See Walter Brueggemann, "David and His Theologian," in *The Vitality of Old Testament Traditions*, ed. W. Brueggemann and H. W. Wolff (Atlanta: John Knox Press, 1975). Brueggemann argues that the passage in its present form may have come from the period of David and Solomon. Read against that background it is seen as a warning not to let pride lead us to disobey God, as our first parents did.

53. Cf. Mouw, *Politics and the Biblical Drama*, p. 37.

54. We can leave aside for the present the question of how this is passed to subsequent generations. While few would accept Augustine's judgment that it occurs through the act of sex, the sense that there is a biological as well as spiritual dimension to sin was sound, as contemporary genetics is suggesting.

55. Levenson, *Creation and the Persistence of Evil,* p. 75. See how the Song of Moses in Exodus 15 ends with Israel being brought into the land, "the place, O Lord, that you made your abode, the sanctuary, O Lord, that your hands have established" (v. 17).

56. Interestingly, both biblical words for worship can mean either worship or work in servanthood—Hebrew, *abarā*; Greek, *latreía*.

57. See, for example, Brevard Childs, *Myth and Reality in the Old Testament,* Studies in Biblical Theology 27 (London: SCM, 1962), which expresses the domi-

nant paradigm. Bertil Albrektson, *History and the Gods: An Essay on the Idea of Historical Events as Divine Manifestation in the Ancient Near East* (Lund: C. W. K. Leerup, 1967) was the first to call this view into question. He says, "The idea of historical events as divine revelation . . . is part of the common theology of the ancient near east" (p. 117).

58. See Michael L. Goldberg, "The Story of the Moral: Gifts or Bribes in Deuteronomy," *Interpretation* 38:1 (1984), pp. 15–25.

59. The point is that in both history and creation God is revealed as *their* God. Albrektson notes that what was unique in Israel's cult was the presence of God in the world in the events celebrated. The "idea of historical events as divine manifestations has marked the Israelite cult in a way that lacks real parallel among Israel's neighbors" (*History and the Gods,* p. 115). This was the point of the celebrations to establish this relationship with God. As Jon Levenson says, in the cult "history is not only rendered contemporary; it is internalized" (*Sinai and Zion: An Entry into the Jewish Bible* [San Francisco: HarperCollins, 1985], p. 39).

60. Levenson, *Creation and the Persistence of Evil,* pp. 85–87; see also his *Sinai and Zion,* pp. 142, 143. Also see Banks, *God the Worker*, who emphasizes God's role in both creation and tabernacle as designer (pp. 315-20).

61. Cf. Levenson, *Creation and the Persistence of Evil,* pp. 78–99 and the literature cited there.

62. Meredith G. Kline made this observation in his book *Images of the Spirit* (Grand Rapids: Baker Book House, 1980).

63. Barr, *Biblical Faith and Natural Theology.*

64. Al Wolters, *Creation Regained: The Biblical Basis for a Reformational Worldview* (Grand Rapids: Eerdmans, 1985), p. 17. Also see "God as Gardener and Orchardist," chapter 4 in Banks, *God the Worker.*

65. G. von Rad, *Wisdom in Israel,* ed. and trans. J. D. Martin (London: SCM, 1972), p. 92. He actually notes in his preface his reason for coming to this new appreciation for creation theology.

66. Wolters, *Creation Regained*, p. 28.

67. Levenson, *Creation and the Persistence of Evil,* p. 57. This reference is part of an extended discussion in which Levenson points out the clear parallels between Psalm 104 and Genesis 1.

68. This link was pointed out long ago by G. F. Oehler, *Biblical Theology of the Old Testament* (Philadelphia: H. B. Garner, 1886).

69. Brown, Driver, and Briggs lists only two references where the literal meaning is intended. Otherwise it refers to what is evanescent, insubstantial, or worthless—even what is absurd or enigmatic (*Hebrew and English Lexicon*).

70. R. K. Johnston, "'Confessions of a Workaholic': A Reappraisal of Qoheleth," *Catholic Biblical Quarterly* 38 (1976), p. 24. I am grateful to Rob for this and the following reference and for stimulating conversation on this point.

71. Larry J. Kreitzer, *The Old Testament in Fiction and Film: On Reversing the Hermeneutical Flow* (Sheffield: Sheffield Academic Press, 1994), p. 212; Kreitzer credits important studies by M. V. Fox and R. N. Whybray, who have argued this way.

72. Quoted in ibid., p. 195.

73. Ibid.

74. The image is Kreitzer's (ibid., p. 220).

75. Cf. Johnston, "Confessions of a Workaholic," p. 19.

76. See E. John Walford, *Ruisdael and the Perception of Landscape* (New Haven: Yale Univ. Press, 1991), pp. 33–38, 143.

77. Moltmann, *God in Creation,* p. 244. He is quoting Oetinger.

78. See Christopher Wright, *Living as the People of God* (Downers Grove: InterVarsity Press, 1983), pp. 46–102.

79. Westermann, *Creation,* p. 46.

80. Levenson, *Sinai and Zion,* pp. 141, 142.

81. Ibid.

82. James McClendon, *Doctrine: Systematic Theology,* vol. 2 (Nashville: Abingdon, 1994), p. 156.

83. H. Berkhof, *The Christian Faith* (Grand Rapids: Eerdmans, 1979), p. 167.

84. Gibbs, *Creation and Redemption.*

85. Irenaeus, *Against Heresies,* V, 19–21 (Richardson, *Early Christian Fathers,* pp. 389-90).

86. Athanasius, *De Incarnatione,* II, 7, in *St. Athanasius on the Incarnation* (London: Mowbray, 1953), p. 33.

87. Gunton, *The Actuality of the Atonement,* esp. chaps. 4 and 5; quotation at p. 89.

88. Ibid., pp. 119, 138–39. Gunton quotes Mary Douglas in connection with his comments on pollution; this will become significant in our discussion of ecology below. Cf. Douglas: "Impurity . . . is clearly subordinate to the positive view of the theistic universe against which it is balanced . . . impurity is the foil for displaying the meaning of righteousness. More than a literary foil it is a statement about the nature of existence in a sacramental universe, a religious ontology" (in *Pomegranates and Golden Bells: Studies in Biblical, Jewish, and Near Eastern Ritual, Law, and Literature in Honor of Jacob Milgrom,* ed. David P. Wright, David Noel Freedman, and Avi Hurvitz [Winona Lake, Ind.: Eisenbrauns, 1995], p. 255).

89. Gunton, *Christ and Creation,* p. 46.

90. Moltmann, *God in Creation,* p. 65.

91. Gunton, *Christ and Creation,* p. 32; he refers to Hebrews 2:18.

92. Ibid., p. 50.

93. Robert Wuthnow, *Communities of Discourse* (Cambridge: Harvard Univ. Press, 1989), pp. 518–27.

94. See Frances Young and David Ford, *Meaning and Truth in Second Corinthians* (London: SPCK, 1988), pp. 168ff.

95. See Ronald Hock, *The Social Context of Paul's Ministry: Tentmaking and Apostleship* (Philadelphia: Fortress Press, 1980).

96. On what follows see Young and Ford, *Meaning and Truth in Second Corinthians,* and Keith F. Nickle, *The Collection: A Study in Paul's Strategy,* Studies in Biblical Theology 48 (London: SCM, 1966).

97. I owe the image of the "cosmic cycle" to Robert Banks in his comments on an earlier draft of this chapter.

98. Moltmann, *God and Creation,* pp. 52–61.

3 CULTURE

1. Augustine, *Confessions,* IV, 7, 10, trans. by R. S. Pine-Coffin (Harmondsworth: Penguin, 1961), pp. 78, 80.

2. John Calvin, *Institutes*, ed. John McNeil (Philadelphia: Westminster, 1960), 2.2.13, vol. 1, p. 272.

3. Ibid., 2.2.17. Calvin goes on to note that this "common grace" of God restrains the evil in culture but does not cleanse it (2.3.3 in McNeil, pp. 276, 292).

4. Francis Bacon, *Selected writings of Francis Bacon*, ed. Hugh G. Dick (New York: Random House, 1955), p. 499. Bacon constantly returns to this theme of wise use of knowledge, not to make us proud, but "to give ourselves repose and contentment" (p. 163).

5. Charles, Taylor, *The Sources of the Self: The Making of the Modern Identity* (Cambridge: Harvard Univ. Press, 1989), pp. 215-221, 271. Robert Wuthnow notes a parallel phenomenon in which commentary on nature came to replace commentary on scripture (cf. Robert Wuthnow, *Communities of Discourse* [Cambridge: Harvard Univ. Press, 1989], p. 324).

6. Michael Buckley, *At the Origins of Modern Atheism* (New Haven: Yale Univ. Press, 1987), p. 356. Taylor says of this move: In denying miraculous intervention history is marginalized; the whole is now the creation of "instrumental reason" (*The Sources of the Self*, pp. 273, 280).

7. Buckley, *At the Origins of Modern Atheism*, p. 358.

8. James Turner, "Secular Justification of Christian Truth Claims: A Historical Sketch," in *American Apostasy: The Triumph of Another Gospel*, ed. R. J. Neuhaus (Grand Rapids: Eerdmans, 1989), p.15.

9. Ibid., p. 18. Turner concludes: "Although Christianity might comprehend the world, the world could not define Christianity nor comprehend God" (p. 19). Cf. also James Turner, *Without God, Without Creed: The Origins of Unbelief in America* (Baltimore: Johns Hopkins Univ. Press, 1985).

10. See Timothy Smith, *Revivalism and Social Concern in Mid Nineteenth Century America* (New York: Abingdon, 1957). For the growing voluntarism see George M. Marsden, *The Evangelical Mind and the New School Presbyterian Experience: A Case Study of Thought and Theology in Nineteenth-Century America* (New Haven: Yale University Press, 1970). Nathan O. Hatch has documented the way American Christianity adapted and molded the democratic spirit of the country's founding in *The Democratization of American Christianity* (New Haven: Yale University Press, 1989).

11. Marsden shows how much of the debate between the New School and Old School Presbyterians centered around the use of culture in evangelism (*The Evangelical Mind*).

12. A good summary is to be found in George M. Marsden, *Fundamentalism and American Culture: The Shaping of Twentieth-Century Evangelicalism 1870-1925* (New York: Oxford University Press, 1980), and Mark Noll, *The Scandal of an Evangelical Mind* (Grand Rapids: Eerdmans, 1994).

13. Ironically, the fundamentals as they were published in 1910 had a much more extensive program of interaction with the current cultural discussions than their descendents have allowed. Members of the Evangelical Theological Society until very recently were asked to sign a doctrinal statement having a single item: the inerrancy of scripture.

14. Marsden, *Fundamentalism and the American Culture*, p. 226. He notes, "Fundamentalism was a loose, diverse, and changing federation of co-belligerents united by their fierce opposition to modernist attempts to bring Christianity in line with modern thought" (p. 4). He sees this militancy against modernism as the key distinguishing factor of the movement.

15. Martin Lloyd-Jones, quoted in Noll, *The Scandal of an Evangelical Mind,* p. 124. While Lloyd-Jones's statement is helpful as far as it goes, Turner notes, it does illustrate the contemporary Christian view that our problems are primarily intellectual. We are arguing that the problems are a larger deficiency in our Christian form of life, including our intellectual and cultural practices.

16. See Michael S. Hamilton, *The Fundamentalist Harvard: Wheaton College and the Enduring Vitality of American Evangelicalism, 1919-1965,* Ph.D. dissertation, Univ. of Notre Dame, 1994. Hamilton argues that an understanding of fundamentalism as defensive and polemic fails to understand the culturally sensitive institutions that developed. As he notes, no fundamentalist leader was less polemic than V. Raymond Edman, the longtime president of Wheaton.

17. John Seel, "Modernity and Evangelicals," in *Christian Apologetics in a Post-Modern World,* ed. Timothy R. Phillips and Dennis L. Okholm (Downers Grove: InterVarsity Press, 1995), p. 291. George Hunsinger has argued that popular doctrines like inerrancy are uniquely reflective of modern intellectual values (see George Hunsinger in *The Nature of Confession,* ed. Timothy R. Phillips and Dennis L. Okholm [Downers Grove: InterVarsity Press, 1996], pp. 134-50).

18. As Seel points out, the danger of this modernism is not simply heresy but idolatry. One does not need to conclude however, as Seel seems to do, that all that modernism offers is a threat. Rather, what is needed in the social realm as in the intellectual is a careful discrimination that is theologically grounded.

19. Medieval believers would be familiar with this image because the word appears in the Vulgate account of Genesis 2. The Latin word, interestingly, also refers to the liturgy of worship, with what we call the *cult.*

20. D. Hymes, ed., *Reinventing Anthropology* (New York: Vintage, 1974), p. 30.

21. Bronislaw Malinowski, *A Scientific Theory of Culture and Other Essays* (Chapel Hill: Univ. of North Carolina Press, 1944), p. 40. In one of the few references to religion Malinowski says, "Magic and religion can be, in my opinion, functionally interpreted as the indispensable complements to pure rational and empirical systems of thought and tradition" (p. 173).

22. I am following the sketch given in Eric R. Wolf, "Perilous Ideas: Race, Culture, and People," *Current Anthropology* 35/1 (1994), p. 5.

23. Clifford Geertz, *Interpretation of Cultures* (New York: Basic Books, 1973), p. 17. Cf. "The concept of culture I espouse . . . is essentially a semiotic one" (p. 5). Religion, he argues, is also a symbolic system that functions to "synthesize a people's ethos . . . their most comprehensive ideas of order." Like other symbols it functions as a cultural operator (see p. 89).

24. Sherry Ortner, "Theory in Anthropology Since the Sixties," *Comparative Studies in Society and History* 26 (1984), p. 131.

25. See Gustavo Gutiérrez, *A Theology of Liberation* (Maryknoll, N.Y.: Orbis Books, 1973; rev. ed. 1988).

26. See the description of these developments in Ortner, *Comparative Studies in Society and History,* pp. 144-51. Ortner sees this as a combination of Weberian and Marxist ideas.

27. Talal Asad, *Genealogies of Religion: Discipline and Reasons of Power in Christianity and Islam* (Baltimore: Johns Hopkins Univ. Press, 1993), pp. 27-54, esp. p. 47. Subsequent page references to this book are in the text.

28. Asad is quoting Harre. Cf. Robert Wuthnow, *Cultural Analysis: The Work of Peter L. Berger, Mary Douglas, Michel Foucault, and Jurgen Habermas* (Boston;

London: Routledge & Kegan Paul, 1984), pp. 250-57. Culture is better thought of as a set of practices rather than simply ideas about it. And, culture is "a form of behavior itself and . . . the tangible results of that behavior" (Wuthnow, *Communities of Discourse*, p. 15).

29. See Jean François Lyotard, *The Post Modern Condition* (Minneapolis: Univ. of Minnesota Press, 1984; originally published in French, 1979).

30. Cf. the discussion of these options in Steven Connor, *Postmodern Culture: An Introduction to Theories of the Contemporary* (Oxford: Blackwell, 1989), pp. 30-36.

31. This was proposed by Karl-Eric Knutsson in a plenary address in the 1993 Congress on Anthropological and Ethnological Science in Mexico City (see *Current Anthropology* 35/2 [1994]), p. 190. A review of programs at recent American Anthropological Association meetings (1994) shows a preference for this kind of cross-cultural study, e.g., tourism or the global city. The AAA meetings in 1995 even included sessions on missions and missionaries (with reasonable Christian involvement) as a typical cross-cultural process.

32. Eric Wolf, 1993 Congress on Anthropological and Ethnological Science in Mexico City, *Current Anthropology* 35/2 [1994], p. 191. We are all at least bicultural, Wolf noted; that is, carrying within us various "cultural repertoires."

33. In this context even the notion of ethnography has become problematic. How can an outsider propose to come and describe (even interpretively) a group of people? One novel solution is proposed by Alma Gottlieb and Philip Graham in *Parallel Worlds: Anthropologist and a Writer Encounter Africa* (Chicago: Univ. of Chicago Press, 1994). Here they describe their own reactions in a parallel text to that which "describes" the Beng people of the Cote d'Ivoire. These texts are parallel; their difference is not meant to imply judgment.

34. Wolf, "Perilous Ideas," p. 6. Subsequent page references to this article are in the text.

35. Gottlieb and Graham, *Parallel Worlds*, p. 139.

36. Cf. John Howard Yoder, "Every morally accountable affirmation of culture discriminates" (John Howard Yoder and Glen Harold Stassen, *Authentic Transformation: A New Vision of Christ and Culture* [Nashville: Abingdon, 1996], p. 24).

37. Emile Durkheim, *The Elementary Forms of Religious Life* (New York: Free Press, 1995). Quoted in S. D. Gaede, *Where Gods May Dwell: On Understanding the Human Condition* (Grand Rapids: Zondervan, 1985), p. 29. Gaede's is a good discussion of the effects of this assumption on the social sciences.

38. Geertz, *Interpretation of Cultures*, p. 30. Eric Wolf responds to Wallerstein's quest for utopistics in a similar vein: "Large scale utopias are now at a discount. Given the pessimism on the part of many about whether anthropology has a future, I would happily settle for the small scale utopias of the discipline that Boas sketched out for us" ("Perilous Ideas," p. 11). Could it be this positivism is itself a construction of a particular cultural tradition?

39. Benjamin Nelson, *On the Road to Modernity: Conscience, Science and Civilizations* (Totowa, N.J.: Rowman and Littlefield, 1981), pp. 80-105. Cf. "Every generation needs access to the entire spectrum of the human spirit: that is its inalienable right and unavoidable responsibility" (p. xv).

40. Gil Baillie, *Violence Unveiled: Humanity at the Crossroad* (New York: Crossroad, 1995), p. 38.

41. See H. Richard Niebuhr, *Christ and Culture* (New York: Harper & Row, 1951).

42. Cf. Karl Marx: "Men make their history, but they do not make it just as they please; they do not make it under circumstances chosen by themselves, but under circumstances directly encountered, given, and transmitted from the past" (from "The Eighteenth Brumaire of Louis Bonaparte," quoted by John Seel in *Faith and Modernity*, ed. Philip Sampson, Vinay Samuel, and Chris Sugden [Oxford: Regnum, 1994], p. 292).

43. Miroslav Volf, "'It Is Like Yeast': How the Gospel Should Relate to Culture," *Theology News and Notes* (October 1994), p. 13.

44. Geertz, *Interpretation of Cultures*, p. 49.

45. P. H. Turner, "Households and Household Codes," in *Dictionary of Paul and his Letters*, ed. G. F. Hawthorne, R. P. Martin and D. G. Reid (Downers Grove: InterVarsity Press, 1993), pp. 417-19. Also see James E. Crouch, *The Origin and Intention of the Colossian Haustafel* (Göttingen: Vandenhoeck and Ruprecht, 1972). Crouch concludes: "The Haustafel calls one, therefore, to give oneself to one's neighbor within the limitations which the social order places on the relationship. Genuine love may transcend the social order, but the forms through which it expresses itself do not" (p. 160).

46. This is especially true in the case of slavery. While the New Testament does not seek to abolish this widely accepted practice, it introduced into it the yeast of the relationships in the body and with Christ through the Holy Spirit, which must have radically changed the institution in practice. See especially Philemon 16, where Paul tells Philemon to receive Onesimus back "no longer as a slave but more than a slave, a beloved brother—especially to me but how much more to you, both in the flesh and in the Lord."

47. Yoder, *Authentic Transformation*, p. 71.

48. Asad, *Genealogies of Religion*, p. 48.

49. Wuthnow, *Communities of Discourse*, pp. 518-27.

50. Miroslav Volf, "Soft Difference: Theological Reflections on the Relation between Church and Culture in 1 Peter," unpublished paper presented at the Symposium on the Theological Interpretation of Scripture, October 1994, p. 3.

51. "Human beings . . . evolve themselves unto God . . . having assumed the task of disclosing the potencies lying dormant in creation and successively coming within reach in the course of the history of the world" (Klaas Schilder, *Christ and Culture* [Winnipeg: Premier, 1977], p. 40, as quoted in William Berends, *The Evaluation of Culture in Missiology: A Topical and Theological Approach to the Value and Significance of Culture in the Context of Mission*, Ph.D. dissertation, Australian College of Theology, Melbourne, 1990, p. 157). This view has been helpfully developed by James Olthuis, who has underlined the connection of this process with the word of God as the means of creation (see *Facts, Values and Ethics* [Assen: Van Gorcum, 1968], chap. 7).

52. Kuyper's most famous treatment of common grace, a three-volume work, has not been translated into English. But see his *Stone Lectures, Lectures on Calvinism* (Grand Rapids: Eerdmans, 1931), pp. 24-31. "We must in every domain, discover the treasure and develop the potencies hidden by God in nature and in human life" (p. 31). Christians (and others) following this mandate have led us, Kuyper believes, to a higher and richer stage of human development.

53. Berends, *The Evaluation of Culture in Missiology*, p. 190. The terms he uses are "yet" and "not yet." See page 147 for what follows.

54. A particular weakness, for example, of the Reformed discussion of these things is the limited role that is given to the Holy Spirit—with the notable exception of Kuyper.

55. Israel herself recognized the cultural uniqueness that resulted from God's instructions: "What other great nation has statutes and ordinances as just as this entire law that I am setting before you today?" (Dt 4:8).

56. Many commentators have pointed out that the notion of the believer's life in Christ becomes, in Paul, the functional equivalent of Christ's central teaching about the Reign of God on earth, which Christ identifies with his own ministry (for references to some of the literature, see William A. Dyrness, *Let the Earth Rejoice* [Westchester, Ill.: Crossways Books, 1983], pp. 159-65).

57. This becomes clear when Ananias fraudulently claims that he has sold a piece of property to give it to God. Peter asks: "Why has Satan filled your heart to lie to the Holy Spirit?" (Acts 5:3).

58. Stanley Hauerwas and William H. Willimon, *Resident Aliens: Life in the Christian Colony* (Nashville: Abingdon, 1989). Subsequent page references to this book are in the text.

59. This is the argument of Sander Griffoen and Richard J. Mouw, *Pluralisms and Horizons: An Essay in Christian Public Philosophy* (Grand Rapids: Eerdmans, 1993), pp. 51, 162.

60. This tendency to flee the world is the opposite danger to the one they attack—Constantinian Christianity, the era they believe ended in 1963. But the solution to that very real danger is not to abdicate responsibility for our corporate life together with our nonbelieving neighbors.

61. See Miroslav Volf, "Soft Difference." Volf argues that the pluralism of life-worlds evident in 1 Peter parallels in important ways our own late-twentieth-century world. He points out that evil in the form of a roaring lion (see 5:8) can appear at any point and constantly challenges our Christian calling. See also John H. Elliot, *A Home for the Homeless: A Sociological Exegesis of I Peter, Its Situation and Strategy* (Philadelphia: Fortress Press, 1981).

62. Colleen McDannell, *Material Christianity: Religion and Popular Culture in America* (New Haven: Yale Univ. Press, 1995), p. 6. McDannell notes that spiritualist and elitist conceptions of religion and culture created an extremely hostile environment for the study of popular religion (p. 10).

63. Sven Birkherts, "The Electronic Hire: Refuse It," *Harpers Magazine* (May 1994), p. 20, quoted in Elizabeth Patterson, "Theological Education by E-mail: The Implications of Distance Education," *Ecumenical People, Papers and Programs* (May 1996), Collegeville, Minn., p. 12.

64. Kathleen Norris, *Dakota: A Spiritual Geography* (New York: Ticknor & Fields, 1993), p. 145. Norris points out that being truly open to a place, letting it work on us, is what makes conversion possible (p. 157).

65. J. H. Bavinck, *An Introduction to the Science of Missions*, ed. and trans. David H. Freeman (Phillipsburg, N.J.: Presbyterian and Reformed Press, 1960), p. 179. Cf. a similar view expressed by the Jesuit Herve Carrier, who argues that the gospel can enrich the culture by showing there is a Christian way of living, "a particular way of working, of resting, of celebrating joys and experiencing sorrows" (Freeman, *An Introduction to the Science of Missions*, p. 71).

66. *Letter to Diognetus* 5, in *Selections from Early Christian Writers*, ed. E. M. Gwatkin (Westwood, N.J.: Fleming H. Revell, n.d.), p. 15.

67. See John R. W. Stott and Robert Coote, eds., *Down to Earth: Studies in Christianity and Culture* (Grand Rapids: Eerdmans, 1980), p. viii. We argue that the basic problem with the contextualization discussion was the failure to see that these two questions are really one and the same. The most important constructive essay on contextualization during this period was Charles Kraft, *Christianity in Culture* (Maryknoll, N.Y.: Orbis Books, 1979).

68. Herve Carrier, *Evangelizing the Culture of Modernity* (Maryknoll, N.Y.: Orbis Books, 1993), p. 67. John Paul II defined the process as the "incarnation of the Gospel message in autochthonous cultures and, at the same time, the introduction of those cultures into the life of the Church" (ibid., p. 156 n.5).

69. See the helpful discussion in William Berends, *The Evaluation of Culture in Missiology*, pp. 108-36. Berends concludes that there is no agreement as to "the identity of the human situation as the context and the Gospel as the text" (p. 136). John Howard Yoder draws a similar conclusion: The contextualization "movement is impressive in its anthropological competence and creativity. It has not been at work long enough for us to determine whether it will develop criteria for defining heresy" (*The Priestly Kingdom: Social Ethics as Gospel* [Notre Dame, Ind.: University of Notre Dame Press, 1984], p. 68). Part of the problem was that the concerns focused too narrowly on communication and thus discussions tended to be constricted by linguistic models (as in the case of Charles Kraft's otherwise excellent book).

70. See the excellent discussion of this problem in Kwame Bediako, *Christianity in Africa: The Renewal of a Non-Western Religion* (Edinburgh: Univ. of Edinburgh Press; Maryknoll, N.Y.: Orbis Books, 1995), esp. chap. 7. He concludes: "The achievement meant here is not to be measured in terms of Western missionary transmission, but rather by African assimilation of the Faith" (p. 119).

71. Lamin Sanneh, *Translating the Message: The Missionary Impact on Culture* (Maryknoll, N.Y.: Orbis Books, 1989). Subsequent page references to this book are in the text.

72. Cf. John Mbiti's statement: "The Gospel enabled people to utter the name of Jesus Christ . . . that final and completing element that crowns their traditional religiosity and brings its flickering light to full brilliance" (quoted in Bediako, *Christianity in Africa*, p. 118).

73. It is an important part of the argument of Ephesians that this involves a breaking down of hostility between cultural groups (see Eph 2:14, 15). Just as we saw in the Colossians passage, then, this reality is to be lived out in terms of the particular culture in which the Ephesians found themselves, but in terms of practices that display internal differences from that culture—these are spelled out in the rest of Ephesians—chapters 4 and 5.

74. Geertz, *Interpretation of Cultures*, p. 30. The intellectualist bias of Geertz is clear here. The assumption is that if those answers are made known, and consulted, we will be better off. Unfortunately, there is not much evidence for the truth of this assumption.

75. James D. Hunter, *Culture Wars: The Struggle to Define America* (New York: Basic Books, 1991). Subsequent page references to this book are in the text. Cf. also his follow up, James D. Hunter, *Before the Shooting Begins: Searching for Democracy in America's Culture War* (New York: Free Press, 1994).

76. Hunter's discussion is more nuanced than I have made it out to be, but the interpretation of the battle, especially by his followers, often leads to the dangers I describe here (see the interchange in *Christianity Today*, March 6, 1995).

77. I have developed these and other values that are central to American culture in *How Does America Hear the Gospel?* (Grand Rapids: Eerdmans, 1989).

78. M. Volf, "It Is Like Yeast," p. 14.

79. Someone might point out how strongly Jesus spoke out against the religious leaders. But this only demonstrates the point I am making: Jesus reserved his strongest rebukes for his own people, his own "side," as it were, of the culture wars. In this he illustrates the argument that Christian love begins with personal and cultural self-criticism—what the Christian scriptures call repentance.

80. See especially the excellent article by John D. Woodbridge, which makes many of the points I am making and which has been important to my thinking through this issue ("Culture War Casualties," *Christianity Today* [March 6, 1995], pp. 21-26). See also the helpful and balanced discussion in Tom Sine, *Cease Fire: Searching for Sanity in American Culture Wars* (Grand Rapids: Eerdmans 1995).

81. As John Woodbridge puts this, if we look around with compassion we "see our neighborhood or local school not as another battle field in the 'culture war' but as a mission field" ("Culture War Casualties," p. 25).

82. See John Howard Yoder's description of the church in these terms in "The Hermeneutics of Peoplehood: A Protestant Perspective," in *The Priestly Kingdom*, pp. 15-45. We develop this idea further in the next chapter.

4 ETHNICITY

1. At the 1993 Congress on Anthropological and Ethnological Science in Mexico City the most ubiquitous words were *ethnicity* and *gender*, which figured in almost every plenary discussion (see *Current Anthropology* 35:2 [1994], p. 190).

2. "'The Lads Who Are Here Are All Kicking': Campus Life Two Centuries Ago, as Revealed in a Cache of Old Letters at Williams College," *New York Times*, November 5, 1995, Educational Supplement, p. 46.

3. Arthur M. Schlesinger, Jr., *The Disuniting of America: Reflections on a Multi-Cultural Society* (New York: W. W. Norton, 1992).Subsequent page references to this book are in the text.

4. Eric R. Wolf, "Perilous Ideas: Race, Culture, and People," *Current Anthropology* 35:1 (1994), p. 2.

5. See Gustavo Gutiérrez, *Las Casas: In Search of the Poor of Jesus Christ* (Maryknoll, N.Y.: Orbis Books, 1993).

6. We follow here the description of these changes in Robert J. C. Young, *Colonial Desire: Hybridity in Theory, Culture, and Race* (London: Routledge, 1995). Subsequent page references to this book are in the text.

7. D. Wheeler, "A Growing Number of Scientists Reject the Concept of Race," *The Chronicle of Higher Education*, February 17, 1995, p. A9. Subsequent page references to this article are in the text. See also Immanuel Wallerstein's response to Eric Wolf: "As Wolf so clearly shows, races, cultures and peoples are not essences. They have no fixed contours. They have no self-evident contours" (in Wolf, "Perilous Ideas," p. 10).

8. See Wendell Wilkie's *One World* (1943) and Edward Steichen's famous exhibition of photographs *The Family of Man* (1955). A good guide to the issue is the discussion in David Hollinger, *Post-Ethnic America* (New York: Basic Books, 1995), pp. 51-68.

9. Richard Herrnstein and Charles Murray, *The Bell Curve* (New York: Free Press, 1994).

10. A similar statement of the executive council of the American Association of Physical Anthropologists said, "The idea of discrete races made up chiefly of typical representatives is untenable" (Wheeler, "A Growing Number of Scientists Reject the Concept of Race," p. A9). A recent survey of physical anthropology textbooks, cited in this article, found that only two of twenty-two used *race* to classify humans.

11. Dinesh D'Souza, *The End Of Racism: Principles for a Multi-Racial Society* (New York: Free Press, 1995), p. 526. In a recent interview D'Souza argued that "the cultural strategy that says racism must be responsible for [black problems] is dysfunctional. It's an obstacle to success" (quoted in Ellen K. Coughlin, "America's Dilemma: New Books Attest to the Intractability of the Race Problem," *Chronicle of Higher Education,* September 8, 1995, p. A10).

12. Stephen Steinberg, *Turning Back: The Retreat from Racial Justice in American Thought and Policy* (Boston: Beacon Press, 1995).

13. It is not always clear how *ethnicity* differs from *race*. As Professor Gail E. Wyatt of UCLA puts it: "A lot of behavioral scientists use the term 'ethnicity,' but I don't think that they have any understanding of how it differs from 'race.' They have just substituted 'ethnicity' for 'race' and moved on" (quoted in David Wheeler, "A Growing Number of Scientists Reject the Concept of Race," p. A15. Robert Young's conclusion is more troubling: "Today's ethnicity, it could be argued, is merely an antithetical version of the same [racial] cultural discourse, albeit positively marked" (*Colonial Desire,* p. 88).

14. Norman Miller and Rodger Yaeger, *Kenya: The Quest for Prosperity,* 2d ed. (Boulder: Westview Press, 1994), p. 72.

15. See Susan Billington Harper, "Ironies of Indigenization: Some Cultural Repercussions of Mission in South India," manuscript of lecture given in 1994 for the Pew Foundation. Harper refers to the obsession outsiders had with ordering the people as the product of "urgent European rationalizing ideologies."

16. Abraham Rosman and Paula G. Rubel, *The Tapestry of Culture: An Introduction to Cultural Anthropology*, 5th ed. (New York: McGraw Hill, 1995), pp. 302-303. Rosman and Rubel note that this process sometimes went to the extent of "inventing" historical items, which they subsequently "discovered," such as the manuscripts "discovered" in 1817 and 1818 in Bohemia.

17. See Samuel P. Huntington, "The Clash of Civilizations?" *Foreign Affairs* (Summer 1993). Huntington predicts that as interactions increase these clashes will intensify.

18. See Donald McGavran, *Understanding Church Growth* (Grand Rapids: Eerdmans, 1970); idem, *Ethnic Realities and the Church* (Pasadena: William Carey, 1979). For a more extensive study, see C. Peter Wagner, *Our Kind of People: The Ethical Dimension of Church Growth* (Richmond: John Knox, 1979).

19. McGavran, *Understanding Church Growth*, p. 183. In what I have read of McGavran, the only definition of *ethnicity* I have seen is the following: "Ethnicity

in its broadest sense is the way different groups act." McGavran, however, does often speak of *endogamy* as a further characteristic (*Ethnic Realities and the Church*, p. 22). His interest in ethnicity is subordinated to what he terms "homogeneous units," which comprise locations where natural community takes place and may include elements of class as well as ethnicity. In his paper at Lausanne he noted: "Most existing congregations are shut up to one language, one ethnic unit, and frequently to one social or economic class" (quoted in Wagner, *Our Kind of People*, p. 20).

20. McGavran, *Ethnic Realities and the Church*, p. 33. Subsequent page references to this book are in the text.

21. The theological grounding of the Church Growth movement has been the subject of consistent criticism (see Sakari Pinola, *Church Growth: Principles and Praxis of Donald A. McGavran's Missiology* [Turku, Finland: Åbo Akademi University Press, 1995], pp. 86-87 and the literature cited there). Pinola is especially helpful in describing McGavran's limitations in terms of his Disciples of Christ background, with its heritage of insisting on "no creed but Christ" (pp. 26, 27). Cf. also Charles Van Engen, *The Growth of the True Church: An Analysis of the Ecclesiology of the Church Growth Movement* (Amsterdam: Rodopi, 1981).

22. Wagner nuances his argument by developing further the idea of the homogeneous unit to what he calls an "ethclass," where social, cultural, and ethnic factors converge to create a natural community (*Our Kind of People*, pp. 61-62).

23. Wolf, "Perilous Ideas," p. 6.

24. Liz McMillen, "Lifting the Veil from Whiteness: Growing Body of Scholarship Challenges a Racial 'Norm,'" *Chronicle of Higher Education*, September 8, 1995, p. A23. McMillen refers to the study of David Roediger, who argues that the black "other" was constructed as "embodying the pre-industrial, erotic, careless style of life the white worker hated and longed for." This is argued in *Shades of Pale*, forthcoming from Free Press.

25. Alex de Waal, "The Genocidal State: Hutu Extremism and the Origins of the 'Final Solution' in Rwanda," *Times Literary Supplement*, July 1, 1994, p. 3. De Waal's article reviews recent scholarship on East Africa: Katsyoshi Fukui and John Markakis, eds., *Ethnicity and Conflict in the Horn of Africa*; Catherine Newbury, *The Cohesion of Oppression: Clientship and Ethnicity in Rwanda, 1860-1960*; and Ronold Cohen, Goran Hyden, and Winston P. Nagan, eds., *Human Rights and Governance in Africa*, all published in 1994. Susan Harper, referring to David Horowitz's analysis of group conflict based on territorial claims (see *Ethnic Groups in Conflict* [Berkeley: Univ. of California Press, 1985]) notes: "This exclusivist aspect to collective 'indigenous' moral claims to legitimacy has led to numerous wars and partitions in this century, not to mention more subtle forms of alienation and discrimination" ("Ironies of Indigenization," p. 2).

26. Rosman and Rubel, *The Tapestry of Culture,* p. 152-53.

27. De Waal, "The Genocidal State," p. 3.

28. David Turton, quoted in De Waal, "The Genocidal State," p. 3.

29. De Waal, "The Genocidal State," p. 3.

30. Jean-Luc Vellut, "Ethnicity and Genocide in Rwanda," *Times Literary Supplement*, July 15, 1994, p. 17. Their differences can be understood as both cultural and political, Christopher Fyfe notes in a further response to de Waal: "Their antagonism, instead of being an antagonism of conquering/conquered peoples, an antagonism expressed in political terms, and perhaps resolvable by political means,

became the antagonism of two races" (*Times Literary Supplement.* August 5, 1994, p. 13).

31. See Robert Bellah, et al., *Habits of the Heart: Individualism and Commitment in American Life* (Berkeley: Univ. of California Press, 1985).

32. Colin Gunton, *The One, the Three, and the Many: God, Creation, and the Culture of Modernity*, the Bampton Lectures 1992 (Cambridge and New York: Cambridge Univ. Press, 1993), p. 194. Gunton sees the Spirit's distinctive role as maintaining the distinctiveness of the creature (see chap. 7).

33. Ibid., p. 118.

34. See Karl Ludwig Schmidt: "From the first patriarchs there does not descend a single humanity, but a group of nations divided according to clans and differing in language, custom and situation. The attempt to resist this in Genesis 11, has its origins in human pride. God intervenes to re-establish the order imposed by him" ("Ethnos," *Theological Dictionary of the New Testament* [Grand Rapids: Eerdmans, 1964-76], vol. 2, p. 367).

35. Karl Barth, *Church Dogmatics*, III/4, p. 315. Herman Bavinck has argued that because of this the image of God must be understood in a corporate sense. It is only when all God's people are together worshiping him that the image is clearly seen (see *Our Reasonable Faith* [Grand Rapids: Baker Book House, 1956], pp. 205-11).

36. Norman Gottwald, *The Tribes of Yahweh: A Sociology of the Religion of Liberated Israel* (Maryknoll, N.Y.: Orbis Books, 1980), p. 688. Much of what Gottwald writes must be critically examined, such as his view that Yahweh was a symbol of Israel's social project (p. 693), but his comments on the social background and make up of Israel have been influential, especially his emphasis that "Israel's reality as a social system must not be confused with a monolithic ethnic identity." See the critical discussion in Christopher Wright, "The Ethical Relevance of Israel as a Society," *Transformation* 1:4 (1984), pp. 11-21.

37. Wright, "The Ethical Relevance of Israel as a Society," p. 12. "The expectation of mutual aid was an authentic feature of early Israelite society" (p. 11). Subsequent page references to this article are in the text.

38. I have explored this dimension of American culture in *How Does America Hear the Gospel?* (Grand Rapids: Eerdmans, 1989), chap. 3, "The Virgin Land."

39. Richard Mouw and Sander Griffoen, *Pluralism and Horizons* (Grand Rapids: Eerdmans, 1993), p. 157.

40. Ibid. This direction is being played on a cosmic field, as Mouw and Griffoen put it, "under an open heaven."

41. See Charles Taylor, *Multiculturalism and the Politics of Recognition* (Princeton: Princeton Univ. Press, 1992), pp. 27, 28. Subsequent page references to this book are in the text.

42. In another place Taylor posits that the two unarguable commitments that go into forming the modern identity are the dignity of rational agents and our feeling with nature and its goodness (*The Sources of the Self: The Making of the Modern Identity* [Cambridge: Harvard Univ. Press, 1989], pp. 313-17).

43. Taylor proposes that religion is one way in which this has been traditionally grounded (as a Catholic it is a way he personally espouses). Mouw and Griffoen also make the point that the positive relativity of cultures must be grounded in some religious commitment, in their view in the Christian view of creation and the Trinity (*Pluralism and Horizons*, pp. 123-26).

44. Africans also have been forced to study alien history and literature by the Colonial (or missionary) powers (see Ngugi wa Thiong'o, *DeColonising the Mind: The Politics of Language in African Literature* [Nairobi: Heinemann, 1986]).

45. Jeremiah Wright, Payton Lectures, Fuller Seminary, February 2, 1995.

46. bell hooks and Cornel West, *Breaking Bread: Insurgent Black Intellectual Life* (Boston: South End Press, 1991), p. 6.

47. Henry Louis Gates, Jr., *Loose Cannons: Notes on the Culture Wars* (Oxford: Oxford Univ. Press, 1992), pp. 49, 98-100.

48. Ibid., p. 50.

49. Miroslav Volf, *Exclusion and Embrace* (Nashville: Abingdon, 1996), p. 207.

50. Paul Gilroy, *The Black Atlantic: Modernity and Double Consciousness* (Cambridge: Harvard Univ. Press, 1993), p. 33. Subsequent page references to this book are in the text.

51. Immanuel Wallerstein, in Wolf, "Perilous Ideas," p. 10. Wallerstein points out that to "make group identity politically efficacious, groups tend to strengthen boundaries, reject overlaps, [and] demand exclusive loyalties."

52. Volf, "Exclusion and Embrace," in W. Dyrness, ed., *Emerging Voices in Global Christian Theology* (Grand Rapids: Zondervan, 1994), p. 23.

53. Emmanuel Levinas, *The Levinas Reader*, ed. Sean Hand (Oxford: Blackwell, 1989), p. 89. Subsequent references in this text to Dr. Lee are taken from this lecture.

54. Volf, "Exclusion and Embrace," p. 38.

55. See Christine D. Pohl, "Hospitality from the Edge: The Significance of Marginality in the Practice of Welcome," *Annual of the Society of Christian Ethics* (1995), pp. 121-36. This all suggests ways in which McGavran's comments on table fellowship need to be rethought.

56. I am dependent here on Dr. Sang Hyun Lee, Princeton Seminary, Payton Lecturer at Fuller Seminary, April 6, 1993. Subsequent references in the text are taken from this lecture.

57. Dieumeme Noelliste, "Faith Transforming Context: In Search of a Theology for a Viable Caribbean," paper given at the World Evangelical Fellowship Theological Commission, April 9-14, 1996, London Bible College, p. 6.

58. As Noelliste puts it in his article, it is God's redemptive superintendence that keeps us from the crippling despair that is so common in the Caribbean region (Noelliste, "Faith Transforming Context").

59. Gil Baillie, *Violence Unveiled: Humanity at the Crossroad* (New York: Crossroad, 1995), p. 40.

60. Colin Gunton, *The Actuality of the Atonement* (Edinburgh: T. & T. Clark, 1988), p. 188.

61. I am indebted for what follows to John Howard Yoder and Glen Stassen, *Authentic Transformation: A New Vision of Christ and Culture* (Nashville: Abingdon, 1996), pp. 45ff.

62. Gunton, *The One, the Three, and the Many*, p. 217.

63. Gunton, *The Actuality of the Atonement*, p. 190.

64. See John Howard Yoder, *The Priestly Kingdom: Social Ethics as Gospel* (Notre Dame, Ind.: University of Notre Dame Press, 1984), p. 47. For Yoder's discussion of the various agents in the church, see pp. 28-33.

65. Gunton, *The Actuality of the Atonement*, p. 193.

66. Yoder, *The Priestly Kingdom*, p. 38.

67. Taylor, *The Sources of the Self*, p. 317.

68. David Hollinger notes the value of ethnic and other groupings in mobilizing people for collective and constructive action. In this he sees that even the idea of nationhood may have an important role to play (see *Post-Ethnic America*, pp. 139, 15, 84, 112, 157).

69. John Milbank, *Theology and Social Theory: Beyond Secular Reason* (Oxford: Blackwell, 1990), p. 5.

70. Volf, "Justice, Exclusion, and Difference," *Synthesis Philosophia* 18 (2/1994), p. 473 (cf. *Exclusion and Embrace*, p. 220). Volf points out that this is not a new meta-language, but rather implies that Christians need to become multilingual (p. 40).

71. Gunton, *The Actuality of the Atonement*, p. 199.

5 ECOLOGY

1. See, for example, the *State of the World*, published annually by the Worldwatch Institute (New York: Norton). The best handbook covering these issues from a Christian perspective is *Earthkeeping in the Nineties: Stewardship of Creation, by the Fellows of the Calvin Center for Christian Scholarship*, 2d ed., ed. Loren Wilkinson (Grand Rapids: Eerdmans, 1991). See also the special issue of *Theology News and Notes*, "A Christian's Ecological Responsibility," ed. W. Dyrness and Rob Cahill (December 1992).

2. See Donella H. Meadows, Dennis L. Meadows, Jorgen Randers, and William H. Berends, III, *The Limits to Growth: A Report for the Club of Rome's Project on the Predicament of Mankind* (New York: Universe Books, 1972). The most striking finding of this study was the impact of the current exponential growth of population and consumption.

3. Lynn White, Jr., "The Historical Roots of Our Ecological Crisis," *Science* (March 10, 1967), pp. 1203-7 (reprinted numerous times).

4. For a good critique of the Wise Use Movement, see Richard Wright, "A Perspective on the Environmental Backlash Movement," *Stillpoint* [Magazine of Gordon College, Mass.] (Winter 1996), pp. 22, 23.

5. A good summary of this debate is found in Riley E. Dunlap, "Ecologist vs. Exemptionalist: The Ehrlich-Simon Debate," *Social Science Quarterly* 64 (March 1983), pp. 200-203. I owe this and the following reference to Sherrie Steiner Aeschliman, a graduate student at Washington State University, who is working on these questions. Christians are to be found on both sides of the debate, as can be seen, for example, in articles appearing in *GreenCross Magazine*, on the one hand, and *World* magazine, on the other.

6. Greg Knill, "Towards a Green Paradigm," *South African Geographical Journal* 73 (1991), p. 58. Knill recognizes that Christianity, while it may have reinforced this paradigm, was not its only source. He notes the important work of C. J. Glacken, who traced the Greek roots for some of these same ideas (*Traces on the Rhodian Shore: Nature and Culture in Western Thought from Ancient Times to the End of the Eighteenth Century* [Berkeley: Univ. of California Press, 1967]).

7. The best discussion of the issues is found in *Western Man and Environmental Ethics*, ed. Ian Barbour (Reading, Mass.: Addison-Wesley, 1973), which also reprints White's essay.

8. John MacQuarrie, "Creation and Environment," *Expository Times* 83 (1971-72), pp. 4-9. I have discussed this in some detail in "Stewardship of the Earth in the Old Testament," in *Tending the Garden,* ed. W. Granberg-Michaelson (Grand Rapids: Eerdmans, 1987), pp. 50-65.

9. H. Paul Santmire, *The Travail of Nature: The Ambiguous Ecological Promise of Christian Theology* (Philadelphia: Fortress Press, 1985). Santmire begins his discussion by noting the mistake of seeing Christian theology as related only to human history and not also as having great implication for the earth. Subsequent page references to this book are in the text.

10. Karl Barth, in spite of the length of his writings, has little to say about human responsibility for the earth and its processes. For him, divine action focuses on humanity: "But man is a creature of earth. Therefore it is for the earth's sake that God fulfills the movement to the world created by him. . . . We are the target of his whole movement to the creature" (*Church Dogmatics*, III/3 [Edinburgh: T. & T. Clark, 1960], p. 431). Barth does point out, however, humanity's dependence on the vegetable kingdom (*Church Dogmatics*, III/1 [1958], pp. 143-44) and its broad calling to serve the earth (*Church Dogmatics*, pp. 235-36) and respect the creatures (*Church Dogmatics,* pp. 350-55). With Teilhard, the whole direction of evolution is toward humanity: "With hominisation, in spite of the insignificance of the anatomical leap, we have the beginning of a new age. The earth 'gets a skin.' Better still, it finds its soul" (*The Phenomenon of Man* [New York: Harper & Row, 1959], pp. 182-83).

11. See Roger D. Sornell, who argues that Francis's attempt to teach people to think of creation with gratitude and appreciation led to a naturalism that paved the way for the Renaissance (*St. Francis of Assisi and Nature* [Oxford: Oxford Univ. Press, 1988], see esp. pp. 124, 143).

12. Santmire, *The Travail of Nature*, p. 121.

13. In spite of his accusations, White himself recognizes that medieval and Franciscan Christian traditions may provide assistance in thinking about our problems (see ibid., pp. 1206-7). Nor can the Reformation be so neatly placed in one category or the other. In a sense, both traditions are represented by the metaphors for creation used by the leading figures of the Reformation. Luther spoke of creation as the "masks of God," while Calvin referred to it as the "theater for God's Glory" (see Susan E. Schreiner, *The Theatre of His Glory: Nature and the Natural Order in the Thought of John Calvin* [Grand Rapids: Baker, 1991]).

14. See Rosino Gibellini, "The Theological Debate on Ecology," in *Ecology and Poverty: Cry of the Earth, Cry of the Poor,* ed. Leonardo Boff and Virgil Elizondo (London and Maryknoll, N.Y: SCM and Orbis Books, 1995), *Concilium* 1995/5, p. 126.

15. Odil H. Steck, *World and Environment* (Nashville: Abingdon, 1980), p. 35.

16. See Raymond Williams, *Culture and Society, 1780-1950* (Harmondsworth: Penguin, 1958). Culture in this sense issued in "an emphasis on the embodiment in art of certain human values, capacities, energies, which the development of society towards an industrial civilization was felt to be threatening or even destroying" (p. 53).

17. Jacques Ellul, *The Technological Society* (New York: Alfred Knopf, 1964), p. 21, quoted in Wilkinson, *Earthkeeping in the Nineties,* p. 263.

18. Ibid., pp. 265-71. There is growing evidence that selective use of technology enables people to continue their more traditional (and environmentally appropri-

ate) way of life (see Arnold Pacey, *The Culture of Technology* [Oxford: Blackwell, 1983], p. 144).

19. Romano Guardini, *Letters from Lake Como*, reprint (Grand Rapids: Eerdmans, 1994; original 1923), p. 46.

20. Julio de Santa Ana, "Socio-Economic System as a Cause of Ecological Imbalance and Poverty," in Boff and Elizondo, *Ecology and Poverty*, p. 5.

21. Charles Taylor, *The Sources of the Self: The Making of the Modern Identity* (Cambridge: Harvard Univ. Press, 1989), p. 370.

22. Jürgen Moltmann, *God in Creation: A New Theology of Creation and the Spirit of God,* ed. and trans. Margaret Kohl (San Francisco: Harper & Row, 1985), p. 86. *Kenosis* speaks of Christ's emptying of himself in becoming human (see Phil 2:6-7).

23. Moltmann argues that the perichoeritic or mutual penetration of the Trinity also applies to the world (ibid., p. 17). We would prefer to say that it is reflected in the world in its own creaturely way. This is an example of Moltmann's tendency to blur the distinctions between God and the world, since he believes all ultimately exists in God. Moltmann associates God's self-limitation with creation so closely with God's suffering that Colin Gunton notes: "There is a thin line between, on the one hand, maintaining systematic links between the doctrines of creation, conservation and redemption, and, on the other, confusing the categories." In this argument, Gunton concludes, Moltmann comes close to crossing this line (Colin Gunton, *Christ and Creation* [Grand Rapids: Eerdmans, 1992], p. 85 n.12).

24. Samuel Terrien, *The Elusive Presence* (New York: Harper & Row, 1978), p. 28.

25. This is why, as many have pointed out, the modern ecological movement, in the end, is just as anthropocentric as its antagonists.

26. Steck, *World and Environment*, p. 87.

27. See Douglas Hall, *The Steward: A Biblical Symbol Come of Age* (Grand Rapids: Eerdmans, 1990).

28. See the discussion of this in Lawrence Osborn, *Stewards of Creation: Environmentalism in the Light of Biblical Teaching* (Oxford: Latimer House, 1990), pp. 26-34.

29. John Calvin, *Institutes,* ed. John McNeil (Philadelphia: Westminster, 1960), 1.5.1, p. 52. Notice the aesthetic dimension of this experience, which will occupy us at length in the next chapter.

30. Steck, *World and Environment*, p. 109.

31. Emmanuel Levinas, *The Levinas Reader*, ed. Sean Hand (Oxford: Blackwell, 1989), p. 100. Levinas notes that this notion of passivity is inherent in the notion of creation *ex nihilo* (p. 103).

32. Larry Rasmussen, "The Integrity of Creation," *The Annual of the Society of Christian Ethics* (1995), p. 165. Rasmussen goes on to describe the recent history of this concept especially in discussions of the WCC.

33. Aldo Leopold, *A Sand County Almanac*, 26th printing (New York: Ballantine, 1989), p. 262, quoted in Rasmussen, "The Integrity of Creation," p. 162. Leonardo Boff and Virgil Elizondo echo this principle in *Ecology and Poverty*. They ask: To what extent does a given activity "help to support or to fracture the dynamic equilibrium that exists in the overall ecosystem"? (p. x).

34. Rasmussen calls this "autopoiesis," ("The Integrity of Creation," p. 172).

35. Ibid., p. 171.

36. See Christopher D. Stone, *Earth and Other Ethics: The Case for Moral Pluralism* (New York: Harper & Row, 1987). The important article "Do Trees Have Standing?" was first published in the *Southern California Legal Review* 450 (1972).

37. Wilkinson, *Earthkeeping in the Nineties*, pp. 250-52. Wilkinson quotes Michael Walzer, who has done more than anyone to help us think about these issues: "[Goods] are not and cannot be idiosyncratically valued. . . . Goods in the world have shared meanings because conception and creation are social processes" (ibid., p. 250). The implications of this for business are developed in Paul Hawken, *Ecology and Commerce: A Declaration of Sustainability* (San Francisco: HarperSanFranciso, 1993).

38. José Ramos Regidor, "Some Premises of an Eco-Social Theology of Liberation," in *Ecology and Poverty: Cry of the Earth, Cry of the Poor*, ed. Leonardo Boff and Virgil Elizondo (London and Maryknoll, N.Y: SCM and Orbis Books, 1995), *Concilium* 1995/5, p. 91.

39. Eduardo Gudynas, "Ecology from the Viewpoint of the Poor," in Boff and Elizondo, *Ecology and Poverty*, p. 108.

40. Holmes Ralston, III, *Philosophy Gone Wild* (New York: Prometheus, 1989), pp. 1-3.

41. James Lovelock, *Gaia: A New Look at Life on Earth* (Oxford: Oxford Univ. Press, 1979), p. 11. It is not clear what ethical norms can be derived from this proposal, because Lovelock does not believe human activity is in any way privileged and that natural forms of pollution are much worse than anything humanity can do. He even goes so far as to say that "ecologists know that so far there is no evidence that any of man's activities have diminished the total productivity of the biosphere" (ibid., pp. 120, 145).

42. James Lovelock, *The Ages of Gaia: A Biography of Our Living Earth* (New York: Bantam Books, 1988, 1990), p. 19. In order to mute the personification his earlier statement implied, Lovelock assured readers that the earth is alive in the sense that it is a self-regulating and self-organizing system (p. 3).

43. Ibid., p. 212. As to whether one should take up a religious attitude toward Gaia, Lovelock says only the fact that "Gaia can be both spiritual and scientific is, for me, deeply satisfying" (p. 217).

44. John B. Cobb, Jr., *Sustainability: Economics, Ecology and Justice* (Maryknoll, N.Y.: Orbis Books, 1992), p. 7. Subsequent page references to this book are in the text. Cobb earlier made a more technical argument for the same thesis with economist Herman E. Daly in *For the Common Good* (Boston: Beacon Press, 1989).

45. Max Stackhouse, "Can 'Sustainability' Be Sustained? A Review Essay of John B. Cobb, Jr's., Sustainability," *The Princeton Seminary Bulletin* 15:2 (1994), p. 153.

46. See A. Pacey, *The Culture of Technology*, p. 63. "All processes, of man or of nature, must add to the Global deficit." He concludes, "There is no sustainable lifestyle."

47. Wilkinson, *Earthkeeping in the Nineties*, p. 89. See also the excellent discussion of these issues in pages 68-90.

48. Quoting from a draft summary of a report by the Intergovernmental Panel on Climate and Change, "Experts Confirm Human Role in Global Warming," *New York Times*, September 10, 1995, pp. B1, 6.

49. Quoted in Dyrness, *How Does America Hear the Gospel?* (Grand Rapids: Eerdmans, 1989), p. 32.

50. See the discussion of the following scripture passages in Christoph Uehlinger, "The Cry of the Earth?," in Boff and Elizondo, *Ecology and Poverty*, pp. 43-47.

51. Wilkinson, *Earthkeeping in the Nineties*, pp. 89, 90.

52. John G. Gibbs argues that this cosmic imagery of creator is present in the earliest levels of the New Testament (see *Creation and Redemption: A Study in Pauline Theology* [Leiden: E. J. Brill, 1971]).

53. Moltmann, *God in Creation*, p. 172.

54. Joseph Sittler, "Called to Unity," quoted in Steven Bouma-Prediger, *The Greening of Theology: The Ecological Models of Rosemary Radford Ruether, Joseph Sittler, and Jürgen Moltmann* (Atlanta: Scholars Press, 1995), p. 69.

55. See Gunton, *Christ and Creation*, p. 20 and the references there.

56. Steck, *World and Environment*, pp. 251-52. Subsequent page references to this book are in the text.

57. For a discussion of ways in which creatures are "responsive agents," see Bouma-Prediger, *The Greening of Theology*, p. 282 and the literature cited there.

58. Levinas, *The Levinas Reader*, p. 121 n.12.

59. Carol Gilligan, "Moral Orientation and Moral Development," *Women and Moral Theory*, ed. E. F. Kittay and D. T. Meyers (Totowa: Rowman & Littlefield, 1987), pp. 19-33, 24, quoted in Volf, *Exclusion and Embrace*, p. 225.

60. I have argued that this servant character is implied in the way the image is presented in Genesis 1 (see Dyrness, "Stewardship of the Earth in the Old Testament," pp. 53-55).

61. This role is sometimes rejected in the name of an organic or non-hierarchical view of nature. But nature is itself full of hierarchies—the food chain, for example—that organize its processes. Moreover, as Richard Mouw points out: "The creator-creature distinction is basic to biblical religion; there is no denying the fact that God is in a very crucial sense infinitely 'higher' than we are" (Richard Mouw, *The God Who Commands* [Notre Dame, Ind.: Univ. of Notre Dame, 1990], p. 163). So all hierarchies are not necessarily bad. See also the discussion in Bouma-Prediger, *The Greening of Theology*, p. 281.

62. James Crenshaw, "Wisdom," *Interpreter's Bible Dictionary*, Supplement (Nashville: Abingdon, 1976), p. 954.

63. Christian Link, quoted in Steck, *World and Environment*, p. 169.

64. James Fairhead and Melissa Leach, "Enriching the Landscape: Social History and the Management of Transition Ecology in the Forest-Savahha Mosaic of the Republic of Guinea," *Africa*, 66:1 (1996), p. 21. Subsequent page references to this article are in the text.

65. Charles Richard Hensman, "Principles for a Socio-Environmental Ethic: The Relationship between Earth and Life," in Boff and Elizondo, *Ecology and Poverty*, p. 115.

66. This is an amazing percentage of the 120,000 cultivars in rice-production developed worldwide (ibid., p. 121).

67. Berta G. Ribeiro, "Ecological Consciousness in Amazonia: The Indigenous Experience," in Boff and Elizondo, *Ecology and Poverty*, p. 22.

68. I have developed this relationship in some detail in "Environmental Ethics and the Covenant of Hosea 2," in *Studies in Old Testament Theology*, ed. R. K. Johnston, R. Hubbard, and R. Meye (Dallas: Word, 1992). What follows is adapted from that chapter.

69. Steck, *World and Environment*, p. 292.

70. Frances Young and David Ford, *Meaning and Truth in Second Corinthians* (London: SPCK, 1988), p. 170. See also pp. 170-75.
71. Bruce Malina, *The New Testament World* (Atlanta: John Knox Press, 1981), pp. 71ff.
72. Steck, *World and Environment*, p. 190.
73. Gibellini, "The Theological Debate on Ecology," p. 131. Gibellini mentions especially E. Moltmann-Wendel, *I Am My Body: A Theology of Embodiment* (New York: Continuum, 1995).
74. Mary Douglas, *Purity and Danger* (New York: Frederick Praeger, 1966), p. 50. Cf. Victor Turner, who has spoken of rituals as "transforming performance" and sees in them the generating source of culture ("Body, Brain and Culture," *Cross-Currents* 36 [1986], pp. 156-78). Mary Douglas in an earlier book described the natural world as a code with implicit meanings (*Natural Symbols: Explorations in Cosmology* [New York: Penguin, 1970], pp. 60-64).
75. Mary Douglas, "Poetic Structure in Leviticus," in *Pomegranates and Golden Bells: Studies in Biblical, Jewish, and Near Eastern Ritual, Law, and Literature in Honor of Jacob Milgrom,* ed. David P. Wright, David Noel Freedman, and Avi Hurvitz (Winona Lake, Ind.: Eisenbrauns, 1995). Subsequent page references to this article are in the text.
76. Paul Cézanne, quoted in Gibellini, "The Theological Debate on Ecology," p. 128.
77. William Irving Thompson, quoted in Julia Velásquez, "Spirituality of the Earth," in Boff and Elizondo, *Ecology and Poverty,* p. 66.
78. Moltmann, *God in Creation*, pp. 183-184.
79. "Substantial healing" was a phrase introduced by Francis Schaeffer in his pioneering study of ecological issues (see *Pollution and the Death of Man: The Christian View of Ecology* [Wheaton: Tyndale, 1970], chap. 5).
80. Donald Worster, *The Wealth of Nature: Environmental History and Ecological Imagination* (Oxford: Oxford Univ. Press, 1993).
81. See Susan Power Bratton, *Distinctive Responsibilities for the Environment: A Christian Perspective* (Wheaton: Center for Applied Christian Ethics, 1995).

6 ART

1. Augustine, *Ad. Simpl.*, quoted in Peter Brown, *Augustine of Hippo* (Berkeley: Univ. of California Press, 1967), p. 155.
2. John Calvin, *Institutes*, ed. John McNeil (Philadelphia: Westminster, 1960), 1.14.20 and 1.5.1, vol. I, pp. 179 and 52.
3. Karl Barth, *Church Dogmatics*, III/1 (Edinburgh: T. & T. Clark, 1960), pp. 98, 181.
4. Plato, *Republic,* 377, in *Philosophies of Art and Beauty: Selected Readings in Aesthetics from Plato to Heidegger,* ed. Albert Hofstadter and Richard Kuhns (Chicago: Univ. of Chicago Press, 1976), p. 9.
5. See R. C. Lodge, *Plato's Theory of Art* (London: Routledge & Kegan Paul, 1953), p. 241; and E. C. Keuls, *Plato and Greek Painting* (Leiden: E. J. Brill, 1978), pp. 10ff.
6. Aristotle, *Poetics*, 1451, b9.
7. This has led recent interpreters to point out that Aristotle's famous notion of catharsis is something that happens first in the work before it happens in the spec-

tator, as it "presents something as if it were real" (Suzanne Langer, quoted in Colin Gunton, "Creation and Re-creation: An Exploration of Some Themes in Aesthetics and Theology," *Modern Theology* 2:1 [1985], p. 5).

8. Aristotle, *Poetics*, 1448b, 20.

9. For a further elaboration of these points see W. Dyrness, "Aesthetics in the Old Testament: Beauty in Context," *Journal of the Evangelical Theological Society* 28:4 (1985), pp. 421-32.

10. Cf. H. Ringgren: "Unfortunately we no longer know the concrete meaning of beholding the beauty (*no'am*) of Yahweh (Ps 27:4) . . . [but] what the worshipper experienced in the Temple filled him with joy and strength" (*Israelite Religion* [Philadelphia: Fortress Press, 1966], pp. 154-55).

11. Gerhard von Rad, *Old Testament Theology*, vol. 1, pp. 366-67.

12. Thomas F. Mathews, *The Clash of Gods: A Reinterpretation of Early Christian Art* (Princeton: Princeton Univ. Press, 1993), p. 180.

13. Augustine, *Confessions*, Book X (New York: Washington Square, 1960), p. 203. Understood in its Neo-Platonic setting it is probably unfair to characterize this as a "radically defective theory of sensibility," as Colin Gunton does ("Creation and Re-creation," p. 2). The problem for Augustine is moral and theological not primarily ontological, though this did lead to a low (or at least a cautious!) view of the sensuous.

14. Bernard, quoted in Umberto Eco, *Art and Beauty in the Middle Ages* (New Haven: Yale Univ. Press, 1986), p. 7. Eco notes the irony that these denunciations of art—and the *Confessions* must certainly be included here—are themselves models of literary style that were not without great cultural influence (p. 8).

15. Ulrich Zwingli, quoted in Charles Garside, Jr., *Zwingli and the Arts* (New Haven: Yale Univ. Press, 1966), pp. 173, 175.

16. Colin Gunton has argued that the whole of Western aesthetics is an attempt to escape from Plato's low view of the sensuous, which is clearly another part of the story ("Creation and Re-creation," p. 2).

17. David Richards, *Masks of Difference: Cultural Representation in Literature, Anthropology and Art* (Cambridge Univ. Press, 1994), p. 13.

18. Simone Weil, *Waiting on God,* ed. and trans. Emma Crawford (London: Routledge & Kegan Paul, 1951), p. 101.

19. Julian Schnabel, quoted in *Art News* (April 1985), p. 69.

20. H. R. Rookmaaker, *Modern Art and the Death of a Culture* (Downers Grove: InterVarsity Press, 1970), pp. 9, 10. Though written a generation ago, this is still an impressive study of the development of modern art. Elements of his interpretation have been more recently confirmed by other critics, such as Suzi Gablik, who do not write from a Christian perspective (see Suzi Gablik, *Has Modernism Failed?* [New York: Thames and Hudson, 1984]; Peter Fuller, *Images of God: The Consolations of Lost Illusions* [London: Hogarth Press, 1990]).

21. Frank Burch Brown, *Religious Aesthetics: A Theological Study of Making and Meaning* (Princeton: Princeton Univ. Press, 1989), p. 31.

22. Immanuel Kant, *Critique of Judgment* (1790), Sec. 6 (Meredith translation), as quoted in W. H. Walsh, "Immanuel Kant," *Encyclopedia of Philosophy*, vol. 4, ed. Paul Edwards (London: Macmillan, 1967), p. 319.

23. Nicholas Wolterstorff has described the situation well in *Art in Action: Toward a Christian Aesthetic* (Grand Rapids: Eerdmans, 1980), pp. 21-39.

24. Gablik, *Has Modernism Failed?,* p. 21.

25. Brown, *Religious Aesthetics,* p. 34.

26. Knud Løgstrup, *Metaphysics*, ed. and trans. Russell L. Dees (Milwaukee: Marquette Univ. Press, 1995), vol. 2, p. 293. Colin Gunton goes so far as to say that composers and artists allow the world to come to rational expression. Certainly their work comprehends rather than excludes this dimension (Colin Gunton, *Enlightenment and Alienation* [Blasingstoke: Marshall, Morgan and Scott, 1985] p. 144).

27. This holistic approach is consistent with sociological studies of art—called cultural studies—that have informed our approach to culture throughout our study. This approach focuses on the whole life of cultural objects from their production through to their use rather than focusing reductively on their production (see Richard Johnson, "What Is Cultural Studies Anyway?," *Social Context* 16 [1987], pp. 38-80).

28. Brown, *Religious Aesthetics*, p. 55.

29. Cf. Gregory Baum: "Religious experience, in the great personalities and in ordinary believers, makes the world religions into vital, flexible and creative movements in history. Religious experience, out of changed social and political circumstances, points to a new meaning of inherited symbols and becomes the experiential basis for reinterpreting traditional religious thinking" (*Religion and Alienation* [New York: Paulist Press, 1975], pp. 256-57).

30. C. G. Seerveld, "The Relation of the Arts to the Presentation of the Truth," in *Truth and Reality: Philosophical Perspectives on Reality*, dedicated to D. H. G. Stoker (Braamfotein, S.A.: DeJong's Bookshop, 1971), p. 162. This recalls John Hosper's well-known aesthetic norm. Good art, Hosper said, is "true to (actual or possible) human experience," though he did not see how any transcendent meaning could come to expression there (see *Meaning and Truth in the Arts* [Chapel Hill: Univ. of North Carolina Press, 1964]).

31. See the valuable discussion of this process in D. Bruce Lockerbie, *The Liberating Word: Art and the Mystery of the Gospel* (Grand Rapids: Eerdmans, 1974), chaps. 1, 2; also see Gunton, *Enlightenment and Alienation*, pp. 34-40.

32. Interestingly, "connection" was inherent in the original Latin meaning of religion, which meant to tie together. Margaret Miles has used this notion of connection as fundamental to religion in her recent study of film, *Seeing and Believing: Religion and Values in the Movies* (Boston: Beacon, 1996).

33. Howard Gardner argues for at least seven different "intelligences" or sets of know-how, only two of which—counting and language—are emphasized in traditional schooling (*Frames of Mind: The Theory of Multiple Intelligences* [New York: Basic Books, 1985]. In *To Open Minds* Gardner develops this further by articulating the role arts can play in helping students discover the domain of their strength and interest (*To Open Minds: Chinese Clues to the Development of Contemporary Education* [New York: Basic Books, 1989]).

34. See Martin F. Gardiner, Alan Fox, Faith Knowles, Donna Jeffrey, "Learning Improvement by Arts Training," *Nature* 381 (May 23, 1996), p. 284 and the literature cited there. I owe this reference to Bethany Rogers, a researcher at the Coalition of Essential Schools at Brown University.

35. C. G. Seerveld, *A Christian Critique of Art and Literature* (Toronto: The Association for Reformed Scientific Studies, 1968), p. 32.

36. Weil, *Waiting on God,* p. 102.

37. Wolterstorff, *Art in Action,* p. 121. Cf. pp. 114-21, where Wolterstorff calls artists "workers in fittingness."

38. C. S. Lewis, *An Experiment in Criticism* (Cambridge Univ. Press, 1961), p. 56. Cf. "The more completely a man's reading is a form of egoistic castle building, the more he will demand a certain superficial realism, and the less he will like the fantastic."

39. T. S. Eliot, "Burnt Norton, V.," *Burnt Norton* (London: Faber and Faber, 1941).

40. Vincent Van Gogh, *Dear Theo: The Autobiography of Vincent Van Gogh*, ed. Irving Stone (New York: New American Library, 1937), pp. 122, 123, 176.

41. Løgstrup, *Metaphysics*, vol. 2, p. 296.

42. Gunton, *Enlightenment and Alienation*, pp. 49-54.

43. T. S. Eliot, "Religion and Literature," *Selected Essays* (London: Faber and Faber, 1934), p. 429. Eliot argues in this essay that whatever modern people say, criticism must always be completed from a definite ethical and theological standpoint. Even Baudelaire, he says, was man enough for damnation.

44. Herbert Marcuse, *The Aesthetic Dimension* (Boston: Beacon Press, 1978), quoted in Wolterstorff, *Art in Action*, p. 152.

45. Peter Fuller, *Images of God: The Consolations of Lost Illusions* (London: The Hogarth Press, 1990), p. 311. Cf. Suzi Gablik, *The Reenchantment of Art* (London: Thames and Hudson, 1991).

46. George E. Marcus and Fred R. Myers, eds., *The Traffic in Culture: Refiguring Art and Anthropology* (Berkeley: Univ. of California Press, 1995). Subsequent page references to this book are in the text.

47. Merold Westphall, *Suspicion and Faith: The Religious Uses of Modern Atheism* (Grand Rapids: Eerdmans, 1993), p. 288.

48. Wolterstorff, *Art in Action*, p. 123.

49. Emmanuel Levinas, "Reality and Its Shadow," *The Levinas Reader*, ed. Sean Hand (Oxford: Blackwell, 1989), pp. 129-43. Subsequent page references to this article are in the text.

50. George Steiner, *Real Presences: Is There Anything in What We Say?* (London: Faber and Faber, 1989). Subsequent page references to this book are in the text.

51. An influential voice of this kind is Watchman Nee, *Love Not the World* (London: Victory Press, 1968).

52. Steiner, *Real Presences*, p. 226. This is also an argument that Etienne Gilson makes in *Painting and Reality* (Cleveland and New York: Meridian-World Publishers, 1957).

53. Steiner refuses to be more explicit about the "transcendence" on which we must wager, even appearing to allow the epiphany to be either Judeo-Christian or Platonic.

54. Colin Gunton, *Christ and Creation* (Grand Rapids: Eerdmans, 1992), p. 118, quotation at p. 121. Gunton refers especially to T. F. Torrance, *Transformation and Convergence in the Frame of Knowledge* (Belfast: Christian Journals, 1984).

55. David Malouf has the protagonist of his book *Remembering Babylon*, Lachlan Beattie, admit the source of his fear: "Not at what he might have to face—he would face anything, he was brave enough—but at what he might have to admit of the way the world was, and how his failure to see it was a weakness in him" (*Remembering Babylon* [New York: Vintage Books, 1993], p. 160).

56. Rookmaaker, *Modern Art and the Death of a Culture*, p. 228.

57. Hans-Georg Gadamer, *Truth and Method*, ed. and trans. by Garret Barden and John Cumming (New York: Seabury Press, 1975), p. 63.

58. John Taylor, *The Go-between God* (London: SCM, 1974), p. 19, quoted in Jeremie Begbie, *Voicing Creation's Praise: Towards a Theology of the Arts* (Oxford: Blackwell, 1991), p. 227. Begbie's study is a rich expression of a trinitarian view of Christian art.

59. Weil, *Waiting on God*, p. 101.

CONCLUSION: HUMAN LIFE AS EMBODIED WORSHIP

1. Catherine LaCugna, *God for Us: The Trinity and the Christian Life* (New York: Harper, 1991), p. 357. LaCugna references the work of A. Kavanagh.

2. Ibid., p. 358.

3. Dante was able to see "all of creation [as] a constant reduplication and emanation of the active love of God . . . [the] timeless affecting all phenomena at all seasons" (Erich Auerbach, *Mimesis: The Representation of Reality in Western Literature* [Princeton: Princeton Univ. Press, 1953; New York: Anchor Books, 1957], pp. 169-70).

4. Ibid., p. 138.

5. Victor and Edith Turner, *Image and Pilgrimage in Christian Culture: Anthropological Perspectives* (New York: Columbia University Press, 1978), p. 237. The phrase "extroverted mysticism" is their description of pilgrimages (see p. 31).

6. Colin Gunton, *The One, the Three, and the Many: God, Creation, and the Culture of Modernity*, the Bampton Lectures 1992 (Cambridge and New York: Cambridge Univ. Press, 1993), p. 227.

7. Luke Johnson notes that these instructions presuppose embodied existence: "Human 'owning' is not itself a result of the sin but the consequence of being a body. Humans therefore cannot become completely dispossessed without losing their identity" (*Sharing Possessions: Mandate and Symbol of Faith* [Minneapolis: Fortress Press, 1981], p. 114).

8. Gunton, *The One, the Three, and the Many*, p. 231.

9. Jon Levenson, "The Eighth Principle of Judaism and the Literary Simultaneity of Scripture," in Jon Levenson, *The Hebrew Bible, the Old Testament, and Historical Criticism: Jews and Christians in Biblical Studies* (Louisville: Westminster/ John Knox Press, 1993), p. 74.

10. Levenson argues for "the simultaneity, the self-referentiality and mutual implication of all its [Torah's] parts" (Levenson, "The Eighth Principle of Judaism and the Literary Simultaneity of Scripture," p. 75; also see Michael Lieb, who describes the way biblical images can inexhaustively enlarge and recreate themselves (*The Visionary Mode: Biblical Prophecy, Hermeneutics and Cultural Change* [Ithica, N.Y.: Cornell Univ Press, 1991]).

11. Dante Alighieri, *The Paradiso*, ed. and trans. John Ciardi (New York: New American Library, 1970), canto xxxiii, lines 133-46.

General Index

Scripture Index

OLD TESTAMENT

NEW TESTAMENT